FRUITS OF PERSEVERANCE

MCGILL-QUEEN'S FRENCH ATLANTIC WORLDS SERIES
SERIES EDITORS: NICHOLAS DEW AND JEAN-PIERRE LE GLAUNEC

The French Atlantic world has emerged as a rich and dynamic field of historical research. This series will showcase a new generation of scholarship exploring the worlds of the French Atlantic – including West Africa, the greater Caribbean region, and the continental Americas – from the sixteenth century to the mid-nineteenth century. Books in the series will explore how the societies of the French Atlantic were shaped and connected by trans-oceanic networks of colonialism, how local and indigenous cultures and environments shaped colonial projects, and how the diverse peoples of the French Atlantic understood and experienced their worlds. Especially welcome are histories from the perspectives of the enslaved and dispossessed. Comparative studies are encouraged and the series will accept manuscript submissions in English and in French. Original works of scholarship are preferred, though translations of landmark books in the field will be considered.

Le monde atlantique français est devenu un domaine de recherche riche et dynamique au sein de la discipline historique. La présente collection a pour vocation d'accueillir une nouvelle génération d'ouvrages explorant les espaces de l'Atlantique français – y compris l'Afrique de l'Ouest, la grande région des Caraïbes et les Amériques continentales – du début du XVIe siècle jusqu'au milieu du XIXe siècle. Les œuvres qui y sont publiées explorent de quelles manières les sociétés de l'Atlantique français sont façonnées et reliées par les réseaux transocéaniques issus du colonialisme, de quelle manière les cultures locales et leurs environnements influencent les projets coloniaux, et comment les divers peuples de l'Atlantique français comprennent et expérimentent leurs mondes. Les ouvrages donnant la parole aux esclaves ou aux acteurs traditionnellement dominés sont particulièrement bienvenus, tout comme les recherches comparées. La collection est ouverte aux manuscrits rédigés en anglais ou en français, de préférence des monographies originales, ainsi qu'aux traductions de livres ayant marqué le domaine.

1 Architecture and Urbanism in the French Atlantic Empire
  State, Church, and Society, 1604–1830
  Gauvin Alexander Bailey

2 Flesh Reborn
  The Saint Lawrence Valley Mission Settlements through the Seventeenth Century
  Jean-François Lozier

3 Power and Subsistence
  The Political Economy of Grain in New France
  Louise Dechêne

4 Fruits of Perseverance
  The French Presence in the Detroit River Region, 1701–1815
  Guillaume Teasdale

Fruits of Perseverance

The French Presence in the Detroit River Region, 1701–1815

GUILLAUME TEASDALE

McGill-Queen's University Press
Montreal & Kingston · London · Chicago

© McGill-Queen's University Press 2018
ISBN 978-0-7735-5500-6 (cloth)
ISBN 978-0-7735-5501-3 (paper)
ISBN 978-0-7735-5575-4 (ePDF)
ISBN 978-0-7735-5576-1 (ePUB)

Legal deposit first quarter 2019
Bibliothèque nationale du Québec

Printed in Canada on acid-free paper that is 100% ancient forest free (100% post-consumer recycled), processed chlorine free

This book has been published with the help of a grant from the Canadian Federation for the Humanities and Social Sciences, through the Awards to Scholarly Publications Program, using funds provided by the Social Sciences and Humanities Research Council of Canada. Funding was also received from the University of Windsor.

Parts of this book have appeared in the *Michigan Historical Review* 38, no. 2 (2012): 35–62.

We acknowledge the support of the Canada Council for the Arts, which last year invested $153 million to bring the arts to Canadians throughout the country.

Nous remercions le Conseil des arts du Canada de son soutien. L'an dernier, le Conseil a investi 153 millions de dollars pour mettre de l'art dans la vie des Canadiennes et des Canadiens de tout le pays.

Library and Archives Canada Cataloguing in Publication

Teasdale, Guillaume, author
    Fruits of perseverance: the French presence in the Detroit River Region, 1701–1815 / Guillaume Teasdale.

(McGill-Queen's French Atlantic worlds series ; 4)
Includes bibliographical references and index.
Issued in print and electronic formats.
ISBN 978-0-7735-5500-6 (hardcover). – ISBN 978-0-7735-5501-3 (softcover). – ISBN 978-0-7735-5575-4 (ePDF). – ISBN 978-0-7735-5576-1 (ePUB)

    1. French – Detroit River Region (Mich. and Ont.) – History – 18th century.
    2. French Americans – Detroit River Region (Mich. and Ont.) – History – 18th century. 3. Canadians, French-speaking – Detroit River Region (Mich. and Ont.) – History – 18th century. 4. Detroit River region (Mich. and Ont.) – History – 18th century. I. Title.

F572.D46T43 2018   977.4'33   C2018-904645-7
                                      C2018-904646-5

This book was typeset by Marquis Interscript in 10.5/13 Sabon.

Contents

Figures vii
Preface ix
Acknowledgments xiii
Introduction 3

1 Early Land Occupation 9

2 Seigneurial Tenure and Landholders 25

3 Trespassers, Aboriginal Deeds, and Taxation 40

4 Contested Public Property Rights 61

5 Private Landowners 72

6 French Orchards 98

7 Divided by the Border 115

Conclusion 137

Notes 141
Bibliography 191
Index 211

Figures

1.1 *Le Mur des Noms* (Wall of Names). Photo credit: Guillaume Teasdale   15

1.2 *Le Mur des Noms* (Wall of Names). Photo credit: Guillaume Teasdale   16

2.1 View of the Moran residence. Courtesy of the Detroit Public Library, Digital Collections, Resource ID EB02c894   27

2.2 Statue of Robert Navarre, the Westin Book Cadillac Hotel, Detroit, Michigan. Photo credit: public domain   29

2.3 Gaspard-Joseph Chaussegros de Léry Jr's map of the Detroit River region, 1754. Taken from Ernest J. Lajeunesse, ed., *The Windsor Border Region: Canada's Southernmost Frontier. A Collection of Documents* (Toronto: University of Toronto Press for the Champlain Society, 1960), lviii   38

3.1 Potawatomi deed to Robert Navarre Jr, Côte des Pous, 26 May 1771. Courtesy of the Burton Historical Collection, Detroit Public Library, Robert Navarre Papers   56

4.1 Belle Isle deed (page 1). Courtesy of the Detroit Public Library, Digital Collections, Resource ID bh009503   65

4.2 Belle Isle deed (page 2). Courtesy of the Detroit Public Library, Digital Collections, Resource ID bh009503   66

5.1 Present-day Essex County, Ontario, ca. 1795. Adapted from Lajeunesse, ed., *Windsor Border Region*, cxvi-a   77

5.2 Lesperance log cabin, Tecumseh, Ontario. Photo credit: Tecumseh Area Historical Society   79

5.3 Man and woman standing on weed-grown ground in front of boarded up clapboard house. Courtesy of the Detroit Public Library, Digital Collections, Resource ID DPA2702   84

5.4 View of the back of the Old Jean-François Hamtramck residence, Detroit, Michigan. Courtesy of the Detroit Public Library, Digital Collections, Resource ID EB02d221   87

5.5 Private claims in Wayne County's District of Hamtramck, 1810. Courtesy of Monroe County Museum, Monroe, Michigan, French Claims File   92

5.6 Private claims in Wayne County's District of Sargent, 1810. Courtesy of Monroe County Museum, Monroe, Michigan, French Claims File   94

6.1 Jesuit pear tree, Windsor, Ontario, date unknown. Courtesy of Museum Windsor, Identifier P6741-72   111

7.1 Former site of Badichon-Labadie windmill (Lassaline-Montreuil), Walkerville, Ontario. Courtesy of Museum Windsor, Identifier M148   122

7.2 French windmill, Walkerville, Ontario, 1893. Source: public domain (accessed through the Centre for Digital Scholarship, University of Windsor)   124

7.3 Marentette homestead, Windsor, Ontario. Courtesy of Museum Windsor, Identifier P5216   136

Preface

My passion for the history of French-speaking communities outside of Quebec stems in part from the fact that I was born in northern Ontario (*le Nouvel Ontario*) to French-Canadian parents. My parents had moved from Quebec to join one of my aunts, who had accepted a position as a French teacher in North Bay. However, shortly after I was born, my parents moved back to Quebec. Although I grew up in Trois-Rivières, Quebec, I maintained my connections with northern Ontario through my aunt and her family. From an early age, I was a Québécois who was quite aware of the existence of French-speaking communities beyond the boundaries of the province of Quebec. Still, I knew next to nothing about their histories. Many years later, while I was pursuing undergraduate studies in history in Montreal, I learned about the waves of French-Canadian emigration to New England and northern Ontario during the second half of the nineteenth century. But it was only after reading Jean-Baptiste Trudeau's *Voyage sur le Haut-Missouri 1794–1796*, published in 2006, that I really began to grasp the scope of the French imprint on North America. From that moment on, I knew I wanted to channel my interest in the history of French-speaking communities outside of Quebec into an academic career. That is when I began my PhD studies in Toronto.

There was no doubt that Trudeau's writings had sparked my interest for the French presence in the Mississippi River valley. However, I rapidly became more curious about the history of French colonial Detroit. In the first summer of my PhD studies, I spent two weeks researching the Burton Historical Collection of the Detroit Public Library to assess the feasibility of writing a doctoral dissertation on that topic. During that stay in Detroit, I collected thousands of pages of archival sources regarding the local French presence, many of which were written in French. These findings far exceeded my expectations, to the point that for a few years I actually felt overwhelmed by the number of sources available. The effort involved in trying to make sense of all these sources and to write a history of French colonial Detroit without being able to build on an already existing historiography proved to be challenging, even discouraging, at times. But it also became a source of motivation.

When I look back at my first experience in the Detroit archives, the discovery of so many documents should not have come as a surprise. The extensive genealogical data on the French presence in the Detroit River region clearly show that hundreds of families lived in the area during the eighteenth and nineteenth centuries. One only needs to browse through Christian Denissen's *Genealogy of the French Families of the Detroit River Region, 1701–1936*, which includes almost fifteen hundred pages, to get a glimpse of that significant presence. Local genealogists, like those of the French-Canadian Heritage Society of Michigan, have always known about this significant French presence. Through their in-depth research they have helped countless residents of Metro Detroit trace their French roots.[1] In addition, retired University of Sudbury professor Marcel Bénéteau, who was born and raised in the Windsor area, has studied the French culture of the Detroit River region for several decades, most notably the local songs and vocabulary.[2] In 2008, with the late University of Windsor professor Peter W. Halford, he published *Mots choisis: Trois cents ans de francophonie au Détroit du lac Érié*, a wide-ranging study of the French lexicon of the Detroit River region.

In the community, on both sides of the border, tens of thousands of people are aware of their French-Canadian background, even those who no longer speak French (that is, the vast majority). I began to realize this when I moved to Windsor in 2012 and spoke to local people who told me stories about their ancestors coming from Quebec and settling on "ribbon farms" along the Detroit River. In 2015, in the context of the celebrations regarding the 400th anniversary of French presence in Ontario, Museum Windsor launched a permanent exhibit entitled "Windsor's French Roots." The creation of this exhibit, on display in the François Bâby House, is probably one of the most important contributions made by the city of Windsor to celebrate its French cultural heritage.

With this book, I wish to recognize these efforts and supplement their findings to enable the tens of thousands of descendants of the eighteenth-century French settlers of the Detroit River region, whether or not they still live in the area, to better understand and appreciate their roots.

Guillaume Teasdale, PhD
15 December 2017
Au Détroit, Pays d'en Haut

Acknowledgments

I first want to thank my wife, Stacie Teasdale, who has been more than supportive throughout the years I have worked on this book. Her passion for the field of urban planning and urban design, one of her areas of professional expertise, had a profound impact on the way I look at the past and question it. From the outset, her influence led me to explore the question of land organization in French colonial Detroit. During this decade-long process, Stacie has also given me three amazing sons. Stacie, I dedicate this book to you, Connor, Quinn, and Aden.

I also wish to acknowledge people who have helped me in this journey. My deepest gratitude goes to Carolyn Podruchny, Marcel Martel, Colin Coates, Yves Frenette, and José António Brandão, who provided insightful comments and suggestions on previous drafts of this manuscript. Susan Amo, thank you for your proofreading services from the beginning to the end of this project. Brian Leigh Dunnigan, thank you for introducing me to the Thomas Gage Papers at the William L. Clements Library many years ago. I think I can say today that this was a major turning point in my research. I would also like to thank Chris Kull, former archivist at Michigan's Monroe County Museum, for her assistance. Thank you as well to the staff of Museum Windsor, especially Heather Butt Colautti, Melissa Phillips, and Madelyn Della Valle, for their assistance in digitizing images for the book. Finally, I am indebted to my editor at McGill-Queen's University Press, Kyla Madden, for her continuous support and guidance through the numerous stages of the publication process, and to my peer reviewers, whose comments and suggestions greatly helped me enhance sections of the book.

This book project would not have been possible without the financial support provided to me over the years by the following institutions: York University, Social Sciences and Humanities Research Council of Canada (SSHRC), the Government of Ontario, the William L. Clements Library, the American Philosophical Society, the Center for French Colonial Studies, the Bentley Historical Library, the University of Windsor, and the Canadian Federation for the Humanities and Social Sciences. In 2016, I obtained a SSHRC Insight Development Grant that allowed me to hire students who gathered helpful information for the writing of chapter 7. My team of research assistants included Salma Abumeeiz, Adam Drouillard, Jason Lavin, John-Michael Markovic, and Shane Miller. Thank you all!

I could not dream of a better working environment than the University of Windsor, where I am surrounded by amazing colleagues (including colleagues from universities in Metro Detroit) and where I am able to share my research findings on the colonial history of the Detroit River region every year with my students. I also feel fortunate to be living in the Detroit River region, where so many associations, on both sides of the border, share a deep passion for the history of their region and provide me with multiple opportunities to interact with and learn from their members. I am truly blessed.

FRUITS OF PERSEVERANCE

Introduction

In 1795, the Detroit River region was one community. There was no border to cross, no duties to pay. Instead of dividing them, the Detroit River was actually bringing people together. Many families had members living on both sides of the river. The vast majority of the locals did not live within Fort Detroit, which had been established as Fort Pontchartrain by French military entrepreneur Antoine Laumet de Lamothe Cadillac in 1701, but on farms fronting the shores of the Detroit River. The towns of Sandwich, Amherstburg, Windsor, and Walkerville did not yet exist, nor did the cities of Dearborn or Mount Clemens. Both sides of the Detroit River were simply referred to as "Detroit" or *le Détroit* in French, meaning "the strait" that connected Lake St Clair to Lake Erie. The physical landscape of the Detroit River region was also very different from what exists today, as farms with orchards fronted the river. Its cultural landscape diverged too, for French was by far the dominant language in the area, on both sides of the Detroit River. In 1795, the Detroit River region was part of British North America, more specifically Upper Canada (created in 1791). However, the following year, when Britain surrendered Michigan to the United States, the Detroit River would become an international border. Still, the physical and cultural landscape of the Detroit River region did not change much until the 1820s; the French farms and the windmills along the Detroit River did not begin to vanish until the 1830s, while for years French remained the most spoken language. On the south shore of the Detroit River (Ontario), where urbanization happened at a much slower pace than on the north shore (Michigan), the French element actually remained dominant well into the second half of the nineteenth century.[1]

These French settlers were single men, married couples, and families who had come from various parts of the Saint Lawrence valley, in present-day Quebec, throughout the eighteenth century.[2] Together, with some support from Versailles and French colonial authorities at Quebec, they had transplanted a French society to the heart of the Upper Country (*pays d'en haut*), as the Great Lakes region was called at that time. Of course, the fur trade played a major role in the local economy of the Detroit River region, and virtually all these settlers were involved to some degree in this industry. The French society of the Detroit River region was not isolated from the rest of the Great Lakes – far from it. Through the fur trade, the French settlers had developed friendly relations with many Aboriginal peoples, including the Huron, Potawatomi, and Ottawa. At times, this led to intermarriages, although this phenomenon was marginal in the Detroit River region compared to other parts of the Upper Country, especially after the 1730s. The main reasons why this phenomenon remained limited in the Detroit River region is that the vast majority of the local French settlers lived on farms, and that hundreds of French women lived in these agricultural settlements. Trading in furs was not their primary economic activity, it complemented agriculture. The story was a little different at Fort Pontchartrain (renamed Fort Detroit after the British conquest) and quite different at posts of the western and northern Great Lakes, where the fur trade was undoubtedly the main economic activity for most of the eighteenth century.

This book will focus on French land occupation in the Detroit River region. Its purpose is not to study the early urbanization of Fort Detroit and/or the fur trade, for several historians have already examined the fur trade in the colonial Great Lakes.[3] Nor is it to attempt to compare Detroit with other French societies like Acadia, the Illinois Country, or New Orleans; such a comparative approach of French land occupation in different parts of North America would deserve to be treated in the scope of a separate project. The main objective of this book is to better explain exactly how a society similar to the rural settlements of the Saint Lawrence valley (land grants, land organization, legal system of the Custom of Paris used for land transactions, marriage contracts, inheritances, etc.) developed in such an isolated place, and survived well beyond the fall of New France.

In the eighteenth-century Saint Lawrence valley most settlers lived in *seigneuries particulières*. These were rural settlements usually owned by nobles or Roman Catholic orders (*particuliers*).[4] After

1663, seigneuries particulières were granted by the governor general of New France on behalf of the French king. In the Detroit River region, French colonial authorities chose instead to establish a *seigneurie directe*, that is, a rural settlement owned by the king himself. This immediately contributed to the growth of the French colonial presence along the Detroit River by standardizing land organization. As a matter of fact, it can be argued that without the creation of this seigneurie directe, French colonial Detroit would have remained nothing more than just another French outpost of the Upper Country, and that French roots in the area would not have been very strong. However, in some ways, it can also be argued that the establishment of a seigneurie directe, rather than seigneuries particulières, in the Detroit River region actually hindered the long-term growth of the local French presence because no nobles or Roman Catholic orders – no seigneurs particuliers – were left to represent the settlers and to defend land property rights after the British conquest.[5]

Both in the Saint Lawrence valley and in the Detroit River region, the settlers who lived in seigneuries particulières or directes did not exactly "own" their tracts of land but "held" them, for they "shared" ownership with their *seigneur*. Since they could buy and sell such tracts, these settlers were not "lease holders" either. In other words, they were "landholders."[6] This system was implemented at Detroit during the French regime, especially between the 1730s and 1750s, but it collapsed after the British conquest. During the decades that followed the fall of New France, British authorities perceived the French settlers of the Detroit River region either as "land squatters" who should not be living in the Great Lakes region or as some sort of "land owners" who should pay property tax. As a result, French land occupation in the Detroit River region became a complicated issue after the demise of the French empire in North America, and this matter was not clarified until the turn of the nineteenth century.

This book will engage with the historiographies of the French Atlantic World, French Canada, and Franco-Ontario. Historians of New France, particularly those working in Quebec, have mostly studied the Saint Lawrence valley itself and have largely forgotten the French presence in the Upper Country, especially the settlements of the Detroit River region.[7] In Ontario, over the last decades, the multiplication of publications on the Franco-Ontarians has not led to a better understanding of the French presence in the province during the preindustrial era, for virtually all these publications have focused on the twentieth century.[8] Therefore, this book will fill major gaps in the literature on the French experience in North America during the eighteenth and nineteenth centuries. Other historiographies with which this book will engage include British North America/Upper Canada, Early American Republic Era/Michigan, Native-Newcomer Relations, and Colonial Borderlands in North America. After the fall of New France, the French of the Detroit River region now lived in an Aboriginal world that would rapidly evolve into a borderland zone between British North America and the United States. Forced to adapt to changing political and legal realities, they did their best to keep their lands and acquire new ones, on both sides of the Detroit River, and therefore on both sides of the future border.

Fruits of Perseverance is a book that will complement other recent historical works on colonial Detroit. In 2014, Catherine Cangany's *Frontier Seaport: Detroit's Transformation into an Atlantic Entrepôt* examined Detroit's role in the Anglo-Atlantic world of the second half of the eighteenth century, through the town's early exportations of manufactured merchandise to Europe and beyond. Her work was not intended to be a study of the local French agricultural settlements, but rather of the development of Detroit into a frontier urban centre connected to the world.[9] In 2017, *Citizens of Convenience: The Imperial Origins of American Nationhood on the U.S.-Canadian Border*, by Lawrence B.A. Hatter, shed light on the challenges that faced the government of the United States regarding citizenship in border zones of the Great Lakes, including the Detroit River region, at the turn of the nineteenth century. Hatter's diplomatic history provided a thorough analysis of how the American government operated to limit the influence of British subjects on the American side of the US-Canada border after the 1794 Jay Treaty.[10] But like *Frontier Seaport*, the purpose of *Citizens of Convenience* was not to offer an in-depth study of the history of the French presence along the Detroit River.

A few works have focused on some aspects of the history of the French presence in the Detroit River region during the New France era and the following decades. About fifteen years ago, in her historical demography PhD dissertation, Lina Gouger studied the migrations of French people from the Saint Lawrence valley to the Detroit River region between 1701 and 1765. Although thorough and supported by multiple statistics, Gouger's work did not look beyond the French regime nor did it carefully analyze the question of French land occupation along the Detroit River.[11] More recently, Jay Gitlin's *The Bourgeois Frontier: French Towns, French Traders, and American Expansion*, published in 2010, brought attention to the fact that French people were already living in the Great Lakes and the Mississippi River valley when the United States took possession of these regions, between the 1780s and 1800s. Gitlin's work demonstrated that several French families, from New Orleans to Detroit (Gitlin coined the term "creole corridor" to describe the stretch of these French settlements in the interior of North America), adapted quite well to the different regime changes that took place after the British conquest of Canada, and that some of them actually became very wealthy. In Detroit, Gitlin gave the example of the Campau family, present in the area since the early eighteenth century. During the British and American regimes, members of the Campau family built impressive fortunes through trade and the acquisition of small tracts of land; Joseph Campau (1769–1863) was undoubtedly the most prominent of them.[12] Still, the Campaus were one family among hundreds of other French families who lived in the Detroit River region before the mid-nineteenth century. Most of these families were not merchants but farmers. *Fruits of Perseverance* will complement the works of Gouger and Gitlin by providing a comprehensive study of French land occupation in the Detroit River region through the French, British, and American regimes.

Lastly, another work that this book will complement is that of Karen Lynn Marrero. French-Aboriginal intermarriage in the Detroit River region has been a taboo topic for a long time. In addition, finding the descendants of such mixed unions in archival records has always been difficult because the vast majority of marriages between French men and Aboriginal women were not ceremonies according to Christian rites and therefore not recorded by Roman Catholic missionaries. Moreover, most of these marriages took place not in Detroit, the French hub of the Upper Country, but at other posts located further south, west, and north, that is, in peripheral regions. As mentioned earlier, Detroit was not isolated from the rest of the Great Lakes. Métis people indisputably visited the Detroit River region throughout the eighteenth century and some, not a large group, seem to have established roots in the area, either within Fort Pontchartrain/Detroit or on farms. Marrero, a native of Windsor and a descendant of French man Pierre Roy and Métis woman Marguerite Ouabankikoue, who married at Fort Miami in 1728 but who obviously maintained strong connections to the Detroit River region, has studied the impact of individuals of mixed ancestry on the early urban development of Detroit.[13] Her work and this book will complete one another on many levels.

I

Early Land Occupation

Historians have long debated about whether or not France controlled the Great Lakes region before 1760. It has been argued that the Upper Country remained an Aboriginal world where the French never succeeded in imposing their will.[1] It has also been argued that despite this apparent lack of control, the French empire was able to put in place an effective system of diplomatic influence that would, in the long run, transform Aboriginal people into loyal subjects of the French king (but that the fall of New France interrupted this process).[2] This chapter examines how, at the turn of the eighteenth century, the French managed to lay the foundations of a settlement along the Detroit River without the necessity of imposing their will on Aboriginal peoples.

CLAIMING THE GREAT LAKES

According to France's official diplomatic policy, Aboriginal peoples were never regarded as the first owners of the land in New France. As a result, the French never considered obtaining treaties of land cession from Aboriginal peoples; instead, they signed treaties of peace and alliance with them.[3] During the period from the sixteenth to the eighteenth centuries, the French Crown never specified that Aboriginal titles to land had to be extinguished prior to land grants being made. Still, as a precaution, colonial administrators were urged to avoid quarrels with Aboriginal peoples at all cost, and to use tact when granting lands for new *seigneuries particulières*.[4] In the Saint Lawrence valley, French authorities always attempted to occupy lands in places where conflicts with Aboriginal peoples would be minimal. For this reason, colonial development in the upper Saint Lawrence valley, west of the island of Montreal, was not particularly encouraged by French colonial authorities.[5] In general, the Aboriginal peoples who welcomed the French onto their lands did so because it was militarily and materially beneficial for their people. In the Saint Lawrence valley, because French land occupation increased slowly before the 1660s, the negative effects of this land encroachment for the Aboriginal peoples were outweighed by the positive aspects of living near French settlers. They enjoyed the benefits of better access to French commodities and presents from the Crown.[6]

In the Great Lakes, as early as 1669, Sulpician missionaries François Dollier de Casson and René de Bréhant de Galinée officially claimed most of the south shore of Lake Erie on behalf of the Crown by planting a cross on which they imprinted the significance of their act.[7] Louis XIV first claimed the shores of the Detroit River itself when French explorer René-Robert Cavelier, Sieur de La Salle, led his expedition from Quebec to the Upper Country and down the Mississippi River in 1682.[8] Four years later, in 1686, French colonial authorities discussed the building of a post in the Detroit River region.[9] They soon assigned trader Daniel Greysolon Dulhut the task of building a fort on the St Clair River, at the southern edge of Lake Huron, where the city of Port Huron, Michigan, stands today.[10] This fort, officially named Fort Saint Joseph, but also known as Dulhut Post, was constructed for the purpose of intercepting British traders on their way to the western and northern Great Lakes.[11] Although its construction was important, it did not carry much political weight with regards to imperialistic claims in North America. It was demolished in 1688 because it lacked the requisite supplies and support it needed to hold out alone.[12] Meanwhile, the Sieur Olivier Morel de La Durantaye, then commander of Fort de Buade, established in 1683 in present-day Saint Ignace, Michigan, was appointed to officially reconfirm France's possession of the Detroit River region. The Sieur de La Durantaye reached the Detroit River on 7 June 1687, and immediately proceeded to fulfill his mission.[13]

FRENCH-ABORIGINAL ALLIANCES

In the late seventeenth century, no Aboriginal villages remained in the vicinity of the Detroit River as a result of raids led by Five Nations Iroquois in the southern Great Lakes throughout the previous decades.[14] Only a few *coureurs de bois* (independent/illegal fur traders) had camps in the area.[15] However, several seminomadic Aboriginal groups undoubtedly hunted in the vicinity. In 1701, military entrepreneur Antoine Laumet de Lamothe Cadillac founded Fort Pontchartrain and immediately "invited" (Cadillac's perspective) Aboriginal peoples such as the Huron, Ottawa, Potawatomi, Miami, and others to settle in the Detroit River region. The establishment of Fort Pontchartrain was similar to the founding of Quebec and Montreal in that it occurred in a territory without a sizeable Aboriginal population.[16] As in the Saint Lawrence valley, several Aboriginal groups initially welcomed the French presence along the Detroit River and relocated closer to the French fort because it offered military protection and/or better access to French goods. A faction of Huron led by Chief Michipichy arrived in December of 1701 and built a village on the southwest side of Fort Pontchartrain, barely a few *arpents* (one arpent equals approximately 58 metres or 190 feet) from it. Cadillac reported that Michipichy told him that his people had been nearly exterminated by Five Nations Iroquois half a century earlier in Huronia because no French were living amongst them to offer protection. He believed that settling at Detroit would prevent such a terrible event from happening again.[17] Parties of Ottawa settled on the south shore of the Detroit River not long after the arrival of the Huron. Their motives for relocating were essentially commercial, for they were assured by Governor General Louis-Hector de Callière (1698–1703) and Cadillac that there would be plenty of French goods for them.[18] A group of Potawatomi from the northwest bank of Lake Michigan landed on the shores of the Detroit River in 1710 and built a village about one kilometre southwest of the fort.[19] Representatives of other Aboriginal peoples such as the Miami, Chippewa, and Fox sporadically inhabited the region, but their presence was never as significant as those of the Huron, Ottawa, and Potawatomi.

During the entire French regime, maintaining peaceful relations with these Aboriginal groups represented a major challenge for French colonial authorities. The French required a constant supply of goods to give away to their Aboriginal neighbours to secure alliances.[20] Gunpowder, guns, bullets, vermillion, knives, and clothes were the goods most sought after by Aboriginal people. They also had to provide services, such as repairing the firearms and tools of their Aboriginal allies. A shortage of such commodities or a failure to provide such services could result in detrimental consequences for the

French in the Upper Country. In 1747, more Aboriginals than usual gathered at Detroit to receive food and goods to hold their allegiance. This led to a significant shortage of supplies. Realizing that this situation could seriously jeopardize French-Aboriginal alliances, Paul-Joseph Le Moyne, Chevalier de Longueuil, commander of Fort Pontchartrain at the time, urged colonial administrators to send more of these commodities to Detroit without delay. In a report signed by Governor General Roland-Michel Barrin de La Galissonière, Marquis de La Galissonière (1747–49), and Intendant Gilles Hocquart (1729–48) in which Longueuil's request was mentioned, it is clear that the commander of Fort Pontchartrain had reason to believe that France's Aboriginal allies in the Detroit River region would soon find out about this shortage.[21] Longueuil understood that alliances in the Upper Country were fragile and could break quickly. A coalition of Huron of Sandusky led by Chief Orontony as well as Potawatomi, Miami, and most likely Ottawa, Chippewa, and Five Nations Iroquois had in fact already attacked Detroit by the time La Galissonière and Hocquart wrote their report.[22] Aware of the raids that were committed against the French settlements of the Detroit River region, Josué Dubois Berthelot de Beaucours, governor of Montreal (1733–48), wrote in a memoir that Aboriginals sneaked from behind the farms of the settlers and killed men, women, and livestock before burning down houses and barns.[23] Although Beaucours slightly exaggerated the outcome of the Aboriginal attacks, at least one French settler was slain while working on his farm.[24] This so-called plot of 1747 helped convince French colonial authorities to strengthen the Detroit settlements throughout the following years.

It is unlikely that the French would have been able to build a fort along the Detroit River without the initial approval of the Aboriginal peoples of the Upper Country, especially the Algonquian nations.[25] Yet, French colonial authorities still did not recognize or acknowledge the Aboriginal peoples of the Upper Country as the first owners of the land. Historian Gilles Havard has rightly specified that French "sovereignty" over the Aboriginal peoples of the Upper Country was primarily a matter of rhetoric aimed at other European empires in the New World, especially that of the British.[26] In other words, this rhetoric was a pretence to dissuade rivals from attempting to establish ties with the Aboriginal peoples of the Upper Country. The lack of French sovereignty over the Aboriginal peoples was certainly clear regarding their status as individuals living within the territory claimed by the French empire. The Aboriginal peoples of the Upper Country were perceived as residents of New France, but they were not subjects of the French Crown; they never gave up their sovereignty. Nor were they considered citizens (*régnicoles*) of the kingdom of France, especially not compared to the French settlers. Nevertheless, some aspects of the French rhetoric seemed to make sense to colonial administrators themselves, particularly the idea that the land in the Great Lakes region, no matter who lived on it, belonged to France as much as the land in the Saint Lawrence valley. For instance, French colonial authorities occasionally associated the Aboriginal people of the Detroit River region with the *domiciliés* of the Saint Lawrence valley, a term referring to Aboriginal people who settled in the Saint Lawrence valley *after* the French had begun to occupy it.[27] In 1721, Governor General Philippe de Rigaud, Marquis de Vaudreuil (1703–25), and Intendant Michel Bégon de la Picardière (1712–26) reported that the lands verbally "granted" to Aboriginal people at Detroit by representatives of the king would be returned to the Crown if their grantees abandoned them, a procedure that was common with the domiciliés in the Saint Lawrence valley.[28] The use of this term in reference to the position of the Detroit Aboriginals reveals how little deference colonial administrators had for their allies in the Upper Country when it came to the issue of land ownership.

The French method of encroaching on Aboriginal land in the Detroit River region was identical to that used in the Saint Lawrence valley. Through an official discourse of peace and alliance the French persuaded their Aboriginal allies to "informally" permit them to occupy lands, even though they did not believe that Aboriginal peoples had any rights over that land. In the short term, the ambiguity regarding land matters did not have dramatic consequences for the Aboriginal peoples. Not only were the alliances, as they existed, beneficial for all of their members, but as historian Robert J. Surtees puts it, the nature of French colonial society "and the nature of the economy which sustained it ... never drew the question of land ownership into sharp focus."[29] However, in the long term, by allowing French settlers to occupy more land, Aboriginal peoples progressively facilitated the expansion of the French colonial presence, even in a remote location like the Detroit River region.

CADILLAC'S DETROIT

The strategic position of the Detroit River, in regards to the establishment of France's claim over the Upper Country, became manifest in the 1680s after two brief English incursions in the area forced French colonial administrators to consider building a fort along the Detroit River. Nevertheless, despite this potential threat, French officials did not proceed to build a fort there for more than a decade. In fact, they closed several military forts and trading posts in the interior in 1696 because the value of the furs was decreasing due to the large numbers being exported to France. Cadillac, who dreamed of laying the foundations of a settlement along the Detroit River, travelled to France both in 1698 and 1699 to discuss his project with French authorities.[30] Cadillac was well acquainted with French interests in the Great Lakes as he had previously served as commander of Fort de Buade. To persuade his addressees, Cadillac stressed the peril of British infiltration in the Upper Country, which, he argued, could ultimately endanger the existence of New France as a whole. In this way, Cadillac convinced the minister of the Marine, Louis Phélypeaux, Comte de Pontchartrain, of the necessity of such an enterprise and ensured financial support for this project from the king.[31]

Between 1626 and 1663, and again between 1664 and 1674, the king of France had granted authority over the Saint Lawrence valley to *compagnies à charte* (or *compagnies propriétaires*), that is, chartered companies (or private companies).[32] These companies held much power. He made one such grant between 1626 and 1663 to the Company of One Hundred Associates (Compagnie des Cents Associés), which owned the Saint Lawrence valley as its *seigneurie, fief et justice*.[33] The term fief referred to the private ownership of the land, seigneurie and justice to public powers (military, diplomatic, legal, and economic). These public powers included the right to grant fiefs within its domain to individuals (*particuliers*), and these individuals would now be considered the *vassaux* of the company. In other words, these new fiefs were to be *seigneuries inféodées*, inferior in status and submissive to the domain of the company. Their owners were expected to show loyalty to the company, for instance, by providing military assistance if required. Legal historian Jean-François Niort explains that the territorial properties of these New France companies looked very much like some large fiefs that existed in France during the late Middle Ages and that were quasi-independent from the authority of the king.[34] Also, the public powers that these companies held (especially the power to create vassaux) meant that their structure was feudal. Up until the mid-sixteenth century, before what is often called the "domanial offensive" of the French monarchy designed to increase

Figure 1.1 *Le Mur des Noms* (Wall of Names), corner of McDougall Avenue and University Avenue East, Windsor, Ontario.

its control over all the territories of the kingdom (in the context of the rise of absolutism), one could find a feudal hierarchy of *seigneurs particuliers* in each region of France: virtually every seigneur particulier was the vassal of another seigneur particulier. During the domanial offensive, the king gradually imposed himself as the *seigneur-suzerain* or supreme lord of the whole kingdom.[35] In the process, French jurists began to make a clearer distinction between private ownership and public powers; indeed, for centuries, much confusion had existed regarding these two interrelated privileges.[36] The owners of fiefs kept the title of seigneurs, but they held fewer and fewer actual public powers. By the early seventeenth century, when France began to colonize the Saint Lawrence valley, the owners of fiefs in France had become subordinated to the state.[37] Therefore, in this context, the implementation by the French government of a feudal structure in New France during the first half of the seventeenth century, especially one quasi-independent from the authority of the king, appears a little surprising.[38]

Between 1649 and 1663, seigneuries particulières in the Saint Lawrence valley were granted by the governor general of New France,

Figure 1.2 *Le Mur des Noms* (Wall of Names), corner of McDougall Avenue and University Avenue East, Windsor, Ontario.

on behalf of the Company of One Hundred Associates.[39] However, starting in 1665, the intendant of New France shared the power to grant seigneuries particulières with the governor general. In seventeenth-century France, the intendants were the main representatives of the king (and absolutism) in the provinces. Therefore, this change was a clear indication that absolutism was now spreading to the New World. After 1674, when the king of France had taken authority over the Saint Lawrence valley away from chartered companies, the governor general and the intendant of New France now reported directly to Versailles, not to intermediaries. Any form of feudalism that had existed during the era of chartered companies vanished because of this centralization of public powers. By the end of the seventeenth century, most public powers were now in the hands of French colonial administrators at Quebec. To be sure, the seigneurs particuliers in the Saint Lawrence valley could no longer endeavour to develop a network of vassaux providing military assistance, for the state now controlled all things regarding military affairs.

By imposing itself as the seigneur-suzerain within its own kingdom in Europe, throughout the sixteenth and seventeenth centuries, the French monarchy was building a "royal domain." From a legal perspective, as historian Rafe Blaufarb writes, "little was written about the royal domain before the seventeenth century."[40] Charles Dumoulin (1500–66) was one of the first French jurists to ever address this question, in the first half of the sixteenth century. To him, the king of France enjoyed "proprietary ownership and supreme jurisdiction over the universality of the kingdom."[41] In other words, as Blaufard explains, Dumoulin's belief "in the paramountcy of the Crown was uncompromising."[42] Other French jurists later built on Dumoulin's ideas. In 1629, the Code Michau, as historian James Lowth Goldsmith writes, "asserted that any allods (unclaimed territories) that were not under the jurisdiction of individual lords came under the direct seigneurial and feudal authority of the king, *la (seigneurie) directe universelle*."[43] Not only did the Code Michau confirm that Louis XIII (1610–40) was the seigneur-suzerain of all the territories located within the kingdom of France, but also that he was the *seigneur direct* of every one of them not already owned by any seigneur particulier. In 1692, Louis XIV (1643–1715) repeated this claim. Now, there would be no land without a lord (*nulle terre sans seigneur*). As Blaufarb remarks, "the Crown offered little theoretical justification for the universal royal *directe*."[44]

On 24 July 1701, Cadillac reached the Detroit River region with a convoy that included twenty-five canoes carrying fifty-two *engagés* or hired men, fifty soldiers, one Recollet missionary, one Jesuit missionary, his son, and a few other men.[45] During the subsequent weeks, Cadillac and his men built a fort large enough to accommodate a church and several other buildings. Once the fort was completed, Cadillac named it Fort Pontchartrain, to honour his main supporter in Versailles.

When the king approved Cadillac's project in 1700, it was decided that the Compagnie du Canada, a chartered company established the same year, would be in charge of the administration of the fort. Cadillac, who was appointed to the position of commander of the fort, would in turn oversee diplomatic relations with Aboriginal peoples. As he wanted to hold both positions, Cadillac hoped that the company would soon encounter financial difficulties and be obliged to pass the administration of the fort on to him. Indeed, by 1703, the company had begun to experience financial difficulties and it became clear that it would have to cede its rights to Fort Pontchartrain.[46] Cadillac immediately seized the opportunity and the company officially handed him the control of Fort Pontchartrain in September 1705.[47]

In 1705, four French families settled at Detroit and the following year Cadillac made a trip to Montreal to organize a convoy of migrants. He came back with 216 people and some livestock.[48] Furthermore, between 1707 and 1709, he granted at least thirty tracts of land northeast of Fort Pontchartrain.[49] All of them measured two arpents wide by twenty arpents deep, which was slightly smaller than in the Saint Lawrence valley, where such tracts generally measured between two and four arpents wide by forty arpents deep.[50] The grantees did not build their houses directly on their lots as in the Saint Lawrence valley but instead inside Fort Pontchartrain.

From available sources, there is no doubt that between 1701 and 1705 the Compagnie du Canada controlled the fur trade at Detroit. However, those sources do not provide any information about the land question. The company did not grant any land to settlers during these years, but had it done so, who would have been considered the seigneur of Detroit? Would it have been the company (as seigneur particulier) or the king (as seigneur direct)? In other words, who "owned" the domain (*le domaine*) of the Detroit River region at that time? Was Detroit a seigneurie particulière (like the seigneuries of the Saint Lawrence valley) or a seigneurie directe, directly under the authority of the king? The 1705 agreement between the Companie du Canada and Cadillac did not include any details that could help shed light on these questions. The only reference to the "land" at Detroit reads as follows: "That in regard to the houses, buildings, warehouses, cleared lands, and other useful and necessary expenditures which the *Compagnie* claims to have incurred at the said place of Detroit, for which the Compagnie asks to be reimbursed by the said *sieur* de Lamothe, who claims he owes it nothing for all these things. They have left this point open and beg *Monseigneur Le Comte* de Pontchartrain [Minister of the Marine] to decide upon it."[51] The minister did address the land question with Cadillac, but not until a few years later.

When Cadillac took charge of the administration of Fort Pontchartrain, not only did he take for granted (or pretended to take for granted) that he was now the seigneur particulier of Detroit, but he also interpreted his "new power" in a feudal way. Fully aware that Versailles heavily relied on "military-entrepreneurs" like himself to expand its influence throughout the interior of North America, Cadillac endeavoured to improve his social status by further controlling the division of land in the Detroit River region.[52] To have any chance of success, he knew that he would have to continue to make his requests directly to the minister of the Marine and bypass French colonial administrators in the Saint Lawrence valley.

Between 1703 and 1710, the year he was appointed governor of Louisiana, Cadillac petitioned the minister on several occasions to be granted a *marquisat* (marquisate) or *comté* (county) in the Detroit River region.[53] In ancien régime France, a marquisat or comté was a seigneurie particulière that enjoyed a special title (*fief de dignité*). It was common for a marquisat or comté to be made up of several seigneuries particulières that had an inferior title or no special title at all.[54] During these years, Cadillac also made many requests to be granted the legal powers of high, medium, and inferior justice (*haute, moyenne, et basse justice*); the high justice essentially concerned serious crimes.[55] This confirmed that Cadillac was trying to replicate seigneurialism as it existed in ancien régime France and not as it had been established in the Saint Lawrence valley since the 1670s, where virtually all seigneuries particulières did not enjoy any special title and where seigneurs particuliers did not hold the power of high justice.

Historians agree that Cadillac did not succeed in getting a marquisat or comté in the Detroit River region. However, they do not agree regarding the question of whether or not Cadillac held the title of seigneur particulier of Detroit. In New France, at least in the Saint Lawrence valley after 1663, the governor general was in charge of granting seigneuries particulières to prominent individuals or Roman Catholic orders. There is no evidence that the governor general ever granted any seigneurie particulière at Detroit during the French regime, not even at the time of Cadillac. But since Cadillac enjoyed a special relationship with Versailles, it is not impossible that he may have received some kind of privilege directly from the king over the land in the Detroit River region.

On 14 June 1704, the minister of the Marine informed Cadillac that the king had given him the power to grant tracts of land to settlers at Detroit "if that helps to the development of the French colonial presence in the area."[56] However, the minister did not specify to whom those settlers would have to pay their seigneurial dues: to Cadillac or to the king? Nor did he mention who was the owner of the Detroit domain: Cadillac or the king? When he granted lands in the following years, Cadillac used a language suggesting that he was the seigneur particulier of Detroit. In his deeds, Cadillac stated that the king had given him the power to grant lands and that the grantees were required to pay their seigneurial dues to him ("*nous payera*") with a range of goods. He also desired that these goods be brought to his "castle" and "main manor" ("*en notre chateau et principal manoir*").[57] Furthermore, Cadillac obliged all grantees to use his seven-metre high windmill on Savoyard River (or "mills," as he seemed to anticipate building more than one) to grind their wheat into flour and, naturally, to pay rights for this.[58] Whether or not it was on purpose, Cadillac did not specify in these deeds if he was collecting taxes on behalf of the king or for himself. Normally, the person in charge of collecting taxes on behalf of the king in a seigneurie directe was the royal notary. However, there was no royal notary at Detroit until 1734.[59] Did the king expect Cadillac to send him the seigneurial dues collected in the Detroit River region? This question remains unanswered. Yet, it seems that the governor general and the intendant, who had not overseen land granting at Detroit, were under the impression that Cadillac owned the Detroit domain. In a letter to the minister of the Marine dated 15 November 1707 both government officials wrote that Cadillac was building a nice domain for himself ("*s'il continue il va s'y faire un beau Domaine*").[60] Although the two colonial administrators were often annoyed by Cadillac's behaviour, their comment in this letter did not suggest that they were surprised by the fact that he was conducting himself as the seigneur particulier of Detroit. As for the king, who was informed of the situation at Detroit by the minister, he seemed quite astonished to learn that Cadillac was "selling" lots within the fort as well as tracts of land around it, as if he were the "proprietor" of the place. Indeed, in 1708 the king required Cadillac to explain his behaviour.[61] Knowing that the king had already given the power to Cadillac to grant tracts of land at Detroit, on 14 June 1704, his reaction is indeed puzzling.

Through the process of land granting, Cadillac continued to use any means available to improve his social status. For example, in 1706 he informed the minister that military officers based at Fort Pontchartrain wished (or Cadillac claimed they wished) to be granted seigneuries particulières in the Detroit River region and to enjoy the powers of high, medium, and inferior justice, before adding that he hoped that "Detroit be erected in his favour."[62] Once again, Cadillac seemed to take for granted (or pretended to take for granted) that he already held the title of seigneur particulier and that he enjoyed the powers of high, medium, and inferior justice. He wanted these future seigneuries particulières to be located within his own property (to be transformed into a marquisat or comté) and their owners to declare an oath of allegiance to him. Clearly, what Cadillac had in mind was to establish a vassal relationship (*relation vassalique*) with these officers, and at the same time free himself as much as possible from the authority of the governor general and the intendant of New France.

In 1708, after finding that his requests to obtain more power and control over the Detroit River region seemed to increasingly fall on deaf ears, Cadillac asked the king for permission to cross the Atlantic and meet with the minister of the Marine; after all, this tactic had paid off in the late 1690s. However, Cadillac's special relationship with Versailles had already started to weaken and the king refused his request.[63] Indeed, the king was more and more irritated by Cadillac's efforts to limit his contacts with French colonial authorities in the Saint Lawrence valley. In addition, coincidentally the same year the king had received the report of François Clairambault d'Aigremont, naval commissary in Canada, whom he had appointed to visit the forts of the Upper Country. In this report, d'Aigremont severely criticized Cadillac's behaviour towards Aboriginal people, local settlers, and colonial authorities.[64] This report had a devastating effect on Cadillac's plans. Yet the minister of the Marine could not simply dismiss Cadillac, because in doing so it would have suggested that he had been wrong in the first place to support his plans in 1698 and 1699. To remedy the situation, he appointed Cadillac to the position of governor of Louisiana in 1710.

However, before Cadillac was removed from the position of commander of Fort Pontchartrain, in 1709, the minister had discussed the land question at Detroit with him. He revealed that the king now seemed to think of Cadillac as the owner of Detroit: "I have given the king an account of your proposal to hand over to him the land of Détroit [to which] His Majesty [replied that he] does not demand this of you, but he desires that you apply yourself to draw from it a large income."[65] If this were the case, Cadillac had clearly succeeded in completely bypassing the authority of both the governor general and the intendant of New France.

After his departure from Detroit, Cadillac put a stop to his requests to be granted a marquisat or comté. However, he did not give up on his pretentions to be the owner of a seigneurie particulière at that location and, as revealed by several sources, some confusion regarding this question of land ownership persisted until the 1720s. For example, in 1718, the Council of the Marine recommended that Cadillac be allowed to enjoy all the rights over the lands he granted at Detroit ("*qu'il jouira des droits sur les terres par lui concédées*").[66] In response to a request to be recognized as the owner and seigneur particulier of the Detroit River region, on 14 June 1720, the Council of the Marine explained to Cadillac that if the king wished to reintegrate Detroit into his domain, it would try to reach an agreement with him based on the 1711 inventory of his possessions at that location.[67] This suggested that Detroit was not under the direct authority of the king between 1705 and 1710, and that it had yet to be reintegrated into the royal domain. In a letter dated 19 May 1722, Cadillac found out that the king had finally proceeded to do just that ("*que Sa Majesté avait [finalement] réuni à son Domaine le fort du Détroit*").[68] Disappointed, Cadillac desperately asked to be granted the Detroit River region and enjoy the powers of high, medium, and inferior justice.[69] However, the king refused to listen to his request.

Detroit's French population decreased sharply during the 1710s. Many of the families that had migrated to Detroit in 1706 and had received a tract of land between 1707 and 1710 either left for other parts of the Upper Country or returned to the Saint Lawrence valley. The outbreak of the Fox Wars in the 1710s certainly had a negative impact on the French colonial presence in the Detroit River region. But the impact of Cadillac's questionable behaviour should not be overlooked. For several years, Cadillac had put in place something that looked like seigneurialism: he had granted lands *en censive* (individual tracts of land within a seigneurie particulière or directe), collected seigneurial dues, etc. However, based on d'Aigremont's report, he was charging taxes that were either illegal or much higher than those collected in the Saint Lawrence valley. Furthermore, it appears that Cadillac had not surveyed any of the lands that he had granted to migrants from the Saint Lawrence valley. In 1716, this reason alone was enough for French colonial administrators to cancel all the land titles granted by him at Detroit.[70] It is unclear whether or not landholders in the Detroit River region had to pay any seigneurial dues to Jacques-Charles Renaud Dubuisson, acting commander of Fort Pontchartrain between 1710 and 1715, or to Jacques-Charles de Sabrevois, commander in 1716. But two things are clear: no settler at Detroit held land titles in the years following the edict of 1716, and seigneurialism collapsed sometime between 1710 and 1716, before being reestablished some years later.

CONCLUSION

Cadillac wanted to control a specific region in the heart of the Upper Country, the Detroit River region. He designed a scheme to bypass the authority of French colonial administrators at Quebec, for he knew they would never agree with his idea of establishing a French settlement so far away from the Saint Lawrence valley, let alone give him power over this settlement. To have any chance to succeed with his project, Cadillac knew he would have to deal directly with Versailles. But for that, he would first have to convince the minister of the Marine of the benefits of his project. With the support of the minister, he obtained financial support from the king to establish Fort Pontchartrain on 24 July 1701. Initially he did not receive full authority over the fort and he immediately began to try to change that. A few years later, "ownership" of the fort was finally transferred to him. Yet, there was confusion at Versailles and Quebec about what this meant exactly. Cadillac did receive the permission to grant lands to French settlers along the Detroit River. However, it was never explicitly stated anywhere that he was allowed to keep for himself the seigneurial dues that he would collect from the settlers. Cadillac took advantage of this ambiguity to attempt to gain much power over the Detroit River region, to be its marquis or comte, and build a feudal hierarchy with himself at the top. Unfortunately for him, his scheme never fully materialized. Before the end of the decade, he lost support from Versailles, and was removed from the position of commander of Fort Pontchartrain in 1710. Moreover, in 1716, the land titles he had granted to settlers were all cancelled by French colonial authorities. Cadillac certainly planted the roots of the French colonial presence in the Detroit River region, but his scheme also convinced French colonial authorities at Quebec to never allow any individual to try to gain power over territory in the Upper Country ever again.

2

Seigneurial Tenure and Landholders

In the early eighteenth century, Cadillac had founded Detroit without any significant support from French colonial authorities at Quebec. Instead, he had dealt primarily with authorities at Versailles. Between the 1730s and 1750s, there was a second attempt at developing the French colonial presence in the Detroit River region. However, in order to prevent the earlier confusion regarding land ownership, this time the governor general and the intendant of New France would play key roles in the venture, notably by overseeing land administration at Detroit on behalf of the king.

THE 1734 RENEWAL OF SEIGNEURIAL TENURE

In the early 1720s, Governor General Vaudreuil and Intendant Bégon wished to strengthen the French colonial presence at Detroit by means of establishing more reliable land administration. However, the behaviour of Cadillac (regardless of whether or not he was truly *seigneur particulier* of Detroit) had convinced them that granting a *seigneurie particulière*, especially so far away from Montreal, was not the best way to proceed. They wanted to avoid a repeat of the situation that had occurred with Cadillac, yet they knew that attempting to increase the French population at Detroit without formally granting tracts of land was futile. Therefore, they proposed to only grant tracts *en censive*. This meant that instead of granting a property to a seigneur particulier who would be responsible for dividing it into smaller lots for prospective settlers, the king would grant individual tracts of land directly to settlers. In addition, as Vaudreuil and Bégon recommended, each grantee would report directly to the king through one of his representatives on the ground instead of reporting to a seigneur particulier.[1] In this way, Vaudreuil and Bégon proposed to convert Detroit into a *seigneurie directe*.

The king had been the *seigneur-suzerain* of New France since 1663 and, as such, all the territories claimed by France that had not been granted to seigneurs particuliers belonged directly to him, at least according to French law. These vast territories were altogether said to be part of the royal domain (*domaine du roi*).[2] The Detroit River region officially became part of the royal domain when René-Robert Cavelier, Sieur de La Salle, took possession of it on behalf of Louis XIV in 1682.

In a seigneurie directe of the royal domain, the local representative of the king was the royal notary.[3] In the Saint Lawrence valley, the first royal notary was appointed in 1663. After that, a clear distinction was established between royal notary (*notaire royal*) and seigneurial notary (*notaire seigneurial*). The first was appointed by the king, or one of his representatives, to oversee legal affairs within a territory directly under royal control. The latter, appointed by a seigneur particulier (or sometimes, in the Saint Lawrence valley, by the intendant, especially during the eighteenth century), worked within a specific seigneurie particulière. Consequently, the geographical jurisdiction of a royal notary was often larger than that of a seigneurial notary.[4]

On 22 May 1734, Intendant Gilles Hocquart appointed Robert Navarre to the position of royal notary at Detroit.[5] Born in 1709 at Villeroy, in France, Navarre was educated in Paris and was already signing legal documents at Detroit at the age of twenty.[6] For Navarre, as Governor General Beauharnois and Intendant Hocquart recorded, this new appointment meant that he was now the receiver of seigneurial dues in the domain of His Majesty at Detroit ("*Receveur du Domaine de Sa Majesté*").[7] As such, Navarre was the person to whom the French settlers of the area were required to pay the *cens et rentes* and other seigneurial dues. Navarre's title of royal notary and the responsibilities that came with it are confirmed in several letters of official correspondence. A memoir dated 16 August 1736, stated that Navarre was the "*Receveur du Domaine au Detroit*" and that his task consisted of receiving all seigneurial dues of the royal domain there.[8] The seigneurial dues that Navarre had to collect were altogether called "the return" (*la recette*).[9] Each spring, Navarre had to total the return and send it to the intendant in Montreal.[10] In addition to his position as royal notary, Navarre was also appointed subdelegate of

Figure 2.1 View of the Moran residence, a one-story wood frame building with garden in front, located on Woodbridge Street between Saint Antoine and Hastings streets, Detroit, Michigan. The house was built in 1734 and was still standing in 1883.

Intendant Hocquart at Detroit in 1743.[11] The role of subdelegate consisted essentially in reporting to the intendant about local civil affairs. Although it was officially the governor general of New France who granted tracts of land at Detroit on behalf of the king through the commander of the fort, it was not the responsibility of the latter to collect seigneurial dues from settlers. The commander of Detroit was changed every three years between 1734 and 1760, and he was solely in charge of granting land.[12] Navarre, as royal notary, was accountable for ensuring the collection of seigneurial dues.

When Robert Navarre moved to Detroit, in the late 1720s, a handful of French *voyageurs* (fur traders who travelled to the interior, usually on behalf of merchants and with the permission of French colonial authorities) from the Saint Lawrence valley also relocated there. Some were accompanied by their spouse and children and others were bachelors. Virtually all of them took up residence inside the fort. Since the cancellation of Cadillac's land grants in 1716 no official grant had been made. Historian Silas Farmer accurately stated that commanders of Fort Pontchartrain such as "La Forest, Tonty, and Sabrevois all made grants [in the 1710s and 1720s]," but that "none of them had authority to do so."[13] Such grants were therefore invalid. In 1730, Commander Henri-Louis Deschamps de Boishébert informed colonial administrators of complaints by French residents of Detroit regarding their inability to secure official land grants.[14] In 1732, both Beauharnois and Hocquart observed that the Detroit settlement had not developed much even though it had been founded more than thirty years earlier.[15] In 1734, they finally acknowledged the limitations of informal land granting.[16] In an effort to resolve this problem, they first strengthened the administrative structure of the Detroit settlement by establishing it as a seigneurie directe and by appointing a royal notary. The next step consisted of giving the commanders of Fort Pontchartrain the power to grant tracts of land en censive on behalf of the king. The plan proposed by Vaudreuil and Bégon in the early 1720s was finally taking form.

SEIGNEURIAL GRANTS

Merely a month after Robert Navarre became royal notary, French settler Charles Chauvin, who then resided within the fort, was officially granted a tract of land along the Detroit River. On 16 June 1734, Beauharnois and Hocquart certified in Montreal that Chauvin had recently obtained a tract of land on the north shore of the Detroit River from the commander of Fort Pontchartrain. Chauvin's deed revealed that most French settlers at Detroit had hesitated to clear the lands in the vicinity of the fort because they did not enjoy official land titles.[17] The tract of land that Chauvin received measured two *arpents* wide by forty arpents deep. To avoid losing his title, Chauvin was required to build a dwelling and maintain it (*"tenir feu et lieu"*). As the settlement grew, he would also be asked to help construct roads (*"les chemins qui seront juger necessaires"*) and erect fences that separated the properties from one another (*"fera les clotures mitoyennes"*).[18] Such obligations bore a resemblance to the *corvée* regularly imposed on holders of censives in the Saint Lawrence valley and in France.[19]

The seigneurial dues that Charles Chauvin had to pay were listed in his deed. His cens was set at one *sol* per fronting arpent and his rente was fixed at twenty sols for every twenty square arpents. In total, Chauvin's annual cens et rente amounted to four *livres* for the size of his land plus two sols and two *minots* of wheat for its frontage. These numbers corresponded to the average cens et rente paid by *censitaires* in the seigneuries particulières of the Saint Lawrence valley.[20] Moreover, the deed mentioned that if Chauvin sold his tract of

Figure 2.2 Statue of Robert Navarre, the Westin Book Cadillac Hotel, Detroit, Michigan.

land to another settler, the king would be entitled to a fraction of the sale price, a tax known as the *lods et ventes* in the Custom of Paris (*Coutume de Paris*). In the seigneuries particulières of the Saint Lawrence valley, the lods et ventes usually amounted to one-twelfth of the total sale price.[21] Robert Navarre later confirmed that it was the same fraction at Detroit.[22]

The deed of Charles Chauvin's land grant further revealed that he was required to grind his flour at the *moulin banal*, that is, at his seigneur's mill.²³ Several windmills had been built on the north shore of the Detroit River prior to the establishment of Detroit as a seigneurie directe in 1734. When he commanded Fort Pontchartrain, Cadillac built a windmill that was supposed to be used as the local moulin banal, but it was abandoned after his departure.²⁴ In 1721, at the age of seventy-four, windmill builder Léonard Paillé dit Paillard was transported from Montreal to Detroit to supervise the construction of a windmill.²⁵ The building of this windmill was probably a private enterprise rather than sponsored by the king.²⁶ Alphonse de Tonty, Baron de Paludy, who commanded Fort Pontchartrain from 1717 until his death in 1727, also built a windmill near the fort. The construction date of this windmill is unknown, but Jean-Frédéric Phélypeaux, Comte de Maurepas, referred to it in the letter he wrote in 1731 to Beauharnois and Hocquart. The widow of Tonty had asked Maurepas to deal with the properties of her defunct husband at Detroit which included two houses and a windmill. Maurepas's letter also revealed that Tonty's widow suggested selling the windmill to the king since the residents of Fort Pontchartrain needed it.²⁷ It is uncertain whether the king had sponsored the construction of a moulin banal at Detroit in 1734 or if he had requisitioned a previously constructed windmill to be used for this purpose. Likewise, Chauvin's deed did not specify the *banalité*. In the Saint Lawrence valley, the banalité had been fixed in 1667 at one-fourteenth of the grain ground.²⁸ The banalité at Detroit was presumably the same after 1734.

Apparently, the only clause of Chauvin's deed that differed from such legal documents produced in the Saint Lawrence valley concerned the possibility of paying his cens et rentes with furs. Given that access to currency was difficult at Detroit, it was not reasonable for the receiver of seigneurial dues to expect being paid this way by the settlers. Therefore, this alternative was offered to the censitaires of the seigneurie directe only until currency would become available.²⁹ On 6 October 1734, after having granted a series of tracts of land along the Detroit River, Beauharnois and Hocquart reported that these grants were almost identical to those made by seigneurs particuliers within their own properties, that only the temporary option of paying the cens et rentes with furs distinguished them.³⁰ In this event, Robert Navarre had been instructed to hire voyageurs to transport these furs to Montreal.³¹ It is notable that paying the cens et rentes with furs remained commonplace at Detroit until the end of the French regime because several settlers had no access to currency.

One seigneurial due about which Chauvin's deed contained no information was the fishing and hunting rights tax, presumably because it did not exist at Detroit. Seigneurs particuliers in the Saint Lawrence valley frequently imposed a fishing and hunting rights tax on their censitaires. This duty was often mentioned in deeds. But as historical geographer R. Cole Harris contends, this tax was "almost impossible to collect, for the seigneur [particulier] had no way of knowing."[32] Trying to keep a close watch on the hunting and fishing activities of the French settlers at Detroit was also likely impossible.[33]

THE NORTH SHORE

In 1734, sixteen other tracts of land were granted on the north shore of the Detroit River.[34] All of their titles were essentially duplicates of Chauvin's deed. The width of these tracts extended from 2 to 5 arpents. They all had a depth of 40 arpents which reveals that the ratio of the frontage to the depth of these properties varied between 1:20 and 1:8. Most censives in the Saint Lawrence valley had a ratio of approximately 1:10.[35] Therefore, holders of land titles at Detroit in 1734 had tracts similar in size to those owned by settlers in the Saint Lawrence valley.[36] The seventeen lots covered altogether 57.5 arpents (3.7 kilometres) of the frontage along the Detroit River east of Fort Pontchartrain. Today, they would stretch from the Detroit-Windsor Tunnel to Picnic Way, the bridge leading to Belle Isle. Similar to the Saint Lawrence valley, where individual tracts of land were aligned perpendicularly to rivers and stretched back from these into the interior between two parallel lines, the seventeen tracts granted in 1734 extended back from the Detroit River through present-day Fisher Freeway in downtown Detroit. In 1736, sixteen additional tracts laid out the same way were granted, all of which measured 4 arpents wide by 40 arpents deep.[37] Combined, the grants of 1734 and 1736 extended more than 120 arpents (7 kilometres) east of the fort. They reached the area where Engel Memorial Park is located today. One tract of land was granted both in 1743 and 1745, also on the north shore of the Detroit River. These tracts were respectively 2 and 3 arpents wide. The former was a tract first granted in 1734 that had been returned to the king because its grantee had failed to build and maintain a dwelling on it.[38] The new holder of this lot was Jean Chapoton, a surgeon who had lived within Fort Pontchartrain for many years. Three more tracts were granted on the north side in

1747. Two of them had a width of 2 arpents whereas the third one measured 3 arpents wide. Robert Navarre received the latter.[39] Of thirty-seven tracts of land granted since 1734, only those of Navarre and Laurent Eustache Gamelin, also granted in 1747, were located on the opposite side of Fort Pontchartrain, between the fort and the Potawatomi village.[40]

During his first visit to Detroit in 1749, military engineer Gaspard-Joseph Chaussegros de Léry Jr observed that French dwellings had been established on the north shore of the Detroit River from the Potawatomi village to a place called Presqu'Isle which corresponded to the location of Engel Memorial Park.[41] Chaussegros de Léry further added that those dwellings, which included houses and barns, were to be found close to the waterway. This meant that every settler living along the Detroit River could easily reach the fort or visit neighbours, as in the Saint Lawrence valley.[42]

Chaussegros de Léry's remarks about Detroit confirmed a new reality: a portion of its French population now lived outside Fort Pontchartrain, on farms located on adjacent tracts of land. The gradual process of transition from a French community confined within the fort to one spreading to the neighbouring lands had begun following the establishment of the seigneurie directe in 1734. In 1740, Pierre-Jacques Payen de Noyan, then commander of Detroit, had already observed this transition when he calculated that about half of the area's one hundred French families lived on farms.[43]

THE SOUTH SHORE

In April of 1749, following the so-called Huron plot of 1747 and the outbreak of King George's War, the Marquis de La Galissonière, then governor general of New France, recommended strengthening the seigneurie directe of the Detroit River region.[44] The plan he proposed involved transporting French families from the Saint Lawrence valley to Detroit through one of the convoys leaving Montreal for the Upper Country each spring. On their arrival, migrants would be granted a tract of land and provided with tools and livestock to cultivate the land. As well, financial assistance would be given to help them become self-sufficient.[45] La Galissonière's plan, advertised in each parish of the Saint Lawrence valley, was aimed at families rather than single men and it stipulated that anyone benefiting from the king's support who traded in furs at Detroit rather than work the land would instantly lose this help. Three convoys carrying French families left Montreal for Detroit between 1749 and 1751.[46] Altogether, 192 French people – 86 adults and 106 children – settled at Detroit as a result of this effort. Most of them were from different areas of the government of Montreal but a handful came from the governments of Trois-Rivières and Quebec. Not only did these convoys have an impact on the Detroit settlements by increasing the local French population, but their arrival also led to the granting of tracts of land on the south shore of the Detroit River for the first time. Still, their importance should not be exaggerated.

By the late 1730s, the French presence in the Detroit River region had become stable as a result of the establishment of the seigneurie directe, which had standardized land administration along the Detroit River. More French people had come to Detroit in 1706 than between 1749 and 1751, but due to the lack of stability with regards to land administration at the time of Cadillac, few of Detroit's first settlers had established roots there. Later, when the convoys reached Detroit, the migrants found themselves not in an unstructured place but in a society that did not differ much from their place of origin. The convoys definitely had a positive impact in settling the area, but rather than representing a turning point in the growth of Detroit they contributed to a movement that was already underway.

When the first convoy reached Detroit in 1749, French authorities were planning on granting each family both a tract of land along the Detroit River and a lot within Fort Pontchartrain to build a house, so that the new settlers would live in a fortified village, even though several settlers had begun to build farms along the Detroit River in the 1730s. From their homes inside the fort they were expected to travel to their respective tracts of land on a daily basis to work their fields and feed their livestock. In the Saint Lawrence valley, as Harris observes, such land organization was not popular among the habitants, who preferred to reside directly on their tracts of land because this way they "were closer to their livestock than if they walked to their farm every day from a compact agricultural village."[47] Still, for reasons of safety French colonial administrators attempted on several occasions to gather the settlers of the Saint Lawrence valley within villages. In the 1660s, Louis XIV advised Intendant Jean Talon (1665–68) that the colony would be safe only once the settlers were brought together in villages.[48] However, such land organization was ill-designed for the physical environment of the Saint Lawrence valley. Following the

Lachine massacre by Five Nations Iroquois in 1689, colonial administrators again promoted without success the construction of villages for settlers. They argued that French houses located along the Saint Lawrence River between Montreal and Trois-Rivières should be gathered within compact villages to reduce the risks of being burned down by Five Nations Iroquois.[49]

At Detroit, the safety issue behind the idea of gathering the migrants of the convoys within Fort Pontchartrain was certainly motivated by the events of 1747. But since the newcomers were accustomed to living directly on their tracts of land, and the geography of the Detroit River region was well suited to replicate the system of land organization of the Saint Lawrence valley, they immediately voiced their refusal to be confined within the fort when they arrived at their destination. Chaussegros de Léry, who had travelled with the migrants, confirmed that it would be difficult to persuade the newcomers not to live on their own lands.[50] The migrants claimed that by not residing on their farms they could not protect their crops and livestock from Aboriginal people and wild animals.[51] In the end, French officials allowed the newcomers to build their houses on their tracts of land.[52] Their decision directly contributed to increasing the number of French houses aligned side by side along the Detroit River.

SEVERAL SETTLEMENTS

Permitting the migrants of the convoys to settle on their own tracts of land also fostered the development of four divisions of French land organization called *côtes* or *rangs*. In the eighteenth-century Saint Lawrence valley, rural areas were predominantly divided into côtes. As Harris puts it, a côte was "a short line of settlement not necessarily on the river."[53] Such a line of settlement generally included dozens of long and narrow tracts of land aligned side by side that often made up a whole seigneurie particulière. These lines of settlement were usually "isolated enough so that its inhabitants thought of the settlement as a distinct community."[54] The oldest côte of the Detroit River region was the Côte du Nord-Est, located northeast of Fort Pontchartrain. Its roots traced back to the Cadillac's grants of 1707. However, it became an actual côte only in 1734, after settlers began to build houses on their tracts of land. This côte extended as far northeast as Grosse Pointe at the end of the French regime.[55] The Côte du Nord-Ouest, created in 1747 from the land grants to Robert

Navarre and Laurent Eustache Gamelin, was situated west of the fort.[56] Due to its proximity to the Potawatomi village, it was often referred to as the Côte des Poutéouatamis or Côte des Pous. In 1764, possibly to accommodate the expansion of the Côte des Pous, the Potawatomi abandoned their village and moved fifty kilometres further south, to the north shore of the River Raisin.[57] Nevertheless, for decades after the departure of the Potawatomi the French interchangeably used these three names to designate this côte. The Petite Côte, located on the south shore of the Detroit River, where the town of La Salle stands today, was established in 1749. The word *petite* in its name is misleading because it was the second longest côte of the Detroit River region after the Côte du Nord-Est. Due to a series of bad crops, it was nicknamed "Côte de Misère" (misery settlement) by its residents.[58] The Côte du Sud, also known as the Côte de la Pointe de Montréal was founded in 1750. It was located north of Petite Côte on the south shore of the Detroit River, across from Fort Pontchartrain. The Huron mission of L'Assomption, established in 1748, bordered the Côte du Sud to the south, therefore separating it from the Petite Côte, and the Ottawa village, established in 1702, bordered it to the east.[59] The residents of Detroit clearly distinguished each of these côtes as testified by the fact that long after the fall of New France land transactions in the area often indicated in which of these côtes the property being sold was located.

Chaussegros de Léry's map of 1754 shows that these four côtes covered more than 430 arpents (twenty-six kilometres) along the shores of the Detroit River. On 14 September 1761, British officer William Johnson wrote that from the fort he "took a ride before dinner up toward the Lake St. Clair" and on his way the "road runs along the river side, which is all settled thickly nine miles."[60] The seigneuries particulières along the Saint Lawrence River usually had a width of less than 168 arpents (ten kilometres).[61] This means that the seigneurie directe of Detroit was larger than most seigneuries particulières fronting the Saint Lawrence River.

In the Saint Lawrence valley, the côtes were also designated as "rows" (rangs).[62] The rows referred to the fact that censives within the seigneuries particulières were aligned in rows (*en rangées*). By the end of the seventeenth century, new rows emerged immediately behind the ones fronting the water. These were called "rear rows" (*arrières-rangs, seconds-rangs,* or *rangs d'arrière-fleuve*). The rows and rear rows of censives were usually separated by a road parallel to the river, to help the settlers living inland to get around. Harris asserts that in the Saint Lawrence valley of the 1750s, "there were second ranges in almost all riparian seigneuries [particulières]."[63] Such settlements were described as "*côtes à deux rangs d'habitations.*"[64] In the seigneurie directe of the Detroit River region, land occupation was not sufficiently developed by the end of the French regime to grant tracts of land behind those facing the water, although the day rear rows of censives would be needed in Detroit did not seem far away. On 12 April 1759, the last commander of Fort Pontchartrain, François-Marie Picoté de Belestre, granted a tract of land to Guillaume Bernard and required him to reserve an eleven-metre-wide parcel behind his tract, extending the entire width of it, for the construction of a road to facilitate transportation for the settlers who would eventually occupy the land at the rear of his farm.[65]

FAMILIES, LIVESTOCK, AND FUTURE PLANS FOR DETROIT

In 1750, 450 French settlers lived along the Detroit River. This total did not include the 100 troops positioned there or the 33 slaves held by the French population. Neither did it count the passing voyageurs.[66] In 1666, the regions of Quebec and Montreal, settled by 1608 and 1642, had populations of 2,135 and 625 people respectively.[67] Detroit experienced a slower demographic growth during its first decades of existence than its counterparts of the Saint Lawrence valley. Yet this discrepancy overshadows two important features of Detroit: its balanced sex ratio and its significant livestock holdings. French females accounted for 46 percent of the population of Detroit in 1750. This was more than the regions of Quebec (36.7 percent) and Montreal (38.6 percent) in 1666. Detroit residents possessed 211 oxen and 471 cows, for a total of 682 cattle. In 1666, 3,107 cattle could be found in the Saint Lawrence valley.[68] Therefore, each French settler held on average more cattle at Detroit in 1750 (1.5 cattle) than in the Saint Lawrence valley in 1666 (1.1 cattle). Furthermore, the French settlers at Detroit had 160 horses in 1750 whereas only 96 horses lived in the entire Saint Lawrence valley in 1681.[69] This balanced sex-ratio and the important presence of livestock explain the fact that 1,070 square arpents were under cultivation at Detroit in 1750, producing altogether 56,200 livres of wheat and 2,681 livres of oats.

Robert Navarre carefully recorded all the French individuals who became landholders in the Detroit River region between 1734 and 1760. Some of the habitants who received a tract of land on the north shore (Côte du Nord-Est and Côte des Pous) in 1750 included, for example: Joseph Cardinal, Gabriel Paillé, Michel Quintin, François Languedoc, Antoine Cueillerier, Guillaume Bernard, Pierre Tremblay, Pierre Tremblay Jr, Ambroise Tremblay, Louis Tremblay Jr, Charles Grimard, Hyacinthe Dehêtres, Gonzague Dehêtres, Jean Fafard, Claude Gouin, Jean Rivard, Antoine Gignac, Joseph La Feuillade, and others. On the south shore (Petite Côte and Côte du Sud), even more French men became landholders that year. The list included, among others: Louis Dehêtres, Pierre La Butte, Jacques Pillette, Joseph Pillette, Laurent Parent, Joseph L'Esperance, Vital Goyau, Baptiste Goyau, Guillaume Goyau, Pierre Réaume, Hyacinthe Réaume, Jacques Gaudet, François Janisse, Joseph Mailloux, Pierre Desnoyers, Louis Gervais, Joseph Poupard, Charles Lamarre, Antoine Robert, Pierre Meloche, Louis Villers, Charles Porlier, Charles Moran, Michel Landry, and Simon Bergeron.[70] Many of them already had roots in the Detroit River region while some were recent migrants. Most married French women, had large families, and have descendants who still live in the Detroit River region today.[71]

In 1749, Chaussegros de Léry proposed that a new "colony" be established at Detroit (*"former une nouvelle colonie au détroit"*), suggesting that a new administrative body be created in the heart of the Upper Country.[72] In 1757, after the outbreak of the Seven Years' War, French military officer Louis-Antoine de Bougainville similarly recommended that the king make Detroit the centre of a new government (*"il faut le mettre en gouvernement"*).[73] Although the plans suggested by Chaussegros de Léry and Bougainville were not carried out before the fall of New France, they revealed that Detroit by the 1750s had begun to emerge as a sizeable French population centre in the middle of the Great Lakes.

CONCLUSION

Up until 1734, the question of landownership at Detroit remained ambiguous and this dissuaded many residents of Fort Pontchartrain from fully engaging in farming activities. The establishment of the seigneurie directe, followed by the appointment of Robert Navarre

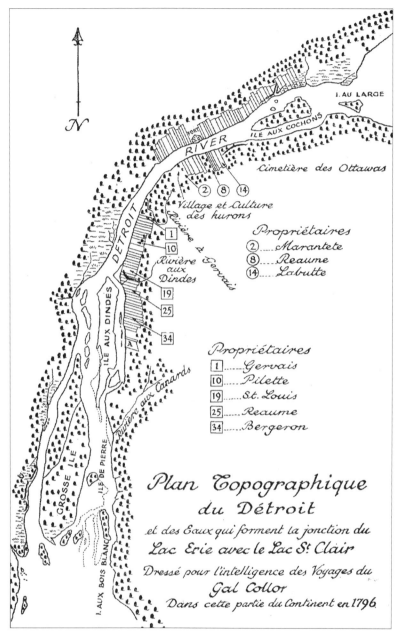

Figure 2.3 Gaspard-Joseph Chaussegros de Léry Jr's 1754 map of the Detroit River region. (Note: Collor simply replicated Chaussegros de Léry's 1754 map in 1796.)

as royal notary, dramatically strengthened the French colonial presence in the Detroit River region. Before long, dozens of French families moved from Fort Pontchartrain to their tracts of land. This process was markedly accelerated between 1749 and 1751 when the king sponsored the transportation of families from the Saint Lawrence valley to Detroit. As a result of this effort, which led to the granting of land titles on the south shore of the Detroit River for the first time, two new côtes were established.

On the eve of the British conquest, Detroit had clearly become a society that resembled many of the rural settlements in the Saint Lawrence valley. Although its status as seigneurie directe certainly distinguished it from all the seigneuries particulières of the Saint Lawrence valley, its fundamental organization was virtually identical. However, as we shall see, because of its remote location, the seigneurie directe of Detroit took a rather different path than that of the seigneuries particulières of the Saint Lawrence valley after the British conquest.

3

Trespassers, Aboriginal Deeds, and Taxation

It may also be proper to erect, as proposed in the report of the governor and chief justice, a court at Detroit, because the settlers there, amounting to about seven thousand persons, are populating very fast, and extending themselves, as the people of New York are, towards each other. An objection may be taken to this, that it is not policy to encourage back settlements.[1]

Sir James Marriott, King of England's advocate-general (1764–1778), 1774

The establishment of a *seigneurie directe* in the Detroit River region in 1734 had an important impact of the growth of the local French population by facilitating land grants. Although they lived on the edge of the French empire, the French settlers at Detroit developed a deep connection to the lands that the commanders of Fort Pontchartrain and the governor generals of New France had granted to them on behalf of the king. This relationship to the land did not disappear after the fall of New France, and the French presence continued to expand along the Detroit River after the British conquest.

On 12 December 1776, George Morgan, an American spy positioned at Fort Detroit, reported that on the north shore of the Detroit River the settlements extended "all the way up to lake Sinclair to a place called Grosspoint which is 9 miles, & down the river on the same side 3 miles to the River Rouge" and that on the south shore it stretched "up the river 3 miles to McDougal's Island (Belle Isle); & down the river 12 miles."[2] According to Morgan, at the beginning of the American Revolution the French farms covered more than forty-three kilometres (up from twenty-six kilometres in 1754) along the shores of the Detroit River. This meant that the four *côtes* in the area had expanded since the end of the French regime. French land occupation in the Detroit River region continued to spread after the British conquest because the French settlers preserved a deep connection to the land. However, with a difference, for now its French population was obliged to stubbornly defend its land rights.

THE BRITISH CONQUEST

In the Saint Lawrence valley of the second half of the eighteenth century, French agriculture was "extensive" as opposed to "intensive." This meant that rather than adopting more effective and productive farming methods, each new generation of farmers sought to acquire more lands within the existing *seigneuries particulières* to cope with the increasing needs of their growing population.[3] French agriculture in the Saint Lawrence valley remained extensive even after the abolition of the seigneurial system of land tenure in Quebec (then known as Canada East) which occurred in 1854.[4] Similarly in the Detroit River region, French agriculture did not evolve towards intensive methods before the second half of the nineteenth century. With every new generation the local French population, as in the Saint Lawrence valley, required more lands to meet its growing needs. However, after the British conquest, the French king could no longer claim the Upper Country as part of his royal domain. This new situation resulted in the sudden demise of the seigneurie directe of the Detroit River region. In these circumstances, the French settlers of Detroit faced problems regarding land matters that their counterparts in the Saint Lawrence valley, who resided in seigneuries particulières, did not encounter following the fall of New France.[5]

During the short period between the capitulation of Montreal, on 8 September 1760, and the Royal Proclamation, issued on 7 October 1763, British officials were not very concerned with the question of French land occupation in the Upper Country. However, the French settlers of the Detroit River region were apprehensive about the future of their settlements under this new regime. Fort Detroit's second British commander, Donald Campbell (1760–62), who was later killed during Pontiac's uprising, wrote on 10 March 1761 to Jeffery Amherst, commander-in-chief in North America from 1760 to 1763, that "the principal inhabitants [at Detroit] have desired me to transmitt to your Excellency an address setting forth the present state of their country."[6] A month later, Amherst replied that the French at Detroit benefitted from all the same rights as those in the Saint Lawrence valley, as stipulated in the articles of capitulation.[7] This indicated, among other things, that their rights to private property were protected. Besides, Amherst himself was not against the colonization of the Upper Country through the establishments of British settlements. Preoccupied by the huge size of the interior of the continent, Amherst actually recommended the establishment of a British colony at Detroit to better ensure its control.[8] John Bradstreet, who briefly served as commander of Fort Detroit in 1764, also advocated for the colonization of the area for a few years.[9] Other British officials also discussed the possibility of colonizing the Detroit River region in the 1770s, but the American Revolution forced them to focus on the colonies of the Atlantic seaboard before encouraging any new colonial endeavours.[10] Yet, such proposals would in reality have been difficult to execute because the British Crown had already determined that the interior of North America would become an Indian Country (or reserve) until the signing of treaties of land cession with the Aboriginal peoples, a process that was expected to take decades to complete.[11]

FRENCH FARMS IN INDIAN COUNTRY

The proposal to prevent encroachment on Aboriginal lands on the western frontier was first considered at the end of the Seven Years' War (1756–63). British military commanders and superintendents of Indian Affairs promised to protect Aboriginal lands from British encroachment after the war.[12] Although this proposal, in all likelihood, was an effort to bring Aboriginal peoples of the interior into the British camp rather than an act of generosity, it evolved rapidly. Both the Board of Trade and the Privy Council approved the creation of Indian Country by 1761.[13] In May 1763, as historian Jack M. Sosin asserts, Charles Wyndham, Second Earl of Egremont and secretary of state for the Southern Department of the Kingdom of Great Britain, made the formal suggestion of "reserving the interior for the use of the Indians for the present."[14] While it was decided that Indian Country would be protected from the establishment of European settlements, for the time being, its civil status had yet to be clarified. A few high-ranking British officials believed that Indian Country had to be part of the civil jurisdiction of one of the four governments of British North America born out of the Treaty of Paris signed on 10 February 1763 (Quebec, East Florida, West Florida, and Grenada).

For instance, Wyndham proposed that Indian Country be related to the government of Quebec for civil legal matters.[15] In the end, however, when the Royal Proclamation was signed, shortly after the outbreak of Pontiac's uprising, which occurred on 9 May 1763, Indian Country was left out of any civil jurisdiction – it was simply depicted as a territory located on the outskirts of the newly created Province of Quebec.[16]

The Royal Proclamation explicitly forbade the establishment of European settlements in Indian Country. The only possible way to settle on portions of its lands was through treaties of land cession signed by both the Crown and the Aboriginal peoples concerned. First and foremost, this decree aimed at British colonists of the Atlantic coast to prevent their invasion of Aboriginal lands, but the French in North America were not exempted from this ruling. In the Detroit River region, this type of treaty of land cession was first signed only in 1786.[17] Therefore, not only was Detroit excluded from the Province of Quebec, the geographical limits of which corresponded roughly to the Saint Lawrence valley, but in theory its very existence became illegal because the British Crown had not yet dispossessed the Aboriginal peoples of the area through treaties of land cession. Besides, by this time the rights to private property of Detroit's French population were not guaranteed because the articles of capitulation no longer applied to the Upper Country.

During the French regime, the only accepted method to acquire a tract of land within the seigneurie directe of the Detroit River region was to address a request to the commander of Fort Pontchartrain. After having approved of the request, the commander would grant the settler a tract of land and then send the deed corroborating the grant to the governor general of New France for approval. Once this deed was confirmed, the grantee was required to pay seigneurial dues to the royal notary of Detroit, Robert Navarre, who collected them on behalf of the king. However, after the British conquest, the French population established along the shores of the Detroit River continued to grow and the community needed more lands. As the French knew of only one method to obtain a land grant (making requests to the commander of the fort), they initially sought to proceed the same way. On 20 April 1762, military officer Donald Campbell reported to Amherst that the French settlers in the vicinity of Fort Detroit frequently solicited him for land grants: "I have been often applyed to by the inhabitants for lands, as severalls of them are too much confined."[18] As he was not particularly preoccupied with the issue of French land occupation at Detroit, Amherst did not give any advice to Campbell on the French settlers' need for more lands.[19] In these circumstances, Campbell likely ended up accommodating those settlers by allowing them to cultivate unoccupied lands of the area, as he had done in 1761 when he gave the permission to George McDougall, a British military officer, to cultivate parts of Hog Island.[20] However, Campbell did not produce any legal documents to authenticate such permissions. Because of these inconsistencies in dealing with requests for lands, soon after the demise of New France the administration of land grants at Detroit became very disorganized, reminiscent of the situation in the 1720s, when French commanders gave informal permissions to settlers to cultivate the lands near Fort Pontchartrain. Although Thomas Gage, commander-in-chief in North America from 1763 to 1774, endeavoured to regulate the land question at Detroit, and to offer better guidance to the commanders of Fort Detroit than had Amherst, his first mandate was to prevent encroachment on Aboriginal lands.

When initially consulted by Detroit commanders and military officers regarding land grants on the western frontier, Gage did not directly prohibit French land encroachment in Indian Country. Rather, he explained that he did not have the power to grant lands. On 14 August 1764, military officer Edward Abbott communicated with Gage regarding the land question at Detroit in order to solicit a tract of land for himself. Gage responded that he wished he could grant him a tract of land, but that he did not have the authority to do so.[21] He added that granting lands at Detroit would in due course become possible as he expected the region to eventually "be assigned to some one of the Governments ... most likely that of Canada."[22] When this occurred, Gage wrote that "it will be in the Governor's power only to make grants of any lands within his jurisdiction."[23] In October of 1765, military officer Deterecht Brehm wanted to develop two salt springs in the neighbourhood of Fort Detroit in order to provide the French settlers with salt. For his project, Brehm hoped to obtain a tract of land on both the River Rouge (then named Rivière Rouge), below the Côte des Pous, and on Lake St Clair, above the Côte du Nord-Est. Brehm was aware of the awkwardness of the position of the Detroit River region when he asked Fort Detroit Commander John Campbell (1765–66) to place his demand "before the Commander in Chief, who will judge of it as he may think best, as this settlement is not included in any government."[24] Replying to Brehm's request, Gage simply reiterated that he did not have the power to grant lands.[25] Nevertheless, Gage encouraged Brehm not to give up his project and to contact the appropriate colonial administrators, whoever they were.

Gage's tolerance for the existence of French settlements in the Detroit River region was pragmatic and can be explained by their convenient location to furnish commodities to British troops stationed in Indian Country. Before the Seven Years' War, Britain did not have troops positioned throughout North America, especially not on the western frontier. After the war, the majority of the troops present on the continent did not return to Britain but were actually employed for the protection of the British colonies against potential troubles by the Aboriginal peoples of the interior.[26] This decision significantly increased Britain's expenses related to its North American empire. In these circumstances, purchasing as many provisions as possible from the French farmers at Detroit to feed the troops stationed there was more economical than importing provisions from the Saint Lawrence valley. Similarly, hiring French settlers to work for the troops represented a less expensive option than transporting a workforce from the east. Amherst and Gage both recognized this fact and, as a result, French farmers at Detroit began to provide a variety of provisions to British troops immediately after the establishment of the new regime. On 23 January 1761, Donald Campbell was pleased to notify Amherst that "the inhabitants do all that I can desire of them, for the good of the service, they continue to supply the troops with flour and Indian corn."[27] On 20 April 1765, replying to a request by John Campbell for the shipping of livestock to Detroit, Gage wrote that he could not send any and, consequently, the French of the area would have to "furnish them, as in all other inhabited countrys of the King's use."[28] One week later, before reading Gage's letter, Campbell declared that he "was obliged to employ the inhabitants with their horses" to build a fenced garden for the garrison.[29] On 5 October 1765, Gage wrote again to Campbell, this time to inquire about the "quantity of provisions that the inhabitants of Detroit would be able to spare for the sustenance of the troops over and above their own consumption, and whether it would be sufficient for a regiment."[30] On 10 April 1766, Campbell notified Gage that the French farmers at Detroit could provide "a sufficiency of flower [sic] to serve this garrison & Michilimakinack."[31] On 22 February 1768, Gage requested Commander George Turnbull (1767–70) to "get early information of the quantity of flour, corn, & fresh meat that the settlement would be able to supply [the] garrison with."[32]

Many French farmers at Detroit were willing to sell their surplus flour to British authorities because it represented an opportunity to earn money in an almost nonexistent local market for commodities. During the 1760s and 1770s, the commanders of Fort Detroit and the French farmers signed a few contracts that listed the quantity of provisions that they could individually provide per annum. On 31 May 1766, habitants François Marsac, Charles Chauvin, Jacques Campau, and Jean Louis Campau, who all received their tracts of land in 1734, could each furnish more than two thousand livres of flour. Another forty-eight farmers, of whom almost all had also obtained tracts of land when Detroit was a seigneurie directe, agreed to supply quantities of flour that varied from two hundred to a few thousand livres.[33] In March 1781, Fort Detroit commander Arent S. de Peyster (1779–84) wrote to Brigadier General H. Watson Powell that he did not anticipate being able to purchase much flour, Indian corn, or heads of cattle from the French because of "the scarcity of crops the year before, and the severity of the weather the winter before which killed most of the hogs and numbers of cattle."[34]

Notwithstanding the signing of contracts and the regular requests by British officials for flour, other French at Detroit were reluctant to develop their farming activities further because they feared they would not get anything in exchange for their surpluses. Those farmers wanted British officials to give better guarantees that they would purchase their flour before they increased their production, as Turnbull reported on 28 August 1768: "If the inhabitants were certain that the produce of their lands would be taken for the use of the garrison they would sow a great deal more grain than they do as present."[35]

ENFORCING THE PROCLAMATION

With time, Gage became more preoccupied with French encroachment on Aboriginal lands in the Detroit River region and, as a result, by the end of the 1760s he began to look more closely at the land question. When he took office, Gage believed that the French commanders at Detroit had never had the authority to grant lands on behalf of the king. On 28 February 1766, he told John Campbell that he was "pretty certain the commanders had no powers vested in them for granting tracts of lands."[36] Gage, who had familiarized himself with the system of French seigneurial tenure in the Saint Lawrence valley when he was governor of the District of Montreal from 1760 to 1763, misinterpreted the relatively different system of land granting that had been used in the Detroit River region during the French regime. Before long though, the commander-in-chief adopted a more conciliatory attitude. Gage changed his view about the role of the French commanders at Detroit after reading the plea written by Robert Navarre in May of 1766. In this plea, Navarre explained that during the French regime he was the receiver of seigneurial dues for the king at Detroit. He further stated that under the French flag the commanders of Fort Pontchartrain had the authority to grant small lots inside the fort as well as tracts of land in the country.[37] After that, Gage did not challenge the property rights of those who could provide evidence that they had obtained their grant from one of the French commanders of Fort Pontchartrain. Still, this compromise apparently eliminated settlers whose land titles were not perceived as fully legitimate according to Gage's new position.

Gage's liberalism regarding the holders of deeds produced by French commanders did not extend to the permissions to cultivate lands granted by most of the eleven British officials who commanded Fort Detroit between 1763 and 1774. To put an end to this illegal practice, Gage evidently needed the collaboration of the commanders themselves. Only British military officer James Stevenson (1770–72) seems to have worked closely with Gage to bring a halt to this practice. On 18 December 1770, after having investigated French land expansion at Detroit, Stevenson corroborated that former Fort Detroit commander Henry Gladwin (1762–64) had informally authorized a few French settlers to occupy new lands and that no deeds were produced for these grants.[38] Predictably, Gage responded that "all grants made by Lieut. Colonel Gladwin, Major Bruce, or any other British commander, are null and void, and of no value."[39] Yet, this practice resumed under the command of Officer Henry Bassett (1772–74). For instance, on 28 February 1773, Bassett gave the permission to Métis Joseph Labadie dit Badichon to cultivate a tract of land of four arpents wide by forty arpents deep in the Côte des Pous.[40]

French land encroachment in Indian Country further enraged Gage when it was revealed that French officials at Detroit had laid out new côtes on the River Rouge and River Ecorse (then known as Rivière aux Écorces) only a few days before the capitulation of Montreal. On 1 September 1760, Commander François-Marie Picoté, Sieur de

Belestre, granted twelve tracts of land on the River Rouge and six on the River Ecorse. All of them measured four arpents wide by forty arpents deep except that of Robert Navarre Jr (nicknamed "Robiche") which had a width of six arpents.[41] On 20 April 1762, Donald Campbell informed Amherst of the grants on the River Rouge and asked for some advice about whether or not to permit the French to cultivate them, but he apparently never received any instructions.[42] On 28 August 1768, Turnbull communicated to Gage that there "are many people who have grants from the French commanding officer towards the River Rouge."[43] In the words of Turnbull, this was controversial not only because of the date those lands were granted, but also because their patents were not "expedited by Bellestre [to the governor general of New France] till the month of November when [British] troops were at the mouth of the [Detroit] River to take possession of the place."[44] Belestre probably knew of the fall of New France when the patents were sent, for Pierre François de Rigaud, Marquis de Vaudreuil-Cavagnal, the last governor general of New France (1755–60), had notified him about the capitulation of Montreal in a letter dated 9 September 1760.[45] On 16 June 1770, Commander Thomas Bruce (1770) also contested the legitimacy of those late grants by Belestre, and let Gage know of his intention to prevent the French from settling on those lands: "Many of the inhabitants here claim lands from grants given [to] them by Mr. Bellestre without being register'd ... I apprehend these grants are not valid, some have been possess'd of these lands ever since he left this, and tho' I have not turn'd them out, I have not allow'd any other to take possession, but I have always told them that their titles are not good, none being so but those approv'd of by Government."[46]

On 14 December 1770, Stevenson established that the grants on the River Rouge and River Ecorse were void and notified the French population of his ruling.[47] Stevenson actually believed that none of the grants of the French regime at Detroit were lawful, and this contention led him to reject Robert Navarre's plea of May 1766 which had already convinced Gage that the French commanders of Fort Pontchartrain had the power to grant lands. By doing so, Stevenson had disregarded Gage's desire to find some compromises in order to keep the land question at Detroit under control, such as recognizing land grants from French commanders or, as discussed below, appointing a public notary. Conscious of his role in fuelling the controversy among the French settlers of the Detroit River region, Stevenson simply invited them "to draw up a memorial stating their case."[48]

On 17 December 1770, three days after Stevenson's statement, Robert Navarre had already written a memorial for Gage. Again, he explained his former role of royal notary and restated that each French official who commanded Fort Pontchartrain (between 1734 and 1760) had been given the power to grant lands.[49] The former royal notary also maintained that if some lands granted by the French commanders had not been confirmed by the governor general of New France, their grantees should not be held responsible because the patents of these grants were sent to Montreal in good faith. To provide further evidence, Navarre declared that on a yearly basis he had posted to the minister of the Marine a complete list of the landholders at Detroit and the seigneurial dues they owed. As for the grants on the River Rouge and River Ecorse, Navarre defended their legitimacy and explained that they did not show in his books because their holders were supposed to pay their seigneurial dues for the first time the following fall. Finally, Navarre added that besides the twelve tracts of land granted by Belestre on the River Rouge, many other individuals had also been granted lands at that location though without having their names recorded.

Gage's response revealed that he had not changed his opinion regarding lands granted by the French commanders of Fort Pontchartrain along the Detroit River. He continued to assert that they were valid as long as their owners could provide evidence of their grants. In this regard, Gage did not sanction Stevenson's belief that virtually all French grants at Detroit were illegitimate. However, he refused to acknowledge the grants on the River Rouge and River Ecorse, which he described as "fraudulent," given the time they were issued.[50] Even though Stevenson had already invalidated the grants, Gage insisted – again – that these be nullified upon reception of his letter. In 1770, although none of these lands on the River Rouge and River Ecorse had been cultivated yet, it would be just a matter of time before French settlers occupied them.

THE DESIRE FOR A CIVIL GOVERNMENT

All through the period during which their community was located in Indian Country, the French of the Detroit River region petitioned British officials to become part of the Province of Quebec, or at least to have a civil government. On 15 May 1772, Gage wrote to Stevenson that he had received an address from the French of Detroit "setting forth many grievances, chiefly in their mode of government which they want much to be changed."[51] While on leave to Britain in 1774, Gage met William Legge, Second Earl of Dartmouth and secretary of state for the Colonies (1772–75), with whom he discussed the case of Detroit. Gage confirmed that the French settlers there wished for civil government.[52] The French of the Detroit River region were aware that the newly created Province of Quebec ensured that long-time residents were able to keep their rights to the private property they had "held" since the French regime. On 7 December 1763, James Murray, governor of the Province of Quebec (1763–68), had been instructed to notify all the French landholders in the Saint Lawrence valley to register with the secretary's office the land titles they had been granted before 2 November 1762.[53] This directive to Murray represented further evidence that having a civil government provided better guarantees regarding private property rights. On 16 April 1768, just as Detroit appeared to be one step closer to becoming part of a civil government, a decree pertaining to the rights to private property at Detroit ordered "all those who have any such deeds or grants of land to bring them before the first of June next to Philippe Dejean esquire in order to have them registered." The decree further stated that "any person refusing to comply with this order will be looked upon to hold their lands or lotts without proper titles."[54] Although Gage had previously insisted that only the deeds granted by French commanders before the capitulation of Montreal (except those on the River Rouge and River Ecorse) were valid, the decree omitted to clarify this detail. Turnbull had appointed Philippe Dejean to the position of public notary and justice of the peace on 28 April 1767, notably to elucidate the land question at Detroit.[55] Therefore, the French at Detroit had good reasons to think that their conditions with regards to land matters would improve by being incorporated into a civil government, particularly if they already held deeds to their lands. Whether or not the governor of a civil government would actually recognize private property rights to the Detroit French was not certain, but the latter had no other option: under these circumstances it appeared that having any kind of deed was better than no deed at all.

ABORIGINAL DEEDS

Although Gage appeared powerless in his attempt to prevent further French land expansion in the Detroit River region, the Royal Proclamation nonetheless had a major impact because the need for new land titles could no longer be fulfilled through requests to the commanders of the fort. Many French settlers had obtained permissions from British commanders to cultivate unoccupied lands on different watercourses in the area, but it was known that such sanctions carried no legal weight. Since the late 1720s, the majority of the French established on lands in the Detroit River region wanted deeds that authenticated their property rights. In this way, the Royal Proclamation, which confirmed that the seigneurie directe had vanished, threatened the future of the French settlements of the Detroit River region. However, rather than accepting confinement within the limits of the lands they already occupied, the French population progressively looked towards its Aboriginal neighbours to acquire new parcels of land and, more importantly, to obtain deeds.

In the months following the end of Pontiac's War, in 1766, Gage was disturbed by the story of a French man at Detroit who had apparently received an Aboriginal deed before the British conquest. Gage suddenly worried that such land grants were common during the French regime and that they would simply continue. On 6 May 1767, he told Turnbull that he was not aware of "any example before this, that any Canadian laid claim to Lands by virtue of Indian gifts." He instructed him to "enquire into this affair, and report whether such things were customary amongst the French," before adding that he was "pretty sure of the contrary."[56] Turnbull replied that he knew of only one instance of an Aboriginal land grant prior to the British conquest. As Turnbull explained, an old Aboriginal "dead some years ago" had granted a small piece of land at the time of New France, but the grant "was never even ratified by the commanding officer [and] never was taken possession of."[57] In 1770, Stevenson informed Gage that there were settlers at Detroit "who have no other rights but such as has been given them by the Indians."[58] Stevenson specified that these settlers had begun to cultivate their lands shortly before his arrival at Fort Detroit.

The first Aboriginal deeds were granted by Ottawa chief Pontiac around the time of the peace treaty he signed with British officials at Detroit on 4 September 1765. Pontiac first granted a tract of land to British military officer George McDougall the day before the signing of the treaty, on the south shore of the Detroit River.[59] This Ottawa deed granted directly to McDougall was never sanctioned by the Crown. Following the signing of the treaty, Pontiac granted four more tracts of land of which apparently only that of British military officer

Edward Abbott, who had in vain requested from Gage a tract of land for himself in 1764, was subsequently approved by the Crown. On 30 July 1766, the king acknowledged that Abbott owned "those islands lying between the lakes Erie and St. Clair ceded to his Majesty by the Treaty of Peace concluded with the Indians."[60] This suggested that Pontiac had ceded to Britain all the islands of the Detroit River in 1765. However, Abbott never made use of these islands and, as later events revealed, this alleged land cession by the Aboriginal people was rapidly forgotten. The other early grantees of Ottawa deeds were settlers Alexis Loranger dit Maisonville, Pierre Chêne dit Labutte, and German-born George Christian Anthon.[61]

These five Ottawa deeds were granted more than two years before the decree of 16 April 1768, which required all persons holding land titles at Detroit to register them before 1 June of that year. Undoubtedly they were related to the negotiations of the peace treaty of 1765; it is known, for instance, that Maisonville had played a role in these discussions.[62] The phenomenon of Aboriginal deeds granted directly to settlers, without the endorsement of the king, actually began throughout the weeks following the decree of 16 April 1768. This new practice rapidly caught the attention of Gage who, on 14 June 1768, sent a Copy of Order to Detroit informing the locals that they could not acquire land titles through Aboriginal deeds.[63]

In 1770, Stevenson recorded that seven settlers, all of them French, held Aboriginal deeds to lands along the Detroit River. Three of the men listed by Stevenson were the descendants of grantees from the era of the seigneurie directe. Three others were the heirs of settlers who had moved to Fort Pontchartrain before the British conquest.[64] In 1771, Stevenson listed another thirteen French settlers who had been granted Aboriginal deeds, all by the Ottawa except one.[65] Nine of these settlers were the sons of grantees of the 1730s or 1750s.[66] Of the others, two were the descendants of French who had moved to Detroit before 1734.[67] The tracts of land that Stevenson listed in 1770 and 1771 had a width that varied between two and six arpents and a length of either forty or eighty arpents. In 1771, Robert Navarre Jr, who was not included in Stevenson's lists, also received a tract of land.[68] Some of these grantees possibly received Aboriginal deeds for tracts of land that they had in fact previously been informally authorized to cultivate by British commanders.

On 8 April 1771, Gage requested that Stevenson revoke all property rights obtained directly from Aboriginal people.[69] On 25 June 1771,

Stevenson wrote to Gage that he had publicly "annull'd every grant agreeable to your Excellency letter of the 8th of April & warn'd the people to remove as soon as they reap their harvest," adding that "many are the complaints against this order." Maisonville was particularly outraged by this ruling, as testified by Stevenson, who informed Gage that "mons. Maisonville, who is a partly concern'd & will be the greatest sufferer."[70] Maisonville no longer owned the land that Pontiac had granted to him, for he had sold it to Bonaventure Réaume in 1769 in order to purchase that of George Christian Anthon, who had also obtained his from the Ottawa chief in 1765.[71] Maisonville's worries about losing his property led him to travel to New York to meet with Gage. On 15 August 1771, Gage wrote to Stevenson that he had recently received a visit from Maisonville and that having looked at his titles he could not acknowledge them: "He has shown me his titles, which consist of an Indian gift to another person of whom he, Maisonville, says he purchased it."[72] Despite Gage's refusal to recognize Maisonville's land titles, the persevering French man did not leave his tract of land and actually went on to become one of the most productive farmers of the Detroit River region by the end of the 1770s. The other French grantees of Aboriginal deeds who complained to Stevenson about his order did not abandon their lands either.

DETROIT AND THE QUEBEC ACT

In 1774, the Quebec Act expanded the geographical limits of the Province of Quebec to include most of Indian Country. Four judiciary districts were created on the western frontier out of this act: Illinois, Vincennes, Detroit, and Michilimackinac. As the Quebec Act was not intended to favour the establishment of European settlements in the new territories of the Province of Quebec, it did not specifically address French land occupation in Indian Country. While in the making, the third (and eventually final) draft of the bill specified that "all His Majesty's Canadian Subjects, within the Province of Quebec, & the Territories thereunto belonging, may also hold, and enjoy their Property & Possessions."[73] However, Wills Hill, the Earl of Hillsborough, who had served as secretary of state for the Colonies between 1768 and 1772, disagreed with the idea of settling the territories to be annexed to the Province of Quebec. William Legge, who had succeeded him as secretary of state for the Colonies, reassured him that the members of cabinet "are unanimously of opinion that the extension of the Province to the Ohio & Mississipi, is an essential & very useful part òf the Bill; it provides for the establishment of civil government over many numerous settlements of French subjects, but does not by no means imply an intention of further settling the lands included in this extension."[74] In 1775, King George III instructed Sir Guy Carleton, First Baron Dorchester, who had been appointed governor of the Province of Quebec in 1768, that the limits of the French settlements "in the interior Country should be fixed and ascertained; and that no settlement be allowed beyond those limits."[75] This decree was contrary to what Gage had told settlers at Detroit on several occasions: that the governor of the civil government in which they would eventually be included would be responsible for granting lands within the geographical limits of his jurisdiction. Therefore, the Royal Proclamation continued to oversee land issues in the Detroit River region after the Quebec Act, and the signing of treaties of land cession between the Crown and the Aboriginal peoples was still required prior to the establishment of any new settlements. It remained this way on the western frontier of British North America for more than a century after the adoption of the Royal Proclamation, for well into the nineteenth century Britain used this framework to acquire Aboriginal lands in other parts of the present-day province of Ontario.[76]

MORE ABORIGINAL DEEDS

Despite the Quebec Act, the French of the Detroit River region could still not obtain new land titles other than through unlawful Aboriginal deeds. As a result, more French settlers acquired Aboriginal deeds over the following years. On 10 June 1776, the Ottawa granted a tract of land of 3 arpents wide to settler Charles Réaume whose father, Hyacinthe Réaume, was a grantee of 1750.[77] On 6 January 1777, the Potawatomi granted a tract of land to Isidore Chêne beside the one they had granted in 1771 to Robert Navarre Jr, in the Côte des Pous.[78] Isidore Chêne was the fifth son of Charles Chêne, who had also received a tract of land at Detroit in 1750.[79] On 26 July 1780, a French man whose surname was Adhémar, possibly Toussaint Antoine Adhémar dit St-Martin, obtained from the Potawatomi a tract of land that measured 4 arpents wide by 120 arpents deep.[80] All of these tracts of land were located along the Detroit River. Following Pontiac's uprising, the residents of the Ottawa village of the south shore had moved further south and built two new villages, one at the mouth of the Maumee River, also known as Presqu'Isle, about ninety kilometres south of Fort Detroit, and the other one along the River Raisin, halfway between Fort Detroit and the mouth of the Maumee River.[81] For their part, the residents of the Potawatomi village of the north shore had relocated to the River Raisin.[82] The deeds the Ottawa and the Potawatomi granted between 1765 and 1780 related to the lands where their respective villages had stood before they were abandoned.

French farms came to occupy most of the shores of the Detroit River by the end of the 1770s and, as a result, dozens of French settlers began to look for land grants on other rivers of the area, as well as along Lake St Clair. On 24 July 1780, settler Joseph Réaume, the older brother of Charles Réaume mentioned above, received from the Ottawa a tract of land of twenty arpents wide by fifty arpents deep on the Maumee River, near the new Ottawa village.[83] Joseph Réaume never resided on this land, however. In 1796, he sold it to Scottish merchant and land speculator John Askin.[84] On 28 July 1780, the Potawatomi granted a tract of land of three arpents wide both to settlers Gabriel Jacques Godfroy and Nicholas Lacelle Jr on the River Rouge.[85] The father of Gabriel Jacques, Jacques Godfroy, had received from Belestre a tract of land on the River Ecorse in 1760.[86] As for Nicholas Lacelle Jr, his father had obtained from the last French commander a tract of four arpents wide on the River Rouge.[87] On 7 May 1781, several children of Antoine Louis Descomps dit Labadie and his Chippewa wife together received from the Chippewa a tract of land at the mouth of the Thames River (then known as Rivière à la Tranche), about fifty kilometres east of Fort Detroit.[88] Dozens more French settlers, many of whom were the descendants of grantees of the French regime, also obtained Ottawa, Potawatomi, and Chippewa deeds on different watercourses of the Detroit River region before the end of the American Revolution.

THE RIVER RAISIN SETTLEMENT

In the 1770s and 1780s, as the residents of the côtes of the Detroit River began to look for lands in nearby peripheral zones, French land occupation in the Detroit River region significantly expanded. The French settlement of River Raisin, located about sixty kilometres south of Fort Detroit, was founded in this process. On 3 June 1785,

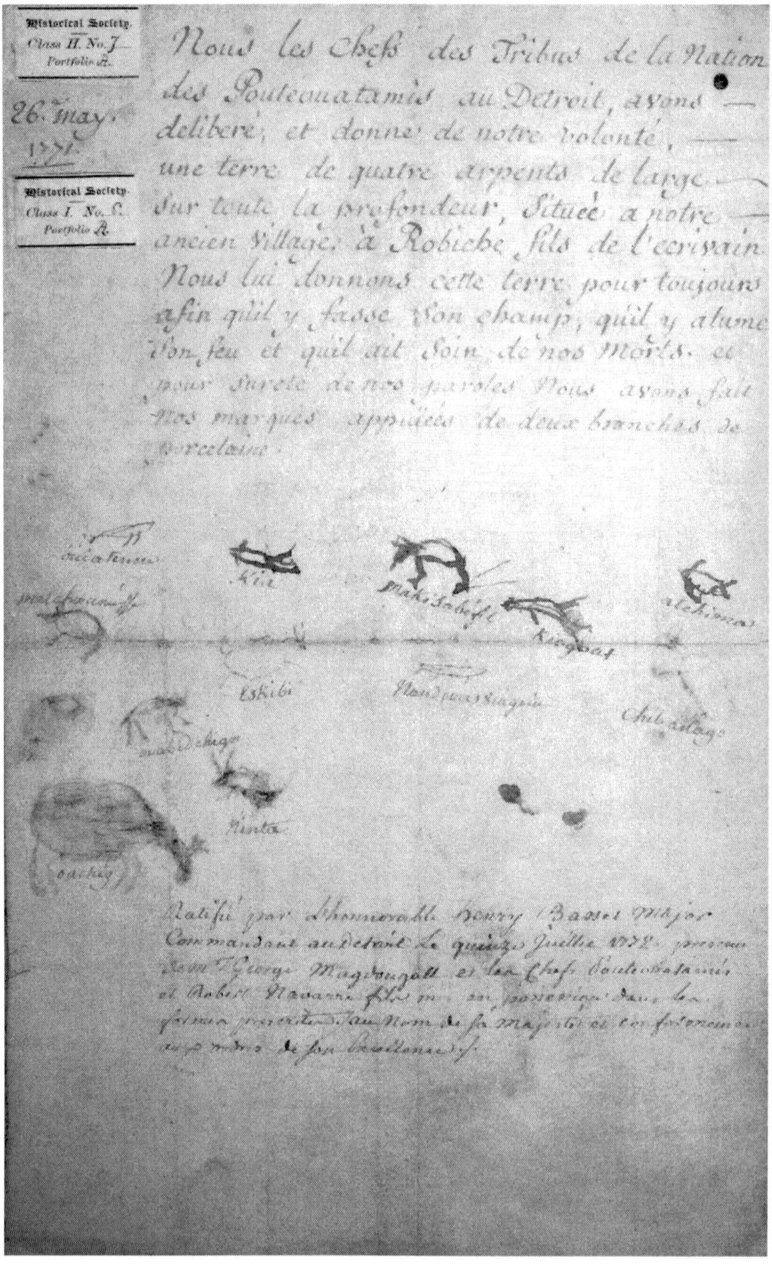

Historical Society. Class II. No. 7 Portfolio R.

26 May 1771.

Historical Society. Class I. No. 6 Portfolio R.

Nous les Chefs des Tribus de la Nation des Pouteouatamis au Detroit, avons deliberé, et donné de notre volonté, une terre de quatre arpents de large sur toute la profondeur, Située a notre ancien village, à Robiche fils de l'ecrivain. Nous lui donnons cette terre pour toujours afin qu'il y fasse son champ, qu'il y allume son feu et qu'il ait soin de nos Morts. et pour sureté de nos paroles Nous avons fait nos marques appuiées de deux branches de porcelaine.

Ratifié par l'honnorable Henry Basset Major Commandant au detroit le quinze juillet 1772, present Sieur George Magdougall et les Chefs Pouteouatamis et Robert Navarre fils mis en possession dans les formes prescrites au Nom de sa Majesté et conformement aux ordres de son Excellence.

Figure 3.1 Potawatomi deed to Robert Navarre Jr, Côte des Pous, 26 May 1771.

François Navarre and his brother Jacques, descendants of former royal notary Robert Navarre, acquired from the Potawatomi a tract of land along the River Raisin. This tract measured twenty arpents wide.[89] Evidently, François and his brother benefitted from the friendship that their ancestors had developed with these Potawatomi. On 26 May 1771, in similar circumstances, the father of François and Jacques had obtained from these Potawatomi a tract of land of four arpents wide in the Côte des Pous, beside the one that his own father had received from the French Crown in 1747.[90] Two Potawatomi chiefs, Askiby and Oüà-Oüi-attenne, were cited in both the 1771 and 1785 deeds which confirmed the history of friendship between these Potawatomi of the Detroit River region and the Navarre family.

François and Jacques Navarre relocated to the River Raisin because the côtes of the Detroit River had already been parcelled out to French settlers in the 1780s. Their relatives who already owned properties in the côtes of the Detroit River did not move to the River Raisin. For instance, their father was still a resident of the Côte des Pous in 1810.[91] From his home at River Raisin, François Navarre remained connected to the French settlements of the Detroit River. Notably, he shipped to the emerging town of Detroit the harvest surplus he had purchased from his neighbours.[92]

QUIT-RENT

By confirming the collapse of the seigneurie directe of the Detroit River region, the Royal Proclamation of 1763 did not only instantly eradicate the French system of land granting there, but it also contributed to the demise of the French seigneurial system of taxation. However, before it disappeared completely, this system somehow survived for several years under the designation of "quit-rent." As historian Beverley W. Bond Jr explains, the quit-rent practice consisted of imposing a feudal due that developed in England throughout the sixteenth and seventeenth centuries as a result "of the movement to transform the peasantry of England, free tenants and villeins, into freeholders and copyholders paying to their lords a fixed money rent."[93] In British North America, the Royal Proclamation of 1763 established that land owners in the Province of Quebec were now obliged to pay quit-rents rather than seigneurial dues.[94] But the presence of more than two hundred seigneuries particulières in the Saint Lawrence valley rendered impossible the conversion from the

French seigneurial system of land tenure and taxation to the English free holding system of quit-rents. As Bond puts it, "the widespread existence of the French tenure of land was especially unfavorable to the development of the quitrents."[95] In 1771, British officials first proposed abandoning the idea of imposing the quit-rent in the Province of Quebec. In 1774, the Quebec Act officially confirmed that the seigneurial system of land tenure and taxation would be preserved in the seigneuries particulières of the Saint Lawrence valley and that censitaires would continue to pay their seigneurial dues to their respective seigneurs particuliers.[96] However, this system was not preserved in the Detroit River region.

The issue of private property taxation at Detroit was only addressed by British authorities after the appointment of Gage as commander-in-chief in North America.[97] On 28 February 1766, Gage wrote to John Campbell that "with respect to the tax paid by the inhabitants to the French king I should be glad to know what that tax was." He directed the commander of Fort Detroit that if, before the British conquest, such a tax pertained to the lands held by the Crown he expected him to "take care that the Kings rights are kept up." In order to facilitate continuity in the payment of such a rent, especially since it had not been paid for a few years, Gage believed it to "be best to keep it in the old channel."[98] On 31 May 1766, after speaking with Robert Navarre, Campbell responded to Gage stating that "taxes paid in the French time were forty one sols for every acre in front & a bundle of wheat each year by every landlord in the country." However, Campbell incorrectly assumed that taxes in the Detroit River region at the time of New France "were by way of quitrent to the King" instead of by way of seigneurial dues.[99] By doing so, Campbell implied that the French settlers who held lands in the Detroit River region were not censitaires who paid annual seigneurial dues (either to a seigneur particulier or to the king as seigneur direct), but owners who were required to pay a yearly feudal rent to a proprietor who happened to be the king. As Bond also explains, in the English system of land tenure, "where these rents were due to the Crown, they were payable either at the exchequer or to the royal receiver."[100] Campbell mistakenly thought that Robert Navarre was the royal receiver of quit-rent at Detroit while he was in fact the royal receiver of seigneurial dues. However, because of the similarities between seigneurial dues and quit-rents, the transition from the former to the latter went unnoticed among the local French. Indeed, they did not react to their status change because their annual dues, as Gage had requested from Campbell, had remained identical to those charged prior to the fall of New France. Furthermore, the French settlers of the Detroit River region actually continued to use the French legal language of the seigneurial system of taxation in their land transactions for several years after the quit-rent was introduced. While British officials designated the annual tax that the French settlers in the Detroit River region had to pay as "quit-rent," the French notaries who produced legal documents of land transactions between 1766 and 1783 generally referred to it as seigneurial obligations (*droits seigneuriaux*). Even the land transactions that British notary Thomas Williams produced specified that the buyer would be required to pay seigneurial dues to the king ("*cens et rentes et droits seigneuriaux envers sa Majesté*").[101] French notaries like Robert Navarre, Jean Baptiste Campau, Philippe Dejean, and Gabriel Legrand at times signed such documents under the title of "royal notary" even though they did not actually work for British authorities and therefore were certainly not royal notaries.[102]

Between 1766 and 1783 (the last year that quit-rents were apparently levied), there were two receivers of the king's revenue at Detroit. In 1766, Irish merchant James Sterling was appointed to this position and sometime in the 1770s Thomas Williams replaced him. Every fall, Sterling and Williams would collect the quit-rent on behalf of the Crown, as Robert Navarre had collected the cens et rentes and other seigneurial obligations on behalf of the French king for a quarter of century.[103]

The Detroit River region was still part of Indian Country when this quit-rent to the British Crown began to be levied. Collecting the quit-rent at Detroit was therefore contrary to the Royal Proclamation because treaties of land cession with the Aboriginal peoples still had to be signed. But since the quit-rent contributed to the reduction of Britain's expenses on the western frontier, the importance of finding solutions to keep the kingdom's finances balanced prevailed over abiding by the proclamation.

In the Detroit River region, the Quebec Act of 1774 did not confirm that the seigneurial system of land tenure and taxation would continue to be used. Historian Melvin G. Holli argues that "seigneurial obligations in land tenure" ended at Detroit when the north shore of the Detroit River was handed over by Britain to the United States in 1796.[104] This is not impossible, although there is little evidence that any quit-rent was collected at Detroit after 1783. Bond argues that in the rest of British North America quit-rents ceased to be collected after the American Revolution because "with feudal dues practically abolished in the United States, it would have been a suicidal policy to have insisted upon a system of quit-rents in Canada."[105] However, no matter when the French of the Detroit River region stopped paying quit-rents that in practice looked like French seigneurial dues, by 1766 they were no longer landholders who paid actual seigneurial dues.

CONCLUSION

After the demise of the seigneurie directe of the Detroit River region, it became virtually impossible for the French of the area to obtain new land titles. Unlike the situation during the French regime, the British commanders of Fort Detroit did not play the role of grantors of lands on behalf of the king. This situation rapidly became problematic because the local French population experienced its most significant demographic growth between 1760 and 1783. The majority of the British commanders at Detroit during this period had agreed to give informal permissions to French settlers to cultivate unoccupied lands. However, these authorizations were not formal land grants. The French who did not enjoy land titles granted by French commanders (along the Detroit River itself) had no other choice than to look towards their Aboriginal neighbours for new land titles even though it was not guaranteed that British authorities would recognize such deeds as valid. Although keeping private property rights was complicated for the local French settlers during the decades that followed the end of the French regime, the situation was even more complicated for those who claimed *public* property rights. The difficulties experienced by these settlers will be expanded upon in the next chapter.

4

Contested Public Property Rights

The British conquest seriously challenged French property rights in the Detroit River region. However, because British authorities found it rather convenient to be able to rely on French farmers on the western frontier to feed troops, the Royal Proclamation of 1763 was not always thoroughly implemented. Despite the lack of official recognition of their land titles by the new government, French settlers in the Detroit River region managed to keep their farms, but the question of *public* property rights at Detroit was interpreted and handled differently by British authorities in Detroit, New York, Quebec, and London. Before the British conquest, public land ownership in the Detroit River region was already ambiguous, and this ambiguity worked against those who claimed such property rights under the new regime.

THE SAINT LAWRENCE VALLEY COMMONS

In France, peasants in rural areas had used commons for pasture since the Middle Ages.[1] The commons (*communes* or *communaux*) were spaces located within *seigneuries particulières* reserved for collective usage by the peasants. In theory, only the peasants who were members of the "community of peasants" (*communauté des habitants*) could keep part of their livestock holdings in the commons of the seigneurie particulière in which they held a *censive*. To become a member of the community of peasants of his seigneurie particulière, and therefore be allowed to use the common, a *censitaire* had to pay an additional rent to his *seigneur particulier*.[2] These communities of peasants can be likened to unions, where all members had the authority to collectively supervise how the common was used. More importantly, these communities of peasants were also responsible for dealing with the seigneurs particuliers with regards to any matter that pertained to the commons.[3]

The first commons in the Saint Lawrence valley were created in the 1620s by the Company of One Hundred Associates. By the 1640s, the creation of commons was either the initiative of the seigneurs particuliers or the censitaires themselves, who generally fashioned them out of portions of their own tracts of land.[4] On a few occasions the governor generals or intendants of New France interceded to create commons within some already existing seigneuries particulières. For instance, on 15 August 1648, Governor General Charles Huault de Montmagny (1636–48) granted a tract of land located within the Jesuit seigneurie particulière of Trois-Rivières for public use.[5] Shortly after New France became a royal colony, in 1663, French colonial authorities acknowledged the convenience of commons and they required settlers to make use of them in order to prevent livestock from roaming everywhere. On 19 August 1669, the Sovereign Council of New France ruled that all the settlers of the emerging *côtes* of the island of Montreal were now required to hold their livestock in commons before and after the sowing season.[6] By the turn of the eighteenth century, one-third of the seigneuries particulières in the Saint Lawrence valley included at least one common. With regards to the censitaire's rights to use commons in the Saint Lawrence valley, R. Cole Harris asserts that the seigneurs particuliers generally charged "a flat rate for the right to use the common regardless of the number of head pastured in it."[7] In this way, they did not have to keep a close watch on their censitaires, who frequently herded their cattle in and out of the commons between March and November. Some "communities of peasants" also existed in the Saint Lawrence valley before 1677.[8]

In the Saint Lawrence valley, commons were often located on islands. In 1712, French military engineer Gédéon de Catalogne observed that most of the islands of the Richelieu River that were part of the seigneurie particulière of Sorel, at the eastern edge of the Government of Montreal, were used as commons for pasture. Catalogne further noticed that islands were also used as commons in the nearby seigneuries particulières of Contrecoeur and Boucherville.[9] In 1815, surveyor Joseph Bouchette noted that islands in the seigneuries particulières of Sorel and Boucherville, as well as of several others of the District of Montreal, still served as commons.[10] In the District of Trois-Rivières, five islands of Lake Saint Pierre were used as commons as late as the 1970s, more than a century after seigneurialism was abolished in the Saint Lawrence valley.[11]

In the Detroit River region, French settlers had already made use of commons for pasture long before the British conquest. There too, they had used islands for that purpose. However, because land granting there did not exactly work the same as in the Saint Lawrence valley during the New France era, this only helped to obscure the question of public property rights throughout the following decades.

THE CLASH OVER HOG ISLAND

The British Proclamation of 1763 disrupted the French claims to public property rights much more than their claims to private property rights. This new reality revealed itself in the dispute regarding the usage of Hog Island (called "Isle aux cochons" by the French; now Belle Isle, Detroit, Michigan). The use of Hog Island as a French common was challenged shortly after the Royal Proclamation, when Thomas Gage, commander-in-chief in North America, instructed military officer John Campbell on 20 November 1764, to "make use of Hog Island and every other part you judge usefull and necessary for the use and convenience of the Garrison."[12] In the next months, British military officer George McDougall, who had recently married Marie France Navarre, the oldest daughter of the notary Robert Navarre, petitioned the king to officially be granted the entire island. McDougall's claim was based, as he himself explained, on the fact that in 1761 "the commanding officer at Detroit [Donald Campbell] granted him leave to cultivate a small island called Hog Island."[13] Although Campbell's permission to cultivate Hog Island was not a land grant, McDougall used it to convince the king and on 4 May 1768, the king informed Gage that he had ruled in favour of McDougall's claim.[14] Gage transmitted the king's ruling to Commander George Turnbull at Detroit no later than on 29 May 1768, and stipulated that McDougall was "allowed a temporary occupation of Hog Island ... upon certain conditions." The occupation of Hog Island depended upon the approval of the Aboriginals from whom, as Gage directed, McDougall had to get "a written acknowledgment of their consenting to the cession of those lands."[15] McDougall obtained such written sanction from the Ottawa and the Chippewa on 5 June 1768. However, many French settlers of the Detroit River region strongly rejected the validity of this land transaction, and argued that as Hog Island was a public property granted a long time ago, it could not be owned by a single individual.

Their claim, however, was open to challenge. In 1749, French military engineer Gaspard-Joseph Chaussegros de Léry Jr reported that both Fighting Island and Turkey Island (then respectively known as Grosse Isle aux Dindes and Petite Isle aux Dindes), in present-day Ontario, were commons where French settlers held livestock.[16] Yet, it is known that Hog Island was also used by French settlers as a common. It is likely that these commons were not created as a result of any official grant but simply out of informal personal initiatives.

This lack of official recognition might explain why the French settlers who used Hog Island as a common were already challenged during the French regime with regard to their public rights to use this island. In the 1720s, while serving as commander of Fort Pontchartrain, Alphonse de Tonty built a house on Hog Island. However, as notary Philippe Dejean, who settled at Detroit only in the 1760s, later reported, "a request of the public forced him immediately to abandon it."[17] At the time, virtually all the French settlers in the Detroit River region lived within the fort and had not yet begun to build farms along the Detroit River. Still, they already possessed livestock that they apparently kept on Hog Island. Once farms had been established on both sides of the Detroit River, the governor general of New France, on 12 June 1752, granted Hog Island to Detroit merchant Louis-Césaire Dagneau Douville de Quindre.[18] But once again, as some French settlers wrote to Guy Carleton, governor of the Province of Quebec (even though Detroit was not part of the Province of Quebec yet), on 16 May 1769, "the earnest representation of the public deprived him of the possession."[19] Therefore, on the eve of the fall of New France, it appears that French settlers in the Detroit River region used islands as commons, although their collective rights to these islands were not supported by any written evidence. After the British conquest, it became very difficult for the users of the common on Hog Island – and probably for the users of any common in the area – to defend their public property rights.

On 14 May 1769, Turnbull publicly announced that Hog Island now belonged to McDougall. Merely a few days later, on 18 May, French settlers shared their discontent with Turnbull.[20] On 24 May, Dejean wrote a petition to Carleton on behalf of ninety-two Detroit French landowners to denounce McDougall's purchase of Hog Island

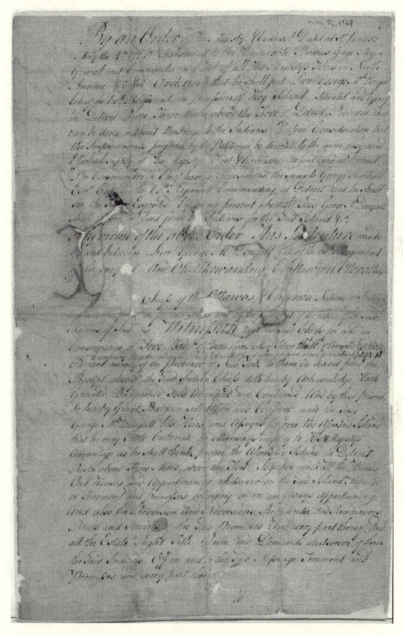

Figure 4.1 Belle Isle deed (page 1). Deed to Belle Isle, formerly known as Hog Island or Île aux Cochon. Belle Isle was purchased from the Chippewa and Ottawa Indians by Lieutenant George McDougall on 5 June 1768 for five barrels of rum, three rolls of tobacco, three pounds of vermillion, and a wampum belt, with an additional three barrels of rum and three pounds of paint to be delivered at the time of possession. Deed is signed by Lieutenant George McDougall and includes pictographic signatures (totems).

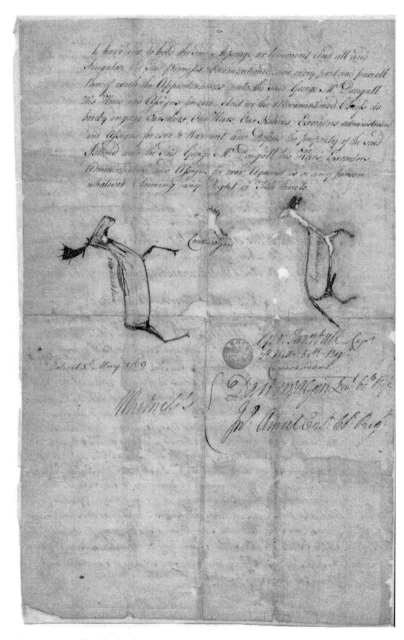

Figure 4.2 Belle Isle deed (page 2).

from the Ottawa and Chippewa.[21] The overwhelming majority of these petitioners were the descendants of settlers who had received lands from French commanders between 1734 and 1760. Former royal notary Robert Navarre did not endorse this petition, most likely because he questioned the legitimacy of the claim that Hog Island had been public property during the French regime (Navarre cannot be portrayed as a traitor and/or pro-British based on the fact that he did not sign this petition or that he was the father-in-law of McDougall, for he did not hesitate to defend the private property rights of his fellow French settlers during the 1760s and 1770s, as discussed in the previous chapter). The aspect of McDougall's acquisition that upset the users of the common on Hog Island the most was the provision that now prohibited them from bringing animals to the island. Dejean explained to Carleton that the common on Hog Island had been "ceded to the public by the late M. de la Motte [Cadillac], first Commandant of the Country, to keep the cattle in safety [and] that this right lasted until now."[22] In a separate letter also submitted to Carleton on 24 May 1769, settlers Jacques Campau, Jean Baptiste Chapoton, Laurent Eustache Gamelin, and Pierre Réaume again repeated that Hog Island was used as a common and added that they would look in the Saint Lawrence valley to find the legal document that confirmed their claim ("*chercher en Canada quelques preuves ou titres par ecrit*").[23] Once this document was found, they would let Carleton see it because their detractors stressed the necessity for them to provide some written proof that Hog Island had indeed been granted status as public property. It is not known if any research was actually conducted in the Saint Lawrence valley to find such evidence. Cadillac did grant tracts of land along the north shore of the Detroit River, in front of Hog Island, between 1707 and 1710. In 1722, he actually claimed that he did grant commons in the Detroit River region.[24] However, since French colonial administrators had cancelled all of his Detroit grants in 1716, the discovery of any written evidence would have been useless.

It is interesting to note that the French settlers who claimed public property rights over Hog Island requested help from Philippe Dejean to write some of their petitions even though he had settled at Detroit *after* the British conquest and, therefore, was probably not familiar with the specifics of land granting and seigneurialism along the Detroit River during the French regime. It is also intriguing that these settlers addressed their petitions to Carleton even though they almost certainly knew that it was Gage who was in charge of dealing with land issues in Indian Country.

On 15 October 1769, Commander Thomas Bruce informed Gage about these new developments. He wrote that "Mons. De La Motte's grant was, according to what discovered, only a verbal one, and [the petitioners] acknowledge[d] that their only pretention is a possession of said island for sixty years, which they seem to think, gives them a very sufficient right."[25] Upon reception of Bruce's letter, Gage notified the king that he "recommended to both parties to decide the dispute by arbitration."[26] On 9 December 1769, William Hill, Second Viscount of Hillsborough, replied to Gage that "the King approves of the method you have recommended for the decision by arbitration of the dispute about the Isle aux Cochons."[27] On 6 April 1770, Gage passed Hill's instructions on to Bruce. Meanwhile, McDougall had built two houses on Hog Island.[28]

The French settlers, upset by the grant of Hog Island to McDougall, continued to communicate their discontent vehemently, to the point that on 31 March 1771, Fort Detroit commander James Stevenson (1770–72) complained that "the people in this settlement want but little encouragement to be the most troublesome set I ever heard of."[29] On 2 April 1771, settlers Jacques Campau, Jean Baptiste Chapoton, and Pierre Réaume, as well as André Charles Barthe and Pierre Laurent St-Cosme, together signed another petition addressed both to Gage and Carleton, in which they declared that day after day they felt the pain of the restriction preventing them from using the island as pasture for their livestock.[30] On 17 June 1771, McDougall and the French settlers who wanted to keep using Hog Island failed to find a compromise and Gage concluded that "the affair [could] be settled by the King and [Privy] Council only."[31]

On 12 June 1772, Robert Navarre and thirty-two other French settlers took position against their fellow settlers who had been claiming public property rights over Hog Island. In their letter to British authorities, they explained that during the French regime the different commanders of Fort Pontchartrain required settlers to keep their horses and other animals on Hog Island or on other islands so they would not cause damage or trouble in settled areas. The petitioners stated that these instructions were not confirmations of any public property rights over Hog Island.[32] This petition revealed that the French community of the Detroit River region was divided regarding the property of Hog Island. The majority of the settlers, supported by newly arrived notary Philippe Dejean, claimed public property rights over the island whereas a minority, led by former royal notary Robert Navarre, who was much more accustomed with local affairs, denied that settlers at Detroit ever held such rights, even prior to the British conquest.

The Quebec Act of 1774, and Thomas Gage's end of tenure as commander-in-chief in North America the same year, did not lead to any kind of compromise regarding the ownership of Hog Island. By the late 1770s, this issue was apparently still not totally resolved. On 12 August 1778, Henry Hamilton, who in 1775 had been appointed first lieutenant-governor of the newly created District of Detroit (part of the Province of Quebec), wrote a letter to Théophile-Hector de Cramahé, who was then lieutenant-governor of the Province of Quebec, in which he sided with the French settlers who opposed McDougall. Hamilton believed that "the claims of [these] inhabitants [were] sufficient to support their claim." He thought that if Hog Island had "ever been granted from the Crown as a common – the inhabitants [had] no power to surrender that right as their property."[33]

In the 1780s, Hog Island definitely became private property. With the arrival of a few British Loyalists to Detroit, as a result of the outbreak of the American Revolution, Hamilton recommended that Hog Island be taken back by the Crown so it could be used as shelter for these families. In 1780, the governor of the Province of Quebec, Frederick Haldimand, granted permissions to Loyalist families to cultivate parts of Hog Island.[34] Meanwhile, McDougall died while away from Detroit. In the following years, his heirs continued to claim private property rights over the island on behalf of the family. On 9 October 1783, George McDougall Jr sent a letter to Haldimand on "behalf of himself, his brother and Mary McDougall relict of the late George McDougall Captain of His Majesty's Eighty fourth Regiment of Foot." He emphasized that, as a result of the American Revolution and, more importantly, the Treaty of Paris that put an end to it (and in theory granted Michigan to the United States), Hog Island "falls within the lines of the United States," before demanding that the island "be put into the full possession of his assigns, for the use and advantage of the widow and orphans heirs and the late proprietor."[35] On 1 October 1784, Major Robert Mathews requested the permission from Lieutenant-Governor Jehu Hay of Detroit to give the island back to the McDougall family, writing that "you will please to permit them to take full possession of the said Island."[36] The petitions of the

McDougall family paid off – not only was their ownership of Hog Island recognized, it was no longer challenged. Intentionally or not, the McDougall family further secured their claim over Hog Island on 5 January 1784, when George McDougall's widow, Marie-France Navarre, married Jacques Campau, a resident of the north shore.[37] In the 1760s and 1770s, through petitions, Campau had opposed the takeover of Hog Island by George McDougall. Now, through his second marriage, he was himself connected to the McDougall family and his descendants stood to benefit from this affiliation, especially regarding the ownership of Hog Island. On 11 November 1793, the McDougall family sold half of Hog Island to Detroit merchant William Macomb.[38] However, when Barnabé Campau, son of Jacques Campau and stepson of Marie-France Navarre, bought back this half in 1817, they became owners of the whole island until his death in 1845, when the island became a city park and was officially renamed Belle Isle.[39] During the first half of the nineteenth century, Hog Island was still used by people with a French cultural heritage, but any French public property rights over it had vanished in the aftermath of the British Proclamation of 1763.

CONCLUSION

During the last decades of the eighteenth century, the British conquest unquestionably affected French society in several ways in the Saint Lawrence valley. However, by virtue of the Articles of Capitulation, French private property rights in the Saint Lawrence valley during the 1760s and 1770s were not challenged. The seigneuries particulières that had been established during the New France era – more than two hundred – remained largely unaltered. Seigneurialism itself was preserved, until 1854. Public properties, notably the commons that had been created within seigneuries particulières, whether on the mainland or on islands, were not altered. In fact, many commons existed until the twentieth century.

The history of the French in the Detroit River region during the first decades of the British regime contrasted sharply with that of the seigneuries particulières of the Saint Lawrence valley. Because Detroit was excluded from the newly created Province of Quebec, by virtue of the British Royal Proclamation that established Indian Country in 1763, French property rights there were no longer protected by the Articles of Capitulation. Moreover, the status of Detroit as seigneurie directe during the French regime only complicated any acknowledgement of property rights after the British conquest, given that there was no seigneur left to defend his rights to private property or those of his censitaires.

The careful recording by French notaries of the numerous land transactions that took place in the Detroit River region during the 1760s, 1770s, and 1780s became crucial for claims to private property rights, especially because of all of the uncertainties regarding land titles.[40] However, the story proved very different regarding public property rights which were already ambiguous under the French regime. It is clear that French settlers had commons which they used for pasture on certain islands of the Detroit River, but the existence of these commons were apparently not stated in any land grants, land transactions, or any type of legal documents. Consequently, during the 1760s and 1770s, their users lacked the necessary documentation to support their claims to public property rights, and this resulted in the loss of such public properties as commons. Although the three decades following the end of New France proved to be frustrating for the French settlers in the Detroit River region, the situation finally began to look up after the American Revolution (1776–83), at least regarding private property rights, when authorities on both sides of the Detroit River at last recognized the private property claims of the settlers.

5

Private Landowners

Between 1734 and 1760, the *seigneurie directe* of Detroit had promoted the growth of French land occupation along the Detroit River through the grants by colonial administrators of tracts of land to families from the Saint Lawrence valley. However, the British conquest had seriously jeopardized the future expansion of the French presence in the Detroit River region. By reserving the entire Great Lakes region for the sole use of Aboriginal peoples, as stated in the Royal Proclamation of 1763, Britain had forbidden the establishment of European settlements in that part of the continent, at least in the short term. By issuing this proclamation, not only had Britain refused to acknowledge the existence of a seigneurie directe at Detroit during the French regime, but it had, in theory, prohibited the presence of French settlers along the Detroit River. The American Revolution (1776–83) would change all this.

PRIVATE CLAIMS ON THE SOUTH SHORE

In theory, the north shore of the Detroit River became part of the United States in 1783, as stated in the Treaty of Paris, which had marked the end of the American Revolution, but Britain did not immediately comply with the terms of the treaty. By the late 1770s, British merchants in Montreal had built strong commercial ties with many Aboriginal nations of the Great Lakes region and these connections favoured the empire as well. In an effort to maintain these ties, Britain initially refused to withdraw its troops from important forts of the western frontier that, according to the treaty, now belonged to the United States. As a result, Fort Detroit and present-day Michigan remained under the British flag beyond 1783. On 19 November 1794, after signing the Jay Treaty with the United States, Britain finally agreed to abandon Fort Detroit by June 1796. Meanwhile, between 1783 and 1796, British authorities began to deal with the land ownership question in present-day Ontario, including on the south shore of the Detroit River.

Due to the arrival of Loyalists in present-day Ontario, Britain's policy preventing the establishment of European settlements in the Great Lakes region changed after the American Revolution. Within the two decades that followed the conflict, as historian Robert Surtees Jr puts it, "Britain acquired the waterfront along the St. Lawrence River, Lake Ontario, the Niagara River, Lake Erie, the Detroit River, Lake St. Clair and the St. Clair River."[1] In conformity with the Royal Proclamation of 1763, these lands were obtained through treaties between the Crown and Aboriginal peoples. This course of action contrasted sharply with the previous two decades, during which the Crown had never seriously considered seeking land cessions from Aboriginal peoples. In fact, the Crown had actually required its representatives in North America to prevent land encroachment in the Indian Country/Province of Quebec. This policy change clearly benefitted the French established on the south shore of the Detroit River.

In the Detroit River region, the first treaty of land cession had taken place on 15 May 1786, but it pertained only to a small tract of land. This treaty stated that the Ottawa and Chippewa nations "granted unto His said Majesty George the Third his heirs and successors" a small tract of land seven miles square below River Canard, south of Petite Côte, on the south shore of the Detroit River, plus Bois Blanc Island (known today as Boblo Island).[2] On 2 September 1789, Carleton notified the Land Board at Detroit that the Crown desired to purchase from the Aboriginal peoples all the lands in present-day southwest Ontario. In order to carry out this plan, Carleton directed the Land Board to contact "[Alexander] McKee the officer of the Indian Department [and use] his knowledge of the temper and disposition of the Indians [to ascertain] what extent of Country it may be proper to treat for with them for the present, consistently with their comfort." Carleton stressed that the lands "possessed or claimed by individuals under pretence of private purchases or grants from Indians, on the side opposite to the Port of Detroit [should] be comprehended within the limits of the general tract." The governor required the board to determine "a proper scite [sic] for a country town for the district on the East side (i.e. south shore) of the streight [*sic*]" once this transaction was completed and then to "direct the surveyor of the district to lay out the township." Following the purchase, Carleton also wanted the board "to receive applications for grants from the claimants or occupants" of lands in the settlements established in the District of Hesse before its creation, and to give "certificates" to those who had improved their lands.[3] On 15 May 1790, George III acquired all of present-day Essex County, Ontario, from the Ottawa, Chippewa, Potawatomi, and Huron nations.[4] This treaty, also known as "surrender no. 2," created two main Aboriginal reserves. The first, Walpole Island, on the north shore of Lake St Clair, in present-day Lambton County, Ontario, was intended for all four nations. The second, the Anderdon Reserve, only intended for the Huron, corresponded to a tract of land south of Petite Côte.[5] To explain the decision of these Aboriginal peoples to sign such treaties of land cession, Aboriginal and treaty rights consultant Victor Lytwyn and founding director of the Walpole Island Heritage Centre Dean Jacobs argue that they "expected the Crown to be more trustworthy in dealing with land-use disputes" than the individuals to whom they had granted tracts of land in the previous years. However, as Lytwyn and Jacobs also point out, unlike deeds to other individuals, those "with the British Crown came to be viewed by Crown officials as agreements extinguishing all Aboriginal interests in the land."[6]

The origins of the Land Board at Detroit can be traced back to 28 July 1788, with the division of the western portion of the Province of Quebec into four districts: Mecklenburg, Luneburg, Nassau, and Hesse. The last comprised most of today's southwest Ontario, including the Detroit River region. Even though Britain was supposed to eventually hand Fort Detroit over to the United States, as stipulated in the Treaty of Paris of 1783, it initially set up the headquarters of the District of Hesse there because towns had yet to be established on the south shore of the Detroit River. On 17 February 1789, a temporary Land Board was appointed in each district to oversee the allocation of land lots to Loyalist immigrants on the waste lands of the Crown. Notably, the boards were directed to hold regular meetings at sites where settlers could petition for land grants. The claimants whose applications were positively received by the boards would take an oath of allegiance to the Crown before receiving a certificate or "ticket of location" which the surveyor-general of their district would use to assign them specific lots (if the claims were not already settled).

The boards would also give a duplicate of these certificates to the office of the governor's secretary.[7] These land boards existed until 6 November 1794, after which applications for land grants had to be made through the clerk of peace of the districts.[8]

On 26 December 1791, the Province of Quebec was divided into two distinct provinces: Lower and Upper Canada. On 16 July 1792, John Graves Simcoe, the first lieutenant-governor of Upper Canada, created nineteen counties in addition to changing the name of the District of Hesse to the Western District.[9] Before its integration into the county of Essex, as a result of the adoption by the Legislative Council of Upper Canada of the Act for the Better Division of the Province, on 1 July 1800, part of the Detroit River region (today's east Windsor, Walkerville, and the City of Detroit) was within Kent County.[10] The Act of 1 July 1800 also subdivided Essex county into six townships: Gosfield, Maidstone, Malden, Mersea, Rochester, and Sandwich.[11] The overwhelming majority of the French population resided in the township of Sandwich, in which nearly half of the lands were occupied by the settlements of Côte du Sud (also known as L'Assomption de la Pointe de Montréal, or simply L'Assomption, at the turn of the nineteenth century) and Petite Côte. Several French families also resided in the other townships, but there they were outnumbered by British settlers.

The British policy regarding the land necessitated some adaptations in the Detroit River region, notably because of the presence of long-established French settlers. Immediately after the American Revolution, Frederick Haldimand, governor of the Province of Quebec, had recommended dividing the colony into counties each made up, as historical geographer John Clarke writes, of townships measuring "six miles square" and including "seven concessions deep and twenty-five lots wide." As well, it had been suggested that these lots be "roughly either 19 by 63 chains or 19 by 105 chains, yielding respective acreages of approximately 120 and 200."[12]

However, as Clarke writes, "the idealized plan envisioned in remote Quebec could not always be met in the light of the physical realities of Upper Canada."[13] On the south shore of the Detroit River, the French method of land organization had been implemented since 1749, and by the late eighteenth century its imprint on the landscape had become too important to be ignored. However, one aspect of British land policy that did not need to be adapted to local constraints in the Detroit River region concerned the size of the lots. Haldimand's suggestion that regular land grants should be two hundred acres per family was incorporated in the acts that created the land boards and Upper Canada, and it proved to work relatively well with the residents of Côte du Sud and Petite Côte.[14]

By August 1789, the French settlers of the district of Hesse began to petition their Land Board for land titles. The bulk of these claimants filled applications for tracts of land located in the "Old Settlement," which corresponded to Côte du Sud and Petite Côte. A few French claimed lands in the "New Settlement" (also known as "Two Connected Townships"), which had been established for disbanded soldiers in 1784, after British military officer William Caldwell had purchased from Aboriginal people a tract of land of twenty-four kilometres along the north shore of Lake Erie.[15] Perhaps because knowledge of the plan suggested by Haldimand in the 1780s for the future organization of townships was not widespread, Caldwell laid out the lots of the new settlement similar to the French farms of the Detroit River (long and narrow rectangle shaped lots rather than squares). On 16 November 1790, Patrick McNiff, deputy-surveyor of the district of Hesse, complained to the board that the lots in the new settlement were not "agreeable to the new plan of survey" and that they were much smaller than the suggested two hundred acres per family.[16] Several other French settlers petitioned the board for land titles beside the Anderdon Reserve on the River Canard, near the mouth of the Thames River, or along the south shore of Lake St Clair, east of the Côte du Sud (that is, where the towns of Tecumseh and Lakeshore are located today).

In the Old Settlement, the front lots had been occupied by French families for generations when the Land Board was created. Originally, the king of France had only granted tracts that measured 40 *arpents* deep in these *côtes*. By the 1790s the majority of the settlers who occupied these tracts had begun to use the lands at the rear of their properties, notably for wood. Some of these settlers also hoped that their descendants would be allowed to settle on these rear lots.[17] In other words, the French had come to perceive these lands as rear rows (*arrière-rangs*) of 40 arpents deep for which the titles had to be clarified. As a matter of fact, most petitioners claimed to possess what they called a "second concession" behind their lots along the Detroit River. Some actually claimed a "third concession" behind their "second concession," for a property of 120 arpents deep. At the meeting of the Land Board held on 27 April 1791, which several French settlers attended, the issue of these rear lands was discussed. Since none of

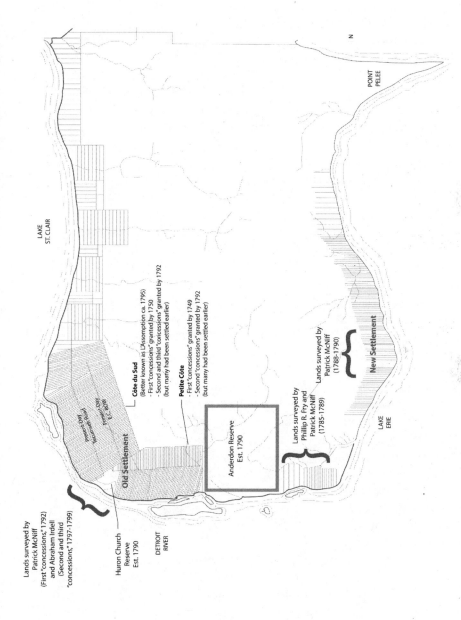

Figure 5.1 Present-day Essex County, Ontario, ca. 1795.

the claimants present understood the English language, Jacques Bâby, himself a member of the Land Board and owner of tracts that included a second and third concession, spoke on their behalf and argued that if these landowners were denied their rights over these rear lands, they would be obliged to get their wood farther away, notably at River Rouge across the Detroit River.[18] On 3 May 1791, McNiff wrote that the French of the Old Settlement "prayed for the 2nd, 3rd & 4th concessions in their respective rears" but that he was personally against the idea of granting these settlers such lands because it would "prevent English farmers from ever settling in the rear of the petitioners."[19] On 6 May 1791, perhaps because they had not heard from the Land Board, forty-four French landowners petitioned Lord Dorchester regarding the question of the rear lands. Their arguments stressed the fact that most of them had large families and that their children would need lands to establish themselves, adding that they would find it convenient to have their children living near them.[20]

On 10 May 1792, the Land Board of the district of Hesse authorized the residents of Petite Côte to claim one additional concession each (either a second or third concession) because two tracts combined would represent about two hundred acres: "The Board does not think the petition unreasonable, so far as it relates to their two concessions, as most of the lots there are about three acres in front, which in the first and second concession together will give little more than 200 acres to each lot."[21] The next day, D.W. Smith, secretary of the Land Board, directed McNiff to begin to survey the second and third concessions of the Petite Côte and to "mark another road between the second and third concessions."[22] On 8 February 1793, the Land Board also positively replied to the residents of the Côte du Sud regarding the possibility of possessing two concessions: "The Board received the claims of the inhabitants of L'Assomption settlement for a second concession in their rear in order the better to supply them with food for the convenience of fencing, as well as for their family purposes, and agreed to grant a second concession to each of the inhabitants possessing the front lots."[23] In the Côte du Sud, eighty-one settlers (eighty French and one British) were thus permitted to own two concessions. Although the board allowed settlers to claim two concessions, it denied them the right to request three concessions in order to prevent them from owning too many acres of land.[24]

In general, the Land Board of the district of Hesse did not challenge the claims made by the French settlers. On 30 April 1792,

Figure 5.2 Lesperance log cagin, Tecumseh, Ontario, built ca. 1800.

they actually recommended to Simcoe that "all these people should be guaranteed in their actual possessions and improvements by receiving some certificate."[25] During the following months, the board granted many certificates to French claimants in which they mentioned that old French titles had been recognized. The majority of the certificates stipulated that their owners had also been granted a second or a third concession. For instance, the certificate of settler Joseph Bondy Sr read as follows: "Joseph Bondy, Senior, the present possessor of Lot No. 51, on the Petite Côte having appeared, the Board confirm him his lot, and having administered the oath of fidelity and allegiance to him as by Law directed, desire a certificate to be made out for him, for a continuation in the second concession of Lots. 23 and 47, which are in his rear."[26] The board also granted certificates for tracts of land in the third concession to French settlers who did not own any other property in the first or second concession. Settler Charles Bernier obtained such certificate: "The Board received the petition of Charles Bernier for the 3rd concession of Lot 89 in the Parish of L'Assomption, improved by him seven years past, and directed a certificate to be granted to him for it, having administered the oath of fidelity and allegiance to him as by law directed."[27] The certificates mentioned virtually no case where the landowner claimed his property by virtue of Aboriginal deed. Yet, it is unquestionable that French settlers had purchased rear lands from Aboriginal people before the creation of the Land Board.

The certificates that the Land Boards granted to settlers between 1789 and 1794 were not final confirmations of land titles. They had certainly helped British authorities to organize the territory, but their holders, known as "original nominees" of the Crown, were required to eventually exchange them for actual patents. Between 1797 and 1805, the Upper Canada government held the Heir and Devisee Commission to facilitate the conversion of these certificates into patents. However, as historian Lillian F. Gates observes, "many persons believed the certificates themselves were valid grants and saw no necessity of exchanging them for patents." As a result, "much land remained on the Surveyor-General's books located but not patented."[28] In the township of Sandwich, as Clarke demonstrates, the first patents were granted in 1797 and by 1817 more than 50 percent of the holders of certificates had obtained patents.[29] A second Heir and Devisee Commission, whose purpose was essentially identical, took place between 1805 and 1911.

Despite the fact that residents of Sandwich Township apparently never exchanged their certificates for patents, many French settlers of Essex County did so during the first and second Heir and Devisee Commissions. The records produced by the administrators of these commissions contained information similar to the notes taken by the Land Board at Detroit prior to 1795. They sometimes stipulated that the holder of the certificate possessed a tract of land that had been occupied since the French regime.[30] Although the certificates granted to the French had been virtually silent about Aboriginal grants in Essex County, the officers of the Heir and Devisee Commissions sometimes indicated that French settlers had been given permission by Aboriginal people to cultivate lands prior to the creation of the Land Board.

Britain's policy change regarding European settlements on the western frontier benefitted the French settlers of the south shore of the Detroit River not only because it led to the recognition of their land titles for lots that fronted the water, but also because it led the members of the local Land Board to agree to grant them certificates for rear lots. During the French regime, unlike in the Saint Lawrence valley, land occupation in the Detroit River region was not yet developed enough for the king to grant rear lots. However, throughout the decades that followed the British conquest the French who resided along the Detroit River came to require more land to support their increasing families. Some left for new settlements, such as those at River Raisin and River Huron (Clinton River), where they had the possibility of owning lots fronting the river. Others stayed at Petite Côte and Côte du Sud and began using the rear lands for firewood, hoping to eventually establish their children there. By having their claims over these rear lands recognized by British authorities, these French settlers reproduced a pattern of land organization that their ancestors in both the Detroit River region and the Saint Lawrence valley had known for generations.

THE NORTH SHORE BEFORE 1796

Between the end of the American Revolution in 1783 and the surrender of Fort Detroit by Britain in 1796, the status of the north shore of the Detroit River remained ambiguous. British authorities generally thought of Fort Detroit and the French settlements of the north shore to be fully part of British North America. On 20 December 1794, Simcoe wrote to William Henry Cavendish Bentinck, Third Duke of Portland, that he "considered the settlement at the River aux Raisins as the [southern] boundary of the territory occupied by His Majesty's subjects, dependant (*sic*) upon Detroit."[31] But a few weeks earlier, on 3 October 1794, British military officer William Mayne reported from Fort Detroit that a French man had beaten to death a Chippewa man at River Raisin and declared that although the Chippewa people wanted this French man to stand trial in Upper Canada, "the Courts of Justice in Canada were too delicate, not wishing to find him guilty as being out of the British domain."[32] Regarding the land question, British authorities could not in theory investigate the land titles of the French settlers of the north shore of the Detroit River after the American Revolution. However, on 17 August 1790, residents of the Côte du Nord-Est expressed their worries to Carleton after noticing a surveyor inspecting the ground near their settlement.[33] They stated that it looked as if this surveyor proposed a new method to lay out their farms, which they argued would seriously disturb their thirty-kilometre-long settlement.[34] On 22 April 1791, D.W. Smith, secretary to the Land Board of the district of Hesse responded to these French settlers about their "memorial to his Excellency Lord Dorchester of the 17th of August last, stating apprehensions of a change of the ancient boundarys (*sic*) of [their] farms."[35] Smith simply informed them that the board would meet "on Wednesday Next, at 10 o'clock A.M., on which day [they were] requested to attend," before adding that he expected them to bring the documents that "best substantiate the assertions contained in the said memorial, particularly [their] original French deeds."[36] Despite Smith's recommendation to the settlers of the Côte du Nord-Est, which was somewhat zealous considering that the Land Board did not necessarily require such documents of the French on the south shore, there was no follow-up by British officials regarding land titles on the north shore of the Detroit River.

PRIVATE CLAIMS ON THE NORTH SHORE

On 1 July 1796, American troops took over Fort Detroit, and the French who lived on the north shore of the Detroit River automatically became citizens of the United States. Although these French settlers had expected this political regime change since the signing of the Treaty of Paris of 1783, it still caused them much anxiety. Overnight they became residents of the Northwest Territory, a territory created in 1787 that included most of today's Midwest. These new citizens of the Republic were particularly worried about their land titles. By 1789, British authorities had begun to give certificates of land occupation to the French settlers established along the south shore of the Detroit River, thereby opening the door to the recognition of the land titles of these people. However, no such certificates had been granted to the French who lived on the north shore. The French of the north shore were conscious of the awkward position in which they found themselves, especially since many of them resided on lands acquired through Aboriginal deeds.

Knowing that it was only a matter of time before they became residents of the Northwest Territory, French residents of the north shore began, even before the regime change, to state their case to the United States government regarding their land titles. In May 1794, François Navarre, grandson of former royal notary Robert Navarre, travelled to Fort Greenville, about 250 kilometres southwest of River Raisin, to meet American military officer Anthony Wayne and implore him to persuade Congress to honour his land titles. During their meeting, Navarre provided Wayne with three documents confirming private property rights. The first document was the deed for a tract of land on the River Rouge that his father Robert Navarre Jr ("Robiche") had received in September 1760 from François-Marie Picoté, Sieur de Belestre, the last French commander of Fort Pontchartrain. The second was a deed for the tract at River Raisin that he and his brother Jacques had obtained from the Potawatomi on 3 June 1785. The third was a Potawatomi deed owned by his friend François de Joncaire de Chabert, who had grown up with him in the Côte des Pous.[37] Although he listened to Navarre, Wayne apparently made no promises that day.

Navarre's journey to Fort Greenville occurred merely weeks before the Battle of Fallen Timbers which took place sixty kilometres south of River Raisin on 20 August 1794.[38] At this battle, Wayne's troops defeated the Aboriginal people who had resisted American expansion in the Ohio valley since the end of the Revolutionary War. On 3 August 1795, Navarre returned to Fort Greenville to sign the Treaty of Greenville as a witness to the peace between the United States and the Aboriginal people.[39] The Treaty of Greenville stipulated that the United States obtained from the Aboriginal people the southern half of present-day Ohio, as well as its northeast portion (then known as the Connecticut Western Reserve). As historian Reginald Horsman puts it, it also specified that "the United States was given sixteen reservations of land on the Indian side of the boundary line to use as posts and was also granted free communication between them."[40] The boundaries of the reservation surrounding Fort Detroit were not clearly defined, but Congress determined that they roughly covered the north shore of the Detroit River from the north shore of River Raisin up to an undetermined point below River Huron (Clinton River), north of the Côte du Nord-Est.[41] These reservations were not land cessions to promote colonization. Despite that, as early as 15 August 1796, Winthrop Sargent, acting governor of the Northwest Territory, signed a proclamation organizing Wayne County, whose initial limits encompassed most of today's lower peninsula of Michigan, and immediately looked into the land question in the vicinity of Fort Detroit.[42] He soon discovered that Aboriginal people had granted lands to settlers in what is today southeast Michigan.[43]

When the United States took possession of Fort Detroit, Congress was already preoccupied by the presence on the western frontier of speculators who sought to purchase vast tracts of lands from Aboriginal people. In the Detroit River region, in the months prior

Figure 5.3 Man and woman standing on weed-grown ground in front of boarded-up clapboard house. Handwritten on card back: "Old [Jean-François] Hamtramck house, about 1881. Jim Scott & wife in foreground. This house was built in 1802, on property purchased by Colonel Hamtramck. In 1892, the house, though still standing, was in a dilapidated condition and was soon demolished. It was located on the river bank between what are now Van Dyke and Baldwin Avenues."

to the change in regime, a syndicate composed of British merchants had attempted to acquire from local Aboriginal people thousands of acres south of Lake Erie with the intention of reselling these lands to the United States government at a later date.[44] The French heard of this plan, and those who lived on lands received from Aboriginal people feared being mistaken for speculators. On 23 March 1799, residents of River Raisin urged Congress to distinguish between themselves and those speculators, because their own parcels were small in size and they had actually cultivated them. They also added that they wished for their land titles to be acknowledged by Congress ("*confirmer leurs droits par de bons contrats*").[45]

On 3 October 1799, military officer Arthur St Clair asked the Potawatomi to stop granting tracts of land to the French settlers in Wayne County because such grants were illegitimate. Regarding their friends, that is the French, St Clair also told the Potawatomi that "the United States will not take their farms from them."[46] Despite St Clair's words of reassurance, a year later the residents of Wayne County still had not heard from Congress regarding their status. On 2 September 1800, 150 of them – 50 Anglo-Americans and 100 French men – petitioned Congress regarding their land titles. The French petitioners explained that they were the "descendants of the first settlers of this country, which was commenced & carried on under the patronage of the French government," and emphasized that back then "the absolute right to, and enjoyment of the soil, which they should settle upon and cultivate, was [already] considered of the first importance."[47] They also stated that during the French regime land titles were granted by the Crown, but that because of "the changes in government, and other accidents, many of the original evidences [were] not to be found."[48] The French settlers declared that following the British conquest most of Fort Detroit's commanders had permitted them to occupy new tracts of land, "but unfortunately for your petitioners no grants were made to them prior to the treaty of peace between that government and the United States."[49] They also contended that because of the growth of their population "during the period 1783 & 1796 ... several of [the] petitioners, at the earnest request of the Indian nations, & patronised by the commandants of this post, made further settlements at great expense."[50] The French pointed out that the lands they had received from Aboriginal people "were generally small being from one to six or eight hundred acres, and actually settled upon and improved by your petitioners, who were induced to proceed therein from a full belief that the United States, when they came into possession, would confirm to them their farms & improvements."[51] Lastly, they asserted that they felt "exceedingly anxious that their rights, titles, & claims to their lands may be speedily settled & confirmed in them & their heirs, should their claims appear sufficient to entitle them thereto, and that they may thereby be relieved from a burdensome litigation."[52]

At the same time that the residents of Wayne County wished for the recognition of their land titles, local representatives of the federal government began to tax their properties. Wayne County was then divided into three districts: Hamtramck (i.e. Côte du Nord-Est, Fort Detroit, Côte des Pous, River Rouge, and River Ecorse), Sargent (i.e. River Raisin area), and St Clair (i.e. River Huron area).[53] In Sargent District, a "territorial tax" was collected as early as 1800, when 154 land owners paid dues of a few dollars.[54] There is also evidence that such tax was collected in all three districts in 1802.[55] Yet, paying a property tax was no confirmation of land titles, for before 1783 British officials at Detroit had collected different taxes (notably a quit-rent, as discussed in chapter 3) without ever acknowledging any private property rights to the French settlers.[56]

In 1802, Henry Dearborn, secretary of the Department of War, gave the directive to the local Indian agent, Charles Jouett, "to investigate and report the titles of this country." As future chief justice of Michigan Territory Augustus Woodward later recounted, when this agent visited the farms of the area "the inhabitants received him with the greatest hospitality [and manifested] their joy at the Government's turning their attention to the titles of that country."[57] In February 1804, this agent reported to Congress on the confusion regarding land titles in the vicinity of Fort Detroit and shortly thereafter measures were taken to clarify this issue. On 26 March 1804, while present-day Michigan was part of Indiana Territory, Congress adopted the Act Making Provision for the Disposal of the Public Lands in the Indiana Territory and for Other Purposes. This act established a Land Office at Fort Detroit.[58] Before the end of the year the office, which was required to report to the secretary of the Treasury, Albert Gallatin (1801–14), observed that many settlers in Wayne County held their lands from Aboriginal grants. On 18 December 1804, Gallatin confirmed that he had been told "that almost every settler at Detroit derive[d] his claim from an Indian title" and added that more information should be gathered on these titles.[59]

On 3 March 1805, Congress voted an Act Supplementary to the Act of 26 March 1804. This act stated that the register and receiver of the Detroit Land Office were to serve as commissioners responsible for examining the claims that pertained to lands possessed and cultivated prior to 1 July 1796. It also directed that the Land Office would "prepare two transcripts of all the decisions made by the said commissioners in favour of the claimants, and to transmit one to the surveyor-general and one to the Secretary of the Treasury." As well, the act stipulated that "it shall also be the duty of the said commissioners ... to make to the Secretary of the Treasury a report of all the claims filed with the register of the land office, which they may have rejected." Finally, the act allowed five hundred dollars to the commissioners to pay for the translation into English of "grants, deeds or other evidences of claims in the French language."[60] On 14 May 1805, a public notice in French was transmitted to the residents of Wayne

Figure 5.4 View of the back of the Old Jean-François Hamtramck residence in Detroit, Michigan.

County. This notice required all landowners to state their case before the commissioners prior to 1 November 1805, regardless of whether they claimed titles from French grants, Aboriginal deeds, or preemption rights.[61] In all three instances, a series of proofs in support of the claim had to be provided to the commissioners. Those who claimed titles by virtue of grants from the French regime were not only expected to show the official deed signed by the governor general of New France, but also the list of all owners of the said tract of land over time. Those who possessed Aboriginal deeds had to present these to the commissioners. If they were not the original grantees, they were also required to provide a list of the previous owners of the said tract of land. Additionally, owners of Aboriginal grants had to provide complete information about the boundaries of their properties, because many Aboriginal deeds lacked such details. The owners of Aboriginal grants who were not able to provide any written document in support of their claim needed at least two witnesses to confirm that they (or previous owners) had cultivated their lands prior to 1 July 1796. Finally, landowners could also claim property rights based on preemption rights. This meant that settlers were authorized to settle on public lands as long as they eventually purchased them from the United States government. Acquiring lands on the western frontier through preemption rights had become legal in 1800, and many Anglo-American settlers took advantage of this type of right, particularly in other territories.[62]

The commissioners appointed to record the private claims no later than on 1 November 1805 were Detroit's registrar of the Land Office, George Hoffman, and receiver of Public Moneys Frederick Bates.[63] During the weeks following this deadline, the two commissioners were instructed to analyze each claim, write a preliminary report in which no decisions were to be made, and finally produce two transcripts, one for the confirmations of titles and the other one for the rejections. On 30 December 1806, several months after the appointments of Hoffman and Bates had ended, Gallatin finally received their transcripts. The secretary of the Treasury immediately transmitted their contents to Congress and wrote, obviously surprised, that the commissioners had "confirmed only six claims" and that "their report of rejections was ... so voluminous."[64] Gallatin had probably expected many more confirmations because Hoffman had told him that there were "at least 1000 claims."[65] Hoffman explained this high number of rejections by stating that virtually all the "claimants were not explicit enough in their notices & did not always bring witnesses from whom the commissioners could ascertain the boundaries, situation, quantity &c of the lands claimed."[66]

In the following months, the adoption of policies addressing questions about the land titles in Wayne County progressed more rapidly. On 3 March 1807, Congress passed an Act Regulating the Grant of Lands in the Territory of Michigan, which instantaneously shifted the significance away from the French grants and the Aboriginal deeds. As long as the land had been occupied and improved before 1 July 1796, the owner was entitled to claim it by virtue of preemption rights. The act notably stated:

> that to every person or persons in the actual possession, occupancy and improvement of any tract or parcel of land, in his, her, or their own right, at the time of the passing of this act, within that part of the territory of Michigan to which the Indian title has been extinguished, and which said tract or parcel of land was settled, occupied and improved by him, her or them, prior to and on the first day of July, one thousand seven hundred and ninety six, or by some other person or persons, under whom he

she or they hold or claim the right to the occupancy or possession thereof, and which said occupancy or possession has been continued to the time of the passing of this act; the said tract or parcel of land thus possessed, occupied, and improved, shall be granted, and such occupant or occupants shall be confirmed in the title to the same.[67]

On 17 November 1807, the United States signed a treaty at Detroit with the Ottawa, Chippewa, Potawatomi, and Huron nations regarding the cession of all of present-day southeast Michigan, which made Aboriginal deeds even more irrelevant in private property claims by the French settlers.

The appointment of new commissioners following the Act of 3 March 1807 also helped resolve the land question in Wayne County because two of them spoke French. Born in France, Peter Audrain had fled to the United States after the outbreak of the French Revolution. In 1796, he had accompanied Anthony Wayne's troops to Fort Detroit and ended up staying there.[68] Fluent in English, Audrain occupied several offices at Detroit until his death in 1820.[69] James Abbott was a Detroit native, proficient in the French language. Moreover, he understood the frustration of many French settlers in the area regarding the land question. In 1780, Aboriginal people had granted two tracts of land to his father in the Detroit River region and, similar to the French who had obtained Aboriginal deeds to lands, the validity of his father's titles had been refuted by British authorities and later questioned by Congress.[70] The third commissioner was Stanley Griswold, secretary of Michigan Territory between 1805 and 1808.

The passing of the Act of 3 March 1807 led the French residents of Wayne County to believe that the recognition of their land titles would soon be resolved. However, as it did not address all of their concerns, on 26 October 1807, more than two hundred French landowners petitioned Congress again. Firstly, they condemned the fact that "only one farm or piece of ground [could] be affirmed to one individual." Some French settlers (i.e. Joseph Campau) owned several tracts of land, acquired from other settlers, but the petitioners stressed that these individuals "plead for no speculative claims, nor for claims to tracts of great extent." Secondly, they acknowledged that "most of the inhabitants in the old settlement on [the] Detroit River have claimed by virtue of ancient written titles only a single piece of ground extending forty arpents in depth," but they added that these settlers had also been using "the lands in rear to supply one of the first necessaries of life in this climate, wood for fuel, for buildings, and for fences." Finally, they disapproved of the clause stipulating that only the settlers who had taken up tracts of land before 1 July 1796 could claim property rights. The petitioners argued that those who had begun to occupy new parcels of land shortly after the change in regime had done so because "their paternal farms were too small to admit of division among several children, and [because] there was no land office [yet]."[71]

Commissioners had already addressed some of these concerns. The first commissioners had notably raised the issue of the rear lands along the Detroit River. On 4 January 1806, Gallatin was notified that the French hoped to have their properties duplicated by the addition of "another farm of exactly the same dimensions in the rear, making the whole depth eighty French acres," and that these extensions were called "second concession" (as on the British side of the Detroit River).[72] For their part, the new commissioners informed Gallatin regarding two of the requests expressed by the French settlers in their petition. On 1 September 1807, they asked him if the French who lived along the Detroit River were allowed to claim "eighty arpents in depth, instead of forty." They had also suggested that Congress adopt "a provision in favor of actual settlers subsequent to the 1st of July 1796."[73] After the request of 26 October 1807, in reply to their plea, Congress adopted a Supplemental to An Act Regulating the Grants of Land in the Territory of Michigan on 25 April 1808. This provision did not explicitly address the issue of the second concessions, but by repealing the "provision which forbade the granting or confirmation of more than one tract of land to any one person" and by granting "pre-emption rights [to] all settlements made subsequent to 1st July 1796, but prior to the 26th March 1804" (i.e. before the Act Making Provision for the Disposal of the Public Lands in the Indiana Territory and for Other Purposes), it indirectly authorized such claims.[74]

After the adoption of the Act of 3 March 1807, the commissioners had received specific instructions from Congress regarding the way to proceed in the study of claims to private property rights in Wayne County. First, they had to receive and investigate the demands of the claimants. Second, they had to determine, according to the notion of preemption rights, whether or not the land claimed had been continuously occupied and improved before 1 July 1796 (or 26 March 1804, as stipulated in the Act of 25 April 1808). Third, once the commissioners had approved the claim, they had to give the applicant a certificate. Such certificates, as Gallatin had directed the commissioners on 25 March 1807, had to be numbered "progressively according to their date, from No. 1 upwards."[75] These certificates were not patents, but simply documents to be shown to the appointed surveyor of Wayne County. Once their properties had been surveyed, the settlers had to return their certificates to the commissioners. Fourth, these commissioners would then recommend Congress to officially grant a patent signed by the president to the said landowner.

The certificates that the commissioners granted to claimants contained details about the location of the said tract of land, its dimensions, and the owners of adjacent lands. In general, requests somewhat explicitly referred to the preemption rights of the landowner, no matter where the tract was located. This confirmed the fact that the commissioners did not make any distinction between the properties that had been granted by the French king in the Côte du Nord-Est or in the Côte des Pous and those granted by Aboriginal people along, for instance, the River Raisin or the River Huron (Clinton River). On 25 June 1808, settler François Rivard registered a claim for the tract of land of two arpents wide by eighty arpents deep he possessed in the Côte du Nord-Est, which received the number 180.[76] Although this tract had obviously been granted by the Crown during the French regime, and that some French deed to this parcel of land perhaps existed, Rivard mentioned nothing on its history in his claim because it was not relevant. Instead, Rivard simply asserted preemption rights: "I claim title to the above tract of land by virtue of possession, and improvements made by me in 1795, and continued to this day."[77] On 3 December 1808, settler Étienne Couture similarly claimed rights to a tract of land near River Raisin. In the request, his witness, Antoine Guy, affirmed that "previous to the 1st of July, 1796, Joseph Deschatelet was in possession and occupancy of the premises, and continued so until he sold his improvements to the claimant eight or nine years ago, who has possessed and occupied the same to this day."[78] This tract, which was given the number 442, had arguably been granted by the Potawatomi. On 29 June 1808, Jacques Allard claimed the tract of land on which he lived north of River Huron, along Lake St Clair. His property, identified as claim number 184, measured three arpents in front by forty arpents in depth. Brought forward as a

Figure 5.5 Private claims in Wayne County's District of Hamtramck, 1810. Surveyed by Aaron Greeley.

witness, Charles Poupard swore that "several years previous to the 1st July, 1796, the claimant was in possession and occupancy of the premises, and has continued so to this day."[79] President James Madison signed the official patent for Allard's tract of land on 1 June 1811, the same day as the commission on private claims in Michigan Territory officially ended.[80]

For some time after the end of the private claims commission, land transactions specified the number that the commissioners had given to the properties being traded. On 17 July 1811, Charles Chauvin (descendant of 1734 grantee Charles Chauvin discussed in chapter 2) sold his tract of land on the south shore of the River Rouge to settler Gabriel Godfroy, and indicated that following the report of the surveyor of the United States ("*suivant le rapport de l'arpenteur des Etats Unis*") his property had been identified as private claim number 37.[81] On 29 August 1818, Laurent Griffard sold his property located on the north shore of Lake St Clair to François Thibault. The transaction stipulated that on 15 June 1812, Congress had recognized the title to said tract of land and that it had then been given the number 183.[82] Others, without specifying the number of their property, mentioned in their transactions that it had been surveyed by Aaron Greeley, a surveyor from Upper Canada.[83]

In total, at least 738 private claims were brought before the commissioners between 1805 and 1811.[84] Apparently, as many certificates were produced and shown to the deputy surveyor of Wayne County. Initially, Congress had appointed Abijah Hull to this position. However, on 1 August 1807, Audrain, Abbott, and Griswold wrote to Gallatin that they were "sorry to say [that] not a single survey had been made and that the person appointed for that purpose was too much occupied in other business to attend to surveying."[85] On 12 November 1807, the commissioners complained that "to this day two surveys only are returned to the register of the land office."[86] Meanwhile, on 16 November 1807, Gallatin had suggested Jared Mansfield, surveyor general of the United States (1803–12), to "appoint another Deputy Surveyor, besides Mr. Hull," so the survey of the lands in Wayne County could be completed.[87] On 14 March 1808, Aaron Greeley, who had recently emigrated from Upper Canada, where he had surveyed many lands near York (Toronto), became the new deputy surveyor of Wayne County.[88] Before the end of 1810, Greeley had surveyed hundreds of tracts of land. His surveys clearly showed the major impact of the French method of land organization,

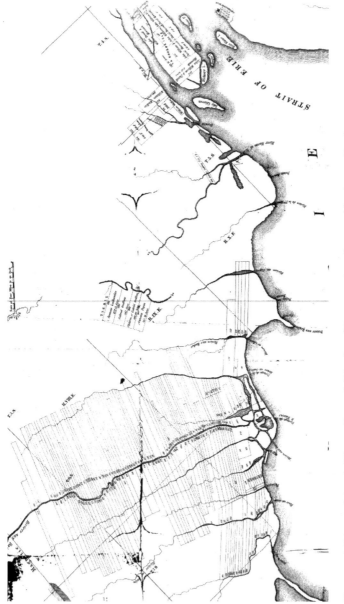

Figure 5.6 Private claims in Wayne County's District of Sargent, 1810. Surveyed by Aaron Greeley.

for only a handful of the tracts of land that Greeley surveyed in the Detroit River region did not have a long and narrow shape.

For the French of Wayne County, the commission on private claims had finally put an end to decades of anxiety regarding their land titles. Besides the fact that the French occupied only a small portion of Michigan Territory, the United States government willingly recognized their claims for two main reasons: 1) the Heir and Devisee Commissions in Upper Canada had already led to the acknowledgement of the land titles of French settlers who lived on the south shore of the Detroit River; and 2) refusing to recognize private property rights to those established on the American side of the border would have been contrary to the ideal of liberty, which all the citizens of the Republic were in theory entitled to enjoy. On 1 December 1805, Hoffman and Bates informed Gallatin regarding the act that had established the first Heir and Devisee Commission in Upper Canada in 1797. They added that they believed that British authorities had "through motives of humanity, expediency, or policy, confirmed the original purchases and claims of almost all descriptions, however irregular or illegal" they were.[89] Although they refused virtually all the claims brought before them, Hoffman and Bates believed that Congress probably had no choice but to imitate British authorities regarding the French settlers: "We will not waste our time nor yours ... by attempting to prove what, indeed, is almost self-evident, that claimants of this description have every thing to hope from the humane benevolence of the Government, but nothing to demand from its justice."[90] On 12 March 1806, a few months after his arrival in Detroit, Augustus Woodward, Michigan Territory's first chief justice, declared with regards to the local farms that "to snatch from the humble Canadian (i.e. French) his little enjoyments, would be an act unworthy the American nation; it would be to treat with unmerited harshness a virtuous citizen, and to inflict a wound on its own prosperity."[91] On 30 January 1807, Commissioner Griswold heartily advocated for the rights of the French of Wayne County in the letter he wrote to President Thomas Jefferson: "Sir, from a thorough acquaintance with the situation of this country and its inhabitants, give me leave to assure you, that it is a matter of considerable importance that the titles to land should be settled without delay, and on principles at least equally liberal as those which have been extended to the other Territories of the United States." He agreed that speculators should not be confirmed in their claims, but felt the need to specify that Detroit was "an ancient settlement, that the farms are cultivated, that the occupants are natives, born on the soil which they now claim, feeling that soil to be their home, as it is indeed the only home they have on earth, and the only source of their subsistence."[92]

The French who lived on the north shore of the Detroit River had worried for decades about the recognition of their land titles. The regime change of 1796 did not have dramatic consequences on their land titles, at least not in the short term. According to the new regime, no matter how they had acquired their properties, the French landowners who had improved their lands would have their rights acknowledged by Congress and their titles officially confirmed by the president, in most cases before the outbreak of the War of 1812. These hundreds of recognitions could only be well received by the French because in addition to giving them long-awaited official land titles, they guaranteed that the layout of their farms would not be changed. In other words, the settlements that they had created along the north shore of the Detroit River as well as at River Raisin and River Huron (Clinton River), and the French society in which most of them had grown up, would not immediately be altered.

CONCLUSION

During the two decades that followed the British conquest, the new regime attempted to prevent the establishment and development of European settlements on the western frontier. After the American Revolution, this situation changed when the British Crown agreed to accommodate the Loyalists who wished to settle in present-day Ontario. As a result, before the turn of the nineteenth century, in accordance with the Royal Proclamation of 1763, the Crown had signed several treaties of land cession with several Aboriginal peoples, and settlers were now authorized to inhabit the areas that had been "ceded." In 1788, four land boards were established to deal with land organization and land titles. One of them was in charge of the territory that included the south shore of the Detroit River. At the time, all the lands along the Detroit River had a long and narrow shape, and almost all of them were owned by French settlers. By 1789, the settlers were able to request that certificates be granted to them that eventually could be exchanged for land titles. Apparently, virtually all of the French landowners of the south shore of the Detroit River applied to obtain such certificates. This process benefitted the French of Essex County, as it allowed them to continue to live on their properties. However, it put an end to the granting of properties which had a long and narrow shape, because beyond their lands British authorities would eventually divide the territory into townships.

In Wayne County, the experience of the French settlers regarding the recognition of their land titles was similar to that of the settlers in Essex County. By 1805, landowners could apply to obtain certificates for their properties which would lead to the recognition of their land titles by Congress and ultimately to the grant of patents by the president. The commission on private claims in Michigan Territory had secured the land titles of hundreds of French settlers. However, when the first auction of the sale of public land in Michigan Territory was held in 1818, authorities in Wayne County began to lay out the territory into square units, putting an end forever to the expansion of the French method of organizing the land in long and narrow lots in the Detroit River region. And yet, throughout the intricate process of trying to have their land titles recognized under the British and American flags, between the 1760s and 1810s, the French continued to transform the physical landscape of the Detroit River region, not only by building farms, windmills, and raising livestock, but also by planting orchards on the very properties they had claimed.

6

French Orchards

After the fall of New France, the deep attachment of the French settlers of the Detroit River region to their lands led them to fight for recognition of their land titles by British authorities. After a few decades of frustrations and disappointments, they were finally, at the turn of the nineteenth century, able to get the recognition they had hoped for, at least regarding private property rights. From the New France era and through the British regime, those French settlers had also further demonstrated their connection with the land by planting fruit trees on their properties. By the early nineteenth century, virtually all of the French farms along the Detroit River and other nearby watercourses had an orchard that usually included apple and pear trees, and sometimes other types of fruit trees as well. These orchards came to symbolize the French roots in the Detroit River region.

FRENCH ORCHARDS IN THE SAINT LAWRENCE VALLEY

In colonial Anglo-America, the act of planting an orchard symbolized the establishment of community roots. Historian William Kerrigan states that this act more precisely "exemplified beliefs about property rights, for a well-ordered orchard was a visible cue of landownership." He also contends that having an orchard "manifested the dominant European subsistence strategy of fixity, as opposed to mobility, on the land," and it "represented a long-term investment in a well-defined place."[1] In this way, the planting of orchards often accompanied Anglo-American colonial endeavours.

For instance, in the 1790s the Loyalists who settled in the Bay of Quinte, Upper Canada, were eager to plant orchards on their new lands, as nineteenth-century Canadian surgeon and amateur historian William Canniff noted: "One of the first considerations, after the settler had attained comfort, at least secured what was requisite for life, was the planting of fruit trees."[2]

Settlers in New France also planted orchards on their properties. Seeds of apple trees imported from France were planted at Quebec in 1617, by the first actual French settler in the Saint Lawrence valley, Louis Hébert.[3] As the region of Quebec began to witness the faster expansion of the French colonial presence, in 1632, French explorer Samuel de Champlain reported that these seeds had become apple trees.[4] In 1664, Pierre Boucher, Sieur de Boucherville, confirmed that apple trees had now been planted further away from Quebec, along the Saint Lawrence River, but also observed the absence of other kinds of French fruit trees in the colony.[5] In the early eighteenth century, French chronicler Claude-Charles Bacqueville de La Potherie affirmed that there were now pear and peach trees at Quebec.[6] In 1749, Swedish botanist Pehr Kalm reported that many French farmers in the Saint Lawrence valley had fruit trees on their properties, but that more dwellers still had not planted any.[7] The growth of fruit trees on French farms of the Saint Lawrence valley continued for several decades after the change in political regime. In 1776, English traveller Thomas Anbury declared that most of the homesteads located along the Saint Lawrence River had no fruit trees, but that overall there were many orchards in the colony.[8]

In the Saint Lawrence valley, Montreal had the best climate for fruit growing. In 1808, English traveller John Lambert confirmed this by writing that at Montreal apples and pears were "in more abundance and in greater perfection than in any other part of Lower Canada."[9] His fellow Englishman and temporary resident Hugh Gray similarly affirmed that the apples from Montreal were "particularly good," before describing them further: "the Pomme de Neige, so called from its being extremely white, and from its having the granulated appearance of snow, when broken; it also dissolves, almost entirely, in the mouth like snow: the Fameuse, Bourassa, and Pomme Gris, are very fine apples."[10] Incidentally, at the time of New France, Roman Catholic orders had several large orchards made up of hundreds of fruit trees in the region of Montreal.[11]

The fruit raised in the orchards of the Saint Lawrence valley was often used to make beverages. The most popular of these beverages was probably apple cider. In 1712, French cartographer Gédéon de Catalogne remarked that the Sulpician superior François Vachon de Belmont, then in charge of the *seigneurie particulière* of Montreal on behalf of his order, had an apple orchard on his property at the Mountain mission, which produced up to 120 barrels of cider annually.[12] In the eighteenth-century Saint Lawrence valley, the making of cider was almost universal among the French farmers who had apple trees on their properties and, in the words of historical geographer R. Cole Harris, this cider "was reported to be equal of that in Normandy."[13]

WILD FRUIT ALONG THE DETROIT RIVER

Several French travel accounts from the late seventeenth century reveal that wild fruit trees were already abundant along the Detroit River before the establishment of Fort Pontchartrain. In the 1670s, Recollet missionary Louis Hennepin was on board the *Griffon*, the first vessel to sail the Great Lakes, when it navigated the Detroit River. Later, the explorer commented on the numerous wild fruit trees he observed.[14] In 1682, René Robert Cavelier, Sieur de La Salle, who had been mandated to take possession of the Great Lakes region on behalf of Louis XIV, was also struck by the significant presence of wild walnut, chestnut, plum, and apple trees along the Detroit River.[15] In the late 1680s, while he held the position of commander of Fort Saint Joseph (Dulhut Post), Louis-Armand de Lom d'Arce de Lahontan, Baron de Lahontan, also observed this significant presence of wild fruit trees in the Detroit River region.[16]

In 1701, after having built Fort Pontchartrain Cadillac gave an identical picture of the surrounding environment by stating that the shores of the Detroit River were bordered by rows of wild fruit trees that had never been taken care of by any gardener. He added that these trees produced so much fruit that their branches bent towards the ground.[17] In 1702, Alphonse de Tonty, then the assistant of Cadillac at Fort Pontchartrain, corroborated the presence in the area of numerous apple trees and of different kinds of plum trees.[18] Positioned at Detroit in 1706, military officer François Dauphin de La Forest reported that his troops agreed with Cadillac's description of the surrounding environment.[19]

GROWING FRUIT TREES AT DETROIT

In regards to the method that the French used to grow fruit trees in the Detroit River region, New York native and author Charles F. Hoffman stated in 1835 that the French orchards of the area were the result of the grafting of roots or plants of fruit trees upon others (native to the place or brought from elsewhere).[20] However, nineteenth-century naturalist Bela Hubbard later contested the idea that the French orchards stemmed from "seedlings raised here and grafted, for the art was then little practised in America, and not at all among the Canadians."[21] Indeed, it is doubtful that French settlers in the Detroit River region ever grafted any plants. The presence of many wild fruit trees in the vicinity of Fort Pontchartrain at the turn of the eighteenth century certainly revealed the high fertility of the soil in the region, making it perfect for the growth of French orchards, but it is unlikely that this led to any grafting experiments, especially not involving these wild trees. Rather, the French initially planted seeds brought from the Saint Lawrence valley and later transplanted small fruit trees from one property to another.

THE ORIGINS OF DETROIT'S FRENCH ORCHARDS: TESTIMONIES

When exactly the planting of French orchards in the Detroit River region began is unknown. There are several conflicting accounts of the dates of these plantings, and the French settlers themselves did not make many notes about the landscape they were changing by planting orchards. Hubbard, whose parents had settled in Detroit in 1835, consulted descendants of the eighteenth-century French settlers about the origin of their orchards in the 1870s. However, the answers he obtained did not entirely elucidate the situation: "Old people will tell you that their ancestors obtained the trees from Montreal, to which place they were brought at a still earlier day from Normandy or Provence."[22] In 1838, a French farmer living on the south shore of the Detroit River told British traveller Anna Jameson that his ancestors had "penetrated into these regions a century ago [and that] they [had] brought with them ... some of their finest national fruits – plums, cherries, apples, pears, of the best quality."[23] J. Bell Moran, descendant of 1734 grantee Claude Charles Moran, stated that of the few orchards that were still standing along the shores of the Detroit

River in the mid-twentieth century, the oldest were certainly two hundred years old.[24] This suggested that these "old" orchards may have been planted in the late 1740s.

THE ORIGINS OF DETROIT'S FRENCH ORCHARDS: CADILLAC

On 30 May 1702, in the letter he addressed to Jesuit missionary Pierre-Gabriel Marest, who was positioned in the Illinois Country, Cadillac said that he was not much concerned about the quality of the soil at Detroit, as long as it produced plenty of good seeds and tasty fruit.[25] The sources pertaining to Cadillac's convoy of 1706, which took French families of the Saint Lawrence valley to Fort Pontchartrain, are vague about the importation of seeds of fruit trees. It is known that one of the canoes of this convoy carried French wheat seeds as well as "other kinds of seeds" ("*toutes sortes d'autres grains*"), but it is not clear exactly what type of seeds the others were.[26] In 1711, after the departure of Cadillac, Recollet missionary Cherubin Deniau listed all the belongings that the first commander of Fort Pontchartrain had left behind, but although his list was exhaustive it contained nothing about seeds or fruit trees.[27] In the 1720s, Cadillac reported on different occasions that he had constructed several buildings at Detroit. However, his statements did not include any information about planting fruit trees.[28] In the early 1730s, Cadillac's oldest son, Joseph de Lamothe Cadillac, declared that his father had gardens at Detroit, though he did not provide any details about them.[29] On 28 August 1738, Joseph sold everything that his late father still owned (or had claimed to own) at Detroit to Bernard Maichens, a merchant based in Marseille, France for twenty-five thousand livres. The certificate that confirmed the sale stated that the Cadillac family possessed lands, fruit, farms, apartments, buildings, and livestock at Detroit.[30] Cadillac, and perhaps a few other settlers, almost certainly had fruit trees within Fort Pontchartrain or nearby, but the sources that relate to the founding of Detroit are lacking clear information regarding the early growth of French fruit trees there.

THE ORIGINS OF DETROIT'S FRENCH ORCHARDS: THE JESUITS

The pear trees that were planted along the Detroit River at the time of New France are sometimes, still today, referred to as the

"Jesuit pear trees" even though their origin is unknown. The first Jesuit missionary in the Detroit River region was Father Armand de La Richardie, who worked among the Huron from 1728 to 1751.[31] When La Richardie arrived at Detroit, the Huron village was located immediately to the west of Fort Pontchartrain, on the north shore (in the future Côte des Pous). It was relocated to Bois Blanc Island in 1742 before being moved again in 1748, this time to the south shore of the Detroit River, near where the University of Windsor stands today. The Jesuit Pierre-Philippe Potier joined La Richardie at the Huron mission on Bois Blanc Island in 1744.[32] Perhaps these missionaries, La Richardie and Potier, played a role in the planting of French orchards at Detroit. If they did, their contribution would most likely have begun before the arrival of the convoys of 1749–51. Military engineer Gaspard-Joseph Chaussegros de Léry Jr planted grape seeds in the "King's garden" ("*jardin du Roy*") at Detroit in 1749.[33] In Montreal, before his departure, he had also prepared a bag of seeds of all kinds to provide to the settlers at Detroit.[34] However, upon his arrival Chaussegros de Léry noted that many French settlers along the north shore of the Detroit River already had small private orchards on their farms. Chaussegros de Léry observed that not only did the French population of Detroit have an abundance of apples, but they also had plenty of pears, peaches, and plums.

CÔTES AND ORCHARDS

By 1734, as a result of the establishment of the *seigneurie directe*, French settlers began to build farms east of Fort Pontchartrain on the north shore of the Detroit River. By 1747, such homesteads started to be laid out west of the fort as well. Up until the early 1730s, practically the entire French population of the Detroit River region had lived within Fort Pontchartrain, but this changed with the formation first of the Côte du Nord-Est and then of the Côte des Pous. Following the convoys of 1749 and 1750, the settlements of Petite Côte and Côte du Sud (or L'Assomption) were created on the south shore of the Detroit River. The growth of this French colonial presence, from its confines within the fortifications to spreading out to the neighbouring lands, had a positive impact on the progression of fruit culture in the area. From this time onward, French farmers began to plant orchards on their properties. Nearly all of the French sources pertaining to the region between the 1730s and 1810s contain no information about fruit trees. Still, a few documents, mainly notarial records, confirmed their growing presence.

On 8 March 1757, settler Jean Baptiste Cardinal Sr sold to Jean Baptiste Rau a property of three arpents wide by forty arpents deep that he had received from the French king in 1750.[35] Royal notary Robert Navarre, who endorsed the transaction between Cardinal and Rau, implied that there was perhaps an orchard on Cardinal's property by stating that the sale included all buildings, fences, and "fruit trees if there are any" (*"arbres fruitiers s'il y en a"*). Navarre's words suggested that the presence of fruit trees on private properties along the Detroit River was not unusual in the 1750s. If Cardinal had fruit trees on his farm, he would have planted them between 1750 and 1757.

On 15 September 1765, the father-in-law of Robert Navarre, François Lootman dit Barrois, who was eighty-six years old, traded his tract of land of three arpents wide by forty arpents deep to settler Charles Denis Courtois. The deed for this land transaction, which had been signed by Navarre, confirmed that the property of Lootman included a fence, gardens, as well as an orchard (*"cloture, jardins & verger"*).[36] Born near Montreal in 1679, Lootman had relocated to Detroit with his wife in the late 1710s, where he later received a piece of land, in 1750.[37] Including Navarre, five of Lootman's sons-in-law were grantees of the French regime, four of whom had received their tract of land along the Detroit River in the 1730s or 1740s.[38] It is plausible that Lootman had obtained seeds of fruit trees or small fruit trees through one of them.

On 8 September 1766, settler Suzanne Pépin and her second husband, François Gervais dit Laderoute, traded the farm they owned at the northeast end of the Côte du Nord-Est, about twelve kilometres from the fort, for that of Jacques Campau, located in Petite Côte. Suzanne Pépin had inherited her property from her first husband, François Godefroy dit St-Georges, who had received it in 1751.[39] Jacques Campau had purchased his property from François Xavier Prud'homme, grantee of 1751.[40] The property of Suzanne Pépin and François Gervais dit Laderoute included buildings, fences as well as an apple tree nursery. In contrast, Jacques Campau had not invested any effort into developing his property, most likely because he had not lived on it.[41] The trade agreement revealed that Pépin and Gervais had required Campau to bring them thirty small apple trees the following spring, so they could begin to grow apples trees on their new property. Gervais had further asked to be able to access a small portion of the nursery after the exchange.⁴² The apples trees of this nursery had obviously been planted by Pépin's first husband between 1751 and his death in 1764.

On 3 April 1770, settler Jean Louis Campau and his wife, Marie Louise Robert, then respectively sixty-seven and seventy-one years old, passed down to their youngest son, Jean Baptiste, a tract of land of three arpents wide by forty arpents deep. The legal document that certified this inheritance, also signed by Navarre, specified that along with the land itself Jean Baptiste's parents had given him all the buildings located on it, all the seeds and fruit trees that already had roots, and all the fences.⁴³

On 1 August 1775, Fort Detroit merchants Collins Andrews and George Meldrum sold to local brothers Jean Baptiste and Antoine Alexis Chapoton a tract of three arpents wide by forty arpents deep that they owned in the Côte du Nord-Est. Neither Andrews or Meldrum had lived on this land which had been purchased from an unidentified grantee of the French regime. Notary Philippe Dejean, who signed the deed for this transaction, testified that the property of Andrews and Meldrum contained a house, barn, fence, and orchard.⁴⁴ In 1775, one of the two properties which bounded that of Andrews and Meldrum belonged to Antoine Boyer, inheritor of Pierre Boyer.⁴⁵ In 1754, the two neighbours of Pierre Boyer were Charles Chauvin Sr and François Nicolas Lauzon. The unidentified grantee of the French regime from which Andrews and Meldrum had purchased the farm was perhaps either Chauvin or Lauzon.⁴⁶ The two men had settled in the Côte du Nord-Est in 1734, after having resided within Fort Pontchartrain for a few years.⁴⁷ There is no evidence that Chauvin and Lauzon had begun to grow fruit trees on their properties in the 1730s or 1740s. However, considering that French farmers in the Côte du Nord-Est already had orchards in 1749, as Chaussegros de Léry reported, it can be argued that Chauvin and Lauzon had likely planted fruit trees before the 1750s. Therefore, the orchard located on the property that Jean Baptiste and Antoine Alexis Chapoton purchased from Collins Andrews and George Meldrum had certainly been planted in the 1760s, perhaps even between the 1730s and 1750s.

On 2 May 1782, Jacques Godfroy, who resided in the Côte des Pous, gave part of his property to his son Gabriel Jacques. On this tract of one arpent wide had been planted an orchard over which, as British notary Thomas Williams reported, Jacques Godfroy had preserved exclusive rights despite his gift of almost the balance of the property.⁴⁸ Born at Detroit in 1722, Jacques Godfroy had apparently lived within the fort until the early 1760s.⁴⁹ It is not clear how and when exactly he had acquired his land in the Côte des Pous, but if he was the first owner of this property then his orchard was less than twenty years old in 1782.

On 20 June 1788, Louis François Suzor sold his property of three arpents wide by forty arpents deep located at Petite Côte to Martin Durocher. Signed by notary Guillaume Monforton, the deed for this transaction revealed that there was an orchard on Suzor's land.⁵⁰ Born near Montreal in 1738, Suzor had acquired his property at Petite Côte either in the late 1750s, through a grant from the commander of Fort Pontchartrain, or in the early 1760s, through a purchase from a grantee who had received it between 1749 and 1760. Therefore, the orchard which Durocher now possessed had likely been planted in the 1760s or 1770s.

In the 1780s, as they acquired lands north of the côtes of the Detroit River, the French also planted orchards in that area. In 1808, twenty-four-year-old Louis Pradet dit Laforge had recently become the owner of a farm located between the Côte du Nord-Est and River Huron (Clinton River), on the west shore of Lake St Clair. On this property was an orchard that had been planted in the 1790s, perhaps a little earlier. It is not known who had owned this property before Louis acquired it. Louis's father had relocated from Quebec to Detroit in the early 1780s, where he married Marguerite Campau, granddaughter of Michel Campau, grantee in 1707 of a tract of land located east of Fort Pontchartrain (in the future Côte du Nord-Est).⁵¹ In 1796, Louis's father was listed as the owner of a tract of land along the River Huron.⁵² However, he was unlikely the first owner of Louis's tract of land. Nevertheless, it is known that the majority of the fruit trees of Louis's orchard were still standing at the turn of the twentieth century.⁵³ Louis died near River Huron in the early 1870s, where most of the children he had first with Thérèse Tremblay and then with Élisabeth Laboursonière established roots.⁵⁴ This suggests that Louis enjoyed this orchard for several decades.

JOSEPH CAMPAU'S ORCHARDS

On 6 October 1808, Joseph Campau, who was among the most prominent Detroit merchants in the first half of the nineteenth century, purchased from Louis Maure Sr a property of five arpents wide located along the River Huron. The transaction stipulated that Maure's property included an old house, barn, fences, as well as fifteen apple trees, nine peach trees, and one cherry tree.[55] Born at Quebec in 1758, Maure had relocated to the Côte du Sud with his wife Marie Moreau sometime between 1782 and 1787. From the Côte du Sud the couple had moved to River Huron. The date of their move to River Huron is not known, but Maure was listed as the owner of a tract of land there in 1796.[56] As a result, it is not clear whether or not Maure himself had planted these fruit trees and if he did, when exactly he planted them. Joseph Campau, for his part, belonged to a family that had been growing fruit in the Detroit River region for at least half a century. In 1769, his grandfather Jean Louis Campau, who was the brother of Jean Baptiste Campau introduced earlier, had inherited a tract of land in the Côte du Nord-Est which most likely included fruit trees planted before the 1760s.

Since the 1790s, merchant Joseph Campau had acquired several other farms, mainly in the Côte du Nord-Est and at River Huron, to lease them to other settlers. Some of his leases mentioned the presence of orchards. In the five-year lease of one of his farms at River Huron to Louis McDougall, dated 24 March 1810, Campau required the leaseholder to stop using everything that was on the property when the contract expires, namely the house, barn, orchard, and fences.[57] On 9 January 1812, Campau used similar language when he leased to Joseph Desnoyers one of his tracts of land located near his home, in the Côte du Nord-Est. However, in this case he restricted the leaseholder from collecting fruit in the orchard during the entire length of their one-year agreement.[58] These leases revealed that Campau had grown fruit trees on his properties or, more likely, that fruit trees had been planted on these lands in the 1780s or 1790s by their first owners.

FENCED PROPERTIES

The French of the Detroit River region generally planted their orchards near their houses, at the end of their tracts of land that fronted onto the river. During the French regime, most farmers built wooden fences around their houses and orchards. In the Detroit River region, this custom traced back to the seigneurial system of French tenure implemented within the seigneurie directe. When French authorities granted tracts of land along the Detroit River between 1734 and 1760, they required their grantees to separate their properties with fences ("*clôtures mitoyennes*").[59] Although they were not obliged to do so, the French also enclosed the dwellings they had built on lands obtained through Aboriginal deeds over the decades following the British conquest.[60] In 1813, Elias Darnell, an American prisoner in the War of 1812, observed that the French settlement of River Raisin was made up of a row of houses near the river banks. More importantly, he remarked that each of these houses was "surrounded with a fence made in the form of picketing, with split timber, from four to five feet high," before adding that this type of fence "was not designed as a fortification, but to secure their yards and gardens."[61] In the 1890s, Charles Moore, whose ancestors were related to Louis Maure Sr introduced earlier, similarly explained that these fences "guarded the farms from the cattle, and especially from the droves of squealing French ponies that dashed up and down the narrow road leading along the river-bank."[62] Not surprisingly, many French settlers of Michigan Territory were upset when their fences were used as firewood by American troops during the War of 1812.[63]

APPLE CIDER

In the early eighteenth century, Cadillac first attempted to produce cider with wild apples that grew near Fort Pontchartrain. French naval commissary François Clairambault d'Aigremont, who had the opportunity to drink some of this cider when he visited Detroit in 1708, wrote that it had a very bitter taste.[64] After the establishment of the seigneurie directe, the French living in the côtes of the Detroit River began to produce a significant quantity of cider from the apples that grew in their orchards. By the 1770s, if not before, many French farmers began to sell some of the apple cider they produced to merchants of Fort Detroit; Jean Baptiste Crête and Jean Baptiste Beaubien are examples of merchants who regularly purchased apple cider from local farmers.[65]

EARLY ANGLO-AMERICAN ACCOUNTS OF THE ORCHARDS

Although it is possible that fruit trees had been raised within Fort Pontchartrain at the time of Cadillac, the French of the Detroit River region only began to plant small private orchards between the 1730s and 1750s, after the establishment of the seigneurie directe. This change in land tenure had encouraged the construction of dwellings along the Detroit River and, as a result, a handful of French settlers planted an orchard on their property. Between the 1750s and 1770s, the planting of fruit trees in the different côtes of the Detroit River had become much more frequent. By the 1780s and 1790s, this practice was extended to the French settlements being established along the other watercourses of the region. Although this development is not explicit in the French sources, the fact that by the early nineteenth century nearly all of the French farmers had guarded their properties from livestock with fences, even though they were not required to do so after the fall of New France, suggests that the number of orchards in the Detroit River region had become quite significant by the early nineteenth century.

Before the nineteenth century, British officials positioned in the Detroit River region paid little attention to the French orchards of the area. This was due mostly to the fact that they had not been instructed to appraise the potential of the area in terms of colonial development, especially not before the American Revolution. In the battle reports of Pontiac's uprising, there were a few allusions to the French orchards. When he described the Battle of Bloody Run on 31 July 1763, after British troops decided to confront Pontiac's warriors about three kilometres east of Fort Detroit, Lieutenant Colonel Henry Gladwin reported that as soldiers retreated to the fort they "were met by the rapid firing of the Indians who had occupied the houses and orchards between the English and the fort."[66] On 8 August 1763, Lieutenant James MacDonald reported to Major Horatio Gages that Captain Alexander Grant of the eighteenth regiment was now "in possession of a very strong orchard."[67] Apparently old, this orchard was almost certainly located in the Côte du Nord-Est. Grant had likely taken possession of it as a military strategy, to prevent Aboriginal people from preparing assaults by hiding behind its trees.

Henry Hamilton, first lieutenant-governor of the District of Detroit after the incorporation of the region in the Province of Quebec, was apparently the only British subject who described the French orchards that grew along the Detroit River before the nineteenth century. On 29 August 1776, he portrayed the French farms of the Detroit River region to William Legge, Second Earl of Dartmouth, as follows: "They build on the borders of the straight, and occupy about 13 miles in length on the north, and 8 on the south side – the houses are all of log or frame work, shingled, the most have their orchard adjoining, the appearance of the settlement is very smiling."[68] Clearly, Hamilton was enchanted by the presence of these French orchards.

During the War of 1812, American military officers briefly mentioned the French orchards on the shores of the Detroit River. Brigadier General Lewis Cass, who became governor of Michigan Territory before the end of the conflict, stated that on 14 July 1812, his troops had left Sandwich, across the Detroit River from Fort Detroit, to move eastward along Lake St Clair on the British side, and that "after marching about eight miles the detachment halted, about an hour before day, in an apple orchard." Cass also reported that on 24 July, he had advanced towards Petite Côte with Major James Denny, where he "halted about three o'clock the next morning, in a wheat field, three fourths of a mile from the bridge over the [River] Aux Canards," and that at sunrise he had "quit the wheat field and formed an ambuscade, in a neighbouring orchard."[69]

During the first half of the nineteenth century, many more British observers commented on the French orchards of the area. Susan B. Greeley, whose father Aaron Greeley had relocated from Upper Canada to Michigan Territory in 1806 to survey private properties, recollected that her father had encountered French orchards at Detroit. "My father," she recalled, "purchased two water lots and a town lot, on Water Street which ran parallel with the Main Street, up the River, through what had been the old French gardens [where] apple trees occupied the sides of the street." Susan's father had particularly been delighted by "two immense pear trees, the admiration of everyone, which had stood here 'time out of mind' and still bore fruit in abundance."[70]

As migration to Michigan Territory increased after the War of 1812, many American observers reported the presence of the French orchards. In 1821, Albert G. Ellis, born and raised in upstate New York, travelled to Green Bay, which was then part of Michigan Territory, and stopped at Detroit. There he found "farms being occupied on the old French plan [where] orchards of apple and pear trees invariably occupied the front – the trees indicating a growth of a hundred years."[71] One afternoon of July 1826, Thomas L. McKenney, who resided in the town of Detroit, where he worked for the United States Indian Department, took a walk through the Côte du Nord-Est and obviously enjoyed the presence of many orchards: "I have just returned from a ride of nine miles up the river to Grosse Pointe …

Figure 6.1 Jesuit pear tree, Windsor, Ontario, date unknown.

the grounds for the whole way are certainly excellent, and are for most part cut up into small farms on which are as fine apple orchards as I have ever seen."[72]

ENDURING IMPERIALIST NARRATIVES

According to historian Edward Watts, in the United States of the early American Republic era (ca. 1789–1823) there were two types of narratives regarding the old French settlements of the trans-Appalachian West. The first type, "imperialist," generally misrepresented these French people by focusing primarily on their "backwardness." The authors of such narratives, Watts argues, purposely minimized the existence of French farms on the western frontier while they overemphasized that of the "more easily removable and exploitable coureurs de bois or voyageurs."[73] When they did acknowledge the presence of French farmers, imperialist narratives denigrated them, notably because they allegedly "refused to focus on material acquisition and competition."[74] For instance, even though the French farmers of Michigan Territory had implored the United States government to recognize their land titles while he was governor of Michigan Territory, William Hull (1805–13) believed these people to be mere traders of the backcountry. In 1824, he described them as "miserable farmers, [who] paid little attention to agriculture, and [who] depended principally on hunting, fishing, and trading with the Indians for support."[75] Their "backwardness" was sometimes illustrated through their ignorance of the benefits of manure as fertilizer. As Detroiter and naturalist Bela Hubbard recollected, many Americans were shocked to witness French farmers in Michigan Territory getting rid of their manure "by carting the encumbrance on to ice in winter."[76] The French in the Saint Lawrence valley were also known for presumably disposing of their manure in the same manner.[77] Practicing such a "backward" custom in Michigan Territory, if true, therefore, does not mean that these French settlers neglected their fields for "frontier activities," and comments such as those of Hull were undoubtedly prejudiced.[78]

Probably the most enduring heritage of the imperialist narratives regarding the French of the southeast part of Michigan Territory is the use of the term "Muskrat French" to label these people.[79] Hubbard asserted that American migrants identified these French as such because of their outward "little degree of mental advancement."[80] Despite the original derogatory connotation of the term "Muskrat French," descendants of these French settlers, especially at River Raisin, came to identify with it as a way to encapsulate their cultural heritage.[81] Although its connotation is obviously not negative anymore, the term "Muskrat French" continues to provide a misleading description of the French of River Raisin because besides suggesting that the habit of eating muskrat was their most important cultural feature, it portrayed them as hunters first and foremost. Yet, the French of River Raisin were not always depicted in that way. In 1820, British traveller Daniel Blowe wrote that the inhabitants of River Raisin "are mostly French, who raise wheat, Indian corn, and potatoes, more than sufficient for their own consumption."[82] Blowe, who never visited River Raisin, had learned about the French of that region through different publications which were obviously not imperialist narratives. Also, it should be noted that the French of River Raisin were not the only French who ate muskrat; this tradition was already popular in every swampy area of the Saint Lawrence valley.[83]

The second type of discourse, "dissident," tended to relate the French farmers of the trans-Appalachian West and their practices to Thomas Jefferson's notion of agrarianism because of the nature of their homesteads. This belief held that rural life based on farming, no matter the scale, was the most virtuous lifestyle in the Republic.[84] In dissident narratives that addressed the presence of French settlers in the southeast part of Michigan Territory, observations regarding the beauty of their orchards abounded.[85] More importantly, during the first half of the nineteenth century dissident narratives praising the French definitely outnumbered imperialist ones. In other words, the French of the Detroit River region were best known for their orchards at that time, not for eating muskrat. Still, perhaps because the orchards that the French planted have progressively disappeared from the landscape, the dissident narratives eventually vanished whereas the imperialist narratives survived. This would explain, for instance, why the term "Muskrat French" rather than an epithet such as the "Orchard French," which certainly portrays the eighteenth-century French settlers of the Detroit River region more accurately, is notably used today by residents of the area to describe the cultural heritage of the descendants of the early residents of a place like River Raisin.

CONCLUSION

Similar to their counterparts in the Saint Lawrence valley, the French settlers in the Detroit River region planted orchards. At Detroit, this process was favoured by the establishment of the seigneurie directe in 1734, which by structuring land organization directly contributed to the building of French farms along the Detroit River. After the British conquest, the French continued to plant orchards as they acquired new tracts of land through Aboriginal deeds. Because they enjoyed an ideal climate for fruit growing, the French of the Detroit River region seemed to have planted many more fruit trees than the French in the Saint Lawrence valley and this might explain why their orchards later drew a lot of attention. In the early nineteenth century, many British and Americans who visited the Detroit River region were delighted by the significant presence of French orchards, and their fascination with them often led to the publication of accounts in which they were either described or mentioned. Yet, the misleading legacy of the "Muskrat French," which developed through imperialist narratives from the nineteenth century, has surmounted the more settled agricultural legacy of the French presence in the Detroit River region, especially on the American side of the border, to this very day.

7

Divided by the Border

This territory is situated on the frontier of a foreign Government, the Province of Upper Canada, belonging to his Britannic Majesty; notwithstanding the difference of Government, the French population which forms the principal part of both [sides of the Detroit River] are [still] one and the same people.[1]
Stanley Griswold, commissioner of Private Property Claims,
Michigan Territory, 1809

When the evacuation of Detroit took place, 1796, few, if any, of the French changed their places of residence. On both sides, the French habitant accepted the rule under which the changing circumstance of the times happened to place him.[2]
Hugh Cowan, 1929

The transformation of the Detroit River into an international border in 1796 did not divide the local French community overnight. After all, for generations, the Detroit River had been used as a conduit that brought people from the north and south shores together. As well, for the locals, "Détroit" had always included both sides of the river, not only the north shore. Therefore, it is not surprising that it took several years for the local French community to fully grasp the consequences of the creation of the border. Between 1796 and 1812, despite the establishment on the south side of the Detroit River of the military town of Amherstburg (est. 1796) and the merchant town of Sandwich (est. 1797), Fort Detroit remained by far the most important economic hub of the region. In this context, the French of the south shore simply continued to visit Fort Detroit for trade purposes during the first decades of the presence of the American regime on the north shore. In addition, in the early nineteenth century, many French individuals, perhaps the majority, had relatives living across the border.[3] Drawing a comprehensive picture of these cross-border family connections represents a difficult task because, at this time, the size of the French community included thousands of individuals on both sides of the Detroit River.[4] Moreover, the Detroit River region was still attracting French people from the Saint Lawrence valley during the first decades of the nineteenth century despite the creation of the border and the War of 1812. However, over time, by the 1830s, the Detroit River had begun to divide the local French community, and by the late nineteenth century there were now two separate French communities in the Detroit River region.

MERCHANT JOSEPH CAMPAU AND THE CROSS-RIVER TRADE

Detroit's wealthiest French man in the early nineteenth century was unquestionably merchant Joseph Campau (1769–1863), whose family's roots in the area traced back to Cadillac's era. He had fostered extensive connections throughout the Detroit River region and beyond, not only among the French but also among other groups, including local Aboriginal peoples. His business activities led him to produce thousands of documents (ledgers, land transactions, personal letters, etc.). These documents, many of which can be found today in the Burton Historical Collection of the Detroit Public Library, are a window into the local French society. For decades, Campau carefully recorded all of his transactions, and the names of his clients are mentioned in his ledgers. At the turn of the nineteenth century, he had dozens of clients, most of whom were French individuals living throughout the Detroit River region.

It is difficult to determine exactly how many of Campau's clients lived on the north shore of the Detroit River (i.e. within Wayne County's districts of Sargent, Hamtramck, or St Clair, altogether encompassing southeast Michigan) in comparison to the south shore (i.e. within Essex County or Kent County, encompassing southwest Ontario). However, it is possible to draw a partial picture of the local French community with regards to cross-river trade. The most obvious cases of cross-border trade involved the clients for whom Joseph Campau explicitly noted that were from *de l'autre bord*, meaning from across the Detroit River, or from a settlement located on the south shore.

Jean-Baptiste Soullière, "habitant des Petites Rivières de l'autre bord," is one such client. Born in the Saint Lawrence valley in 1751, he arrived in the Detroit River region in the 1780s. In 1794, he was living with his wife, Marie Félicité Mornier dit Léveillé, and their children on a farm in the settlement of the Côte du Sud, across the river from Fort Detroit.[5] Campau's 1801–2 ledger includes only a few entries pertaining to Soullière, which suggest that he did not cross the Detroit River on a weekly or monthly basis, at least not to visit the merchant. When the War of 1812 broke out, two of Soullière's sons, Jean-Baptiste Jr and Jean-Bernardin, were enrolled in the Second Regiment of the Essex Militia.[6] By then, the Soullière family was about to expand its presence to both sides of the border, for Jean-Baptiste Jr purchased a property at River Raisin. This occurred sometime during the 1810s, most likely shortly after the war ended as he is not mentioned in Michigan Territory's Commission on Land Titles (1805–11).[7] In 1819, along with dozens of other landowners at River Raisin, Jean-Baptiste Jr signed a petition for relief addressed to Congress.[8]

Jean-Baptiste Meloche, from "[de] l'autre bord fils de François," appeared more often than Jean-Baptiste Soullière in Campau's 1801–2 ledger, but not exactly on a regular basis. The roots of the Meloche family in the Detroit River region go back to the early eighteenth century.[9] His grandfather, Pierre Meloche Sr, had been granted a lot within Fort Pontchartrain in 1726.[10] In 1734, he had received a tract of land in the newly established Côte du Nord-Est.[11] Two years after his passing, in 1762, his sons François (the father of Jean-Baptiste mentioned in Campau's ledger) and Jean-Baptiste still lived on lands in the Côte du Nord-Est. However, Pierre's oldest son, Pierre Jr, now lived on a farm on the south shore, in Petite Côte.[12] Campau's Jean-Baptiste was born in the Côte du Nord-Est in 1773, but his parents sold their property and moved across the Detroit River sometime during the following years, and by 1801 the Meloche family owned properties only on the south shore.[13] Between 1819 and 1849, amid Upper Canada's Second Heir and Devisee Commission, Jean-Baptiste and several of his relatives received official titles for their lands south of the Detroit River.[14]

Charles Cloutier (born 1767), "de la Petite Côte," who did not visit Joseph Campau on a regular basis in 1801 or 1802, also belonged to a family that had roots on both sides of the Detroit River. His father, René, who was born in the Saint Lawrence valley, appeared in the 1762 British census as a resident of Petite Côte. Twenty years later, in 1782, he still resided there.[15] Meanwhile, in the early 1770s, his brother Zacharie (Charles's uncle) also settled in Petite Côte and married Thérèse Campau, a distant relative of Joseph Campau.[16] Sometime between 1785 and 1792, Charles's family moved to River Raisin; his father died there in the spring of 1796.[17] In 1794, only Zacharie apparently still owned property at Petite Côte; he passed away in 1803.[18] After marrying Marie Catherine Bézaire dit Léveillé of Assumption parish in 1795, Charles moved back to Petite Côte, where he died in 1822.[19] However, all his siblings remained at River Raisin. During Michigan Territory's Commission on Land Titles, René's heirs, Charles and his siblings, had the family farm at River Raisin documented as claim number 410.[20]

Many other clients of Joseph Campau, whose places of residence are not specified in the 1801–2 ledger, were also from the south shore of the Detroit River. François Lauzon is one of them. Both his grandfather and father had owned properties in the Côte du Nord-Est, where he was born in 1770.[21] In the 1782 British census, François still lived with his family on the north shore.[22] Between 1792 and 1802, François's father, Jacques, seems to have owned two properties at the same time, one in the Côte du Nord-Est and one in the Côte du Sud.[23] In 1803, when Michigan was part of Indiana Territory, Jacques Lauzon was still living on the north shore for he was among dozens of residents of Wayne County who signed a petition for the creation of Michigan as a new territory.[24] However, the fact that he was buried in the cemetery of Assumption church, on the south shore, in 1806 suggests that he had moved across the Detroit River some time before his death.[25] He may have relocated there to live with his son François and his wife Marie-Joseph Roy, who had married at Assumption church in 1801 and who then raised their children in the Côte du Sud.[26] When he crossed the Detroit River to visit Joseph Campau in 1801 and 1802, François Lauzon did so as a former resident of the north shore. Although most of his siblings also relocated to the south shore of the Detroit River at the turn of the nineteenth century, some members of his extended family continued to live across the border.

Jacques Belleperche, whose place of residence is also not specified in Campau's ledger, was another resident of the south shore. The Belleperches had established roots in the Detroit River region at the beginning of the eighteenth century. Jacques's father, gunsmith Pierre Belleperche, had married Angélique Estève dit Lajeunesse, a distant relative of Joseph Campau on her mother's side, at Fort Pontchartrain in 1727. In 1762, the Belleperches still resided within the fort. However, in 1782, several years after the passing of his father, Jacques now owned a property in the Côte du Sud. The following year, he married Cécile Lauzon. In the early nineteenth century, two of Jacques' siblings, Marie-Anne and Jeanne, lived on the north shore. As for Jacques and Cécile's children, born between 1784 and 1811, almost all of them married French individuals from the south shore and remained on that side of the border their entire lives.[27] In 1840 and 1841, in the context of the Second Heir and Devisee Commission, Jacques's sons, Pierre and Jacques Jr, received official titles for the lands they owned in the Côte du Sud.[28]

Wagon-maker Jean-Baptiste Paré Sr was another of Joseph Campau's clients who lived in Upper Canada at the turn of the nineteenth century. Like others, Jean-Baptiste Sr had lived on the north shore in the past, and some of his descendants would end up settling in Michigan Territory during the first decades of the nineteenth century. From the Saint Lawrence valley, he had settled at Fort Detroit in the early 1760s, where he married Marie-France Pelletier. The first eight children of the couple were born in the Côte du Nord-Est and baptized at Saint Anne's church, while their seven other children were born on the south side of the Detroit River and baptized at Assumption church. The Parés relocated across the river in 1777 or 1778, and Jean-Baptiste Sr was listed as the owner of a property in the Côte du Sud in 1794 where he resided until his death in 1809.[29] Sometime between 1802 and 1808, a Jean-Baptiste Paré, presumably the second youngest child of Jean-Baptiste Sr and Marie-France, born in 1788, claimed a tract of land along the shores of Lake St Clair, north of the Côte du Nord-Est.[30] On 17 June 1808, this lot was recognized by the commissioners of Michigan Territory's Commission on Land Titles as claim number 149. In their report, the commissioners noted that this Paré's tract contained "six arpents in front by forty in depth, bounded in front by lake St. Clair, and in rear by unconceded lands, above by lands claimed by Joseph Dubé, and below by lands claimed by Louis Laforge." They added that "François Dupré was also brought forward as a witness in behalf of the claimant, who, being duly sworn, deposed and said, that he, the deponent, purchased the premises from Cayet, and possessed the same until he sold to the claimant, who has possessed and cultivated the same until this day."[31] It seems that this Jean-Baptiste Paré did not live on this property for very long, if he ever lived on it at all; in the 1820 census of Michigan Territory, no Paré is listed as residing along Lake St Clair.[32] The son of Jean-Baptiste Sr and Marie-France, Jean-Baptiste, who seemingly was the one claiming a property along Lake St Clair before the War of 1812, was married twice. First, he married Angélique Livernois in Detroit's Saint Anne's parish in 1811.[33] The couple had four children between 1813 and 1819. All of them were born on the south shore of the Detroit River and baptized at Assumption church. In 1822, three years after the passing of Angélique, Jean-Baptiste remarried. This time, he was married at Assumption church, to Marguerite Jolibois. Unfortunately for the couple, Jean-Baptiste passed away the following year. He died at River Raisin and was buried in the cemetery of the local church, Saint Antoine's.[34]

These few examples of French men who crossed the Detroit River for trade purposes at the turn of the nineteenth century represent only a small sample of the much larger group of local French settlers who did not think of the newly established border as an obstacle to their economic activities, at least not for several years. For generations, the residents of the Detroit River region had simply crossed the Detroit River when they needed to. However, as historian Lawrence B.A. Hatter explains, "the process of creating a sovereign American state with fixed national boundaries remained unfinished in 1796, despite the transfer of the western posts [like Detroit]."[35] The United States government rapidly became preoccupied with the presence of British merchants on both sides of the border in the Detroit River region. These merchants had strong economic connections with Montreal and London, and many Republican critics believed that this "Laurentine trade threatened the integration of the West into an American national state."[36] Therefore, to the United States government, it became urgent to address this issue by mandating local federal officials in Detroit to strengthen "the authority of the American national state."[37] This would soon have an impact on cross-river trade in the Detroit River region, not only for the local British merchants but also for the French community.

WINDMILLS ON THE BORDER

In 1822, British immigrant to Upper Canada Robert Gourlay counted eight windmills and one watermill in the settlements of Côte du Sud and Petite Côte. He added that there were also two windmills in

Amherstburg.[38] These numbers did not include the windmills along the north shore of the Detroit River or other watercourses of Michigan Territory such as, for example, River Rouge or River Raisin. There had been windmills along the Detroit River since the era of Cadillac. Throughout the eighteenth century, their number had increased along with the growth of the French community. According to early twentieth-century Detroit lawyer and businessman Clarence M. Burton, these windmills "were of circular form with broad, sloping stone foundation and upright wooden body surrounded by a colonial roof, which was turned by a long sweep so as to bring the sails into position."[39] Nineteenth-century politician and Detroit native Thomas W. Palmer (1830–1913) recollected that in 1837 there were still "many of the old French windmills on the river from Amherstburg to St Clair."[40] However, by the 1870s, Detroit naturalist Bela Hubbard noted that "another feature of the old settlements has disappeared, the windmills, which once marked every few miles of river shore, and were an animating part of its picturesque scenery."[41] In the 1880s, a more detailed account of the demise of these French windmills was published in the *Detroit Free Press*: "The French settlers built towers for windmills; the counterparts of those that still grind wheat for the Norman peasants. Probably the last remaining Norman tower on the Canada side is the one by the old Red Tavern down at Petite Cote. A while since there was one on Hiram Walker's property at the upper end of the distillery, but the waves undermined it until at last it answered the call of the waters and sank into the blue Detroit. Further up was one owned by Luc Montreuil. It was of stone and timber, the exact semblance of its brethren in France. After spending a long and useful life in supplying the inhabitants with flour, it, like many another old-fashioned contrivance, gave way to the age of steam."[42]

In the early nineteenth century, when there were still many windmills in the Detroit River region, the local French settlers had several options as to where to take their wheat to be processed. They could take it to the nearest windmill, for convenience, or travel a few kilometres farther away if, for some reason, they had a favourite windmill. Sometimes, this favourite windmill happened to be located across the Detroit River. When the river became a border, in 1796, many French settlers simply continued to cross it as before. However, before long, federal officials in American Detroit began to regulate all types of cross-river trade, including river crossings to grind wheat.

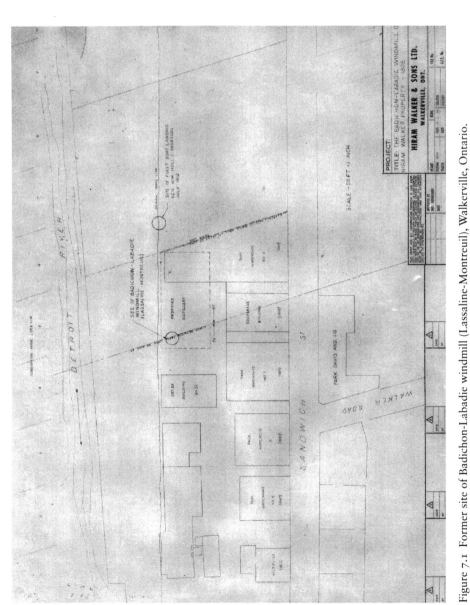

Figure 7.1 Former site of Badichon-Labadie windmill (Lassaline-Montreuil), Walkerville, Ontario.

Historian Catherine Cangany has examined the case of south shore resident Alexis Maisonville, who found himself in trouble for crossing the border to bring his wheat to a windmill in 1808. She writes: "In taking his wheat to a Detroit mill, Maisonville participated in a century-old custom. From the dawn of French settlement in what is today southeastern Michigan, the inhabitants of the Detroit River basin had sent their raw grain for processing into flour to Detroit, where it was milled and then returned. But on that day in July 1808, what should have been a routine commercial transaction escalated into an international legal battle."[43]

Alexis Maisonville was born in Detroit in 1776.[44] As discussed in chapter 3, his father, Alexis Loranger dit Maisonville (1728–1814), was already a resident of the Côte du Sud in the 1760s. In a bold move, Alexis Sr had travelled all the way to New York in 1771 to meet in person with the British commander-in-chief in North America, Thomas Gage, and try to have his land ownership rights recognized. Although he was not successful, because of the clauses of the British Royal Proclamation of 1763 that pertained to land ownership in the Great Lakes, he had not abandoned his property, but had instead continued to farm the land. In 1792, Alexis Loranger dit Maisonville had a windmill on his property in the Côte du Sud. It was located at the corner of today's Riverside Drive and Lincoln Road, in Windsor.[45] It is not known if this windmill still existed a decade later, or if it was still owned by the Maisonville family, but in the early nineteenth century, for some reason, Alexis Maisonville was used to taking his wheat from his property in the Côte du Sud to a windmill on the Michigan side.[46] Like most local French settlers, he did not seem to fully realize that his region was now transforming from one river-based sovereignty to two land-based sovereignties. In 1800, as Cangany explains, "the United States began to rationalize land-based sovereignty through the law, by appointing the first customs collector at Detroit."[47] The first customs collectors were not comfortable "with the new definition of sovereignty and its accompanying restrictions on commerce [so they] partially enforced the law, refusing altogether to levy duties on Canadian wheat landed in town."[48] This changed with the appointment of Reuben Atwater, who was also secretary of Michigan Territory, as Alexis Maisonville discovered in July 1808. When he arrived on American soil with his wheat, Atwater immediately convicted him of "inadvertently defrauding the United States."[49]

Figure 7.2 French windmill, Walkerville, Ontario, 1893.

Like his father had done in 1771, Alexis decided to fight for his rights, this time by suing the Territory of Michigan.

The trial between Alexis Maisonville and the Territory of Michigan took place in 1809. From the beginning, Maisonville argued that members of the local French community had always crossed the Detroit River, free of duty, to take their wheat to windmills, and therefore they should continue to enjoy this customary law. His argument convinced the Michigan Supreme Court and, as Cangany writes, "French residents of British Canada would be allowed to bring grain freely into Detroit for milling and then re-export it for consumption in Canada all free of U.S. duties."[50] However, the successors to Reuben Atwater were apparently not familiar with the 1809 court ruling and, as a result, it was never implemented. This ruling in favour of one of the local French's customary laws was forgotten within a decade. In the 1820s, 1830s, and 1840s, as border-crossing was more controlled, the French of either sides most likely stopped crossing the Detroit River with grain. To be sure, the vanishing of the French windmills from the landscape of the Detroit River region by the 1890s confirmed the end of cross-river milling.

FRENCH MIGRATIONS TO THE DETROIT RIVER BORDER REGION

In the decades between the signing of the Treaty of Paris of 1763, confirming the British conquest of North America, and the admission of Michigan to the Union as the 26th state of the United States in 1837, the migration of French people from the Saint Lawrence valley to the Detroit River region continued undaunted. This reality can be best explained by the fact that until the turn of the nineteenth century, Detroit remained one of the most important locations of the "French river world," along with places like Michilimackinac (Michigan), Saint Louis (Missouri), Sainte Geneviève (Missouri), and other settlements of the interior of North America (i.e. the creole corridor) that as yet had not been integrated into the United States. To explain the survival of this French river world beyond the demise of the French empire in North America, historian Robert Englebert writes that "the social reality on the ground was slow to change, and [that these] French settlements continued much as they had before – tied together by a commercial system of traders and merchants." He adds that "for an entire generation, the numbers of Spanish, British, and Anglo-Americans in the heart of North America remained modest," helping to augment the persistence of the French river world.[51] It is precisely in this context that, between the 1760s and 1840s, thousands of French men from the Saint Lawrence valley worked as voyageurs for Montreal-based British merchants, and travelled to Detroit and other places to acquire peltries from French fur traders or Aboriginal people. During this period of trade, thousands of "voyageur contracts" were produced by Montreal notaries; many of these contracts can be found in Quebec archives. To facilitate their use, historians Nicole St-Onge and Robert Englebert have created the "Voyageur Contracts Database." Accessible through the website of the Société Historique de Saint-Boniface, the database includes data from more than 35,000 contracts signed in front of Montreal notaries between 1714 and 1830. From this database, Englebert has calculated that "between 1763 and 1805 approximately six hundred fur-trade contracts were issued from Montreal for voyageurs bound specifically for the Illinois Country, *an additional six hundred contracts were issued for voyageurs headed to Detroit,* and another three thousand were distributed to voyageurs destined for Michilimackinac."[52] These visits by French voyageurs from the Saint Lawrence valley to the Detroit River region helped the two regions remain connected culturally well beyond the regime changes that followed the fall of New France.

At the turn of the nineteenth century, many French men who were still working in the fur trade as voyageurs decided to leave the Saint Lawrence valley permanently and establish roots in either the Detroit River region or the Illinois Country. These preindustrial migrations have not been studied by historians, and further research needs to be conducted to better understand the context of the departure of these people from the Saint Lawrence valley.[53] Regarding the period extending from the 1840s to the 1920s, several historians have studied the history of the hundreds of thousands of people who left the Saint Lawrence valley for New England, different parts of Ontario, and other regions of North America, such as the prairies and the Pacific coast.[54] They have noticed that many of the migrants were young couples who emigrated because of the lack of available land in the Saint Lawrence valley, and that very often these couples migrated before starting a family.[55] In other words, many people departed because they could no longer replicate their agricultural way of life within the Saint Lawrence valley and were left with two options: to seek work in Montreal factories, New England factories, or in the lumber industry in northern Ontario or northern Michigan, or to try to find a tract of land in northern Quebec (e.g. Saguenay, Lake Saint Jean, Abitibi), southwest Ontario (e.g. Essex and Kent Counties) or in the American Midwest (e.g. Illinois, North Dakota) to farm.[56] However, these migrants from the second half of the nineteenth century were not the first to leave the Saint Lawrence valley. One possible explanation regarding the earlier migrations, at the turn of the nineteenth century, would be that the voyageurs who wished to transition back to a sedentary way of life but did not want to, in the words of Carolyn Podruchny, "farm under the control of a seigneur," saw the agricultural settlements of the Detroit River region and the Illinois Country as attractive destinations.[57] Another possible interpretation would be that, already at the turn of the nineteenth century, lands were increasingly scarce in parts of the Saint Lawrence valley. Finally, a third possible explanation would be the impact of the so-called agricultural crisis that affected the Saint Lawrence valley between 1802 and 1837. Historians have already paid much attention to this crisis, but they have not examined its consequences beyond the boundaries of Lower Canada, for instance, leaving unconsidered the possibility that it encouraged people to look for lands outside of the Saint Lawrence valley. Although the exact circumstances of their departures are still unknown, the fact remains that by the 1840s French people had been leaving the Saint Lawrence valley to relocate to other parts of North America for decades, and that the Detroit River region had been one of the most popular destinations of these migrants.

In 1791, Joseph-Marie Jubinville of the parish of Saint Laurent, on the island of Montreal, signed a voyageur contract before notary Louis Chaboillez, to travel to Detroit and come back on behalf of the merchant company of Todd, McGill & Co.[58] Joseph-Marie, who was born in the parish of Saint Laurent in 1739, was married and had two children when he left for Detroit that year, at the age of fifty-two.[59] Although he did not settle in the Detroit River region, his two sons did. His oldest son, Jean-Baptiste, followed in the footsteps of his father for he signed a voyageur contract to travel to Detroit before the same notary in Montreal in 1804.[60] In 1807, at the age of thirty-five, Jean-Baptiste and his wife, Catherine Dufour, relocated from Montreal to Detroit.[61] As for Joseph-Marie's other son, François, it is not clear whether or not he worked as a voyageur. However, it is known that he settled in the Detroit River region around the same time as Jean-Baptiste and Catherine. In fact, he may have made the trip with them. Single and in his midtwenties, François married Marguerite Réaume at Assumption church in 1808; Marguerite's ancestors had been present in the area for at least two generations.[62] Jean-Baptiste and his brother François were not the first of the Jubinville family to leave the Saint Lawrence valley for the Detroit River region. One of their relatives, Antoine Jubinville, had arrived a decade earlier. Antoine was married twice; the first time, he married Angélique Proulx at Assumption church in 1797, the second time he married Geneviève Campau at Saint Anne's church in 1808. It appears that Antoine first lived on the south shore of the Detroit River, moved to the north shore, and then finally moved back to the south shore.[63] According to the militia rosters of Upper Canada and Michigan Territory, the Jubinvilles' loyalties were divided during the War of 1812. Antoine was enrolled in the First Regiment of the Essex Militia, while Jean-Baptiste was part of the Michigan dragoons of Captain Richard Smyth's Company of Twelve Months Volunteers Calvary.[64] As for François, his case is strange, to say the least. From 9 August to 24 August 1812, he is recorded as a member of the Second Regiment of the Essex Militia, but he is also listed as a member of Smyth's company of Michigan Territory between 26 April and 16 August 1812.[65] The Jubinvilles had probably not chosen one side of the border over the other for political reasons when they settled in the Detroit River region. However, within only a few years they found themselves in the middle of a war which, at least for the duration of the conflict, forced them to choose sides.

Gabriel Ménard, who was born near Montreal, signed a voyageur contract before notary Louis Chaboillez in 1799. This contract stated that Ménard was asked to travel to Detroit.[66] At the time, he was twenty-six years old and single. A few years later, Ménard settled in the Detroit River region, where he married Louise Réaume at River Raisin in 1806. The parents of the bride were Jean-Baptiste Réaume and Marie-Louise Robert, both born in the area.[67] It appears that Gabriel Ménard did not own a property at River Raisin when the War of 1812 broke out, for he is not listed in Michigan Territory's Commission on Land Titles; instead, he may have leased a tract of land from another local French settler. At the beginning of the conflict, he was part of the River Raisin militia, under the command of Colonel John Anderson.[68] He was buried in the cemetery of Saint Antoine's church in 1823.[69]

In 1814, François-Luc Montreuil from La Prairie, located south of Montreal, married Élizabeth Labadie at Assumption church.[70] Élizabeth's ancestors, the Labadie and Barthe families, had been present in the Detroit River region for generations by the early nineteenth century. Between 1814 and 1840, François-Luc and Élizabeth had thirteen children in the Côte du Sud.[71] Prior to settling on the south shore of the Detroit River, François-Luc had worked as a voyageur. In 1801, at the age of sixteen, he was hired to travel from Montreal to Michilimackinac.[72] In 1805, another contract had sent him to the "Upper Countries."[73] François-Luc's family had been involved in the fur trade for generations, for his grandfather, father, and brother Louis had also worked for Montreal merchants and travelled throughout the Great Lakes. His grandfather, Jean-Marie Sédilot dit Montreuil, had travelled from Montreal to Detroit as a voyageur in 1754.[74] François-Luc's father, also named Jean-Marie, had visited the Great

Lakes multiple times between 1795 and 1810.[75] As for his brother Louis, he had travelled to places like Temiskaming, Michilimackinac, Missouri, and Lake Superior between 1800 and 1813.[76] In 1817, following the example of his brother, Louis settled in the Côte du Sud, and married a local French woman, Cécile Soullière, at Assumption church. Between 1818 and 1826, the couple gave birth to five children. In 1830, they had another child, this time at River Raisin.[77] This suggests that after living on the Upper Canada side of the border for thirteen years, Louis and Cécile moved to Michigan Territory. However, François-Luc continued to live in the Côte du Sud for the rest of his life. In 1842, he received an official land title from the Upper Canada government for his property on the south shore of the Detroit River and, after his passing in 1850, he was buried in the cemetery of Assumption church.[78]

Born in Berthier en Haut, located halfway between Montreal and Trois-Rivières, Joseph-Ambroise Généreux settled at River Raisin in 1817. A few years earlier, he had been hired as a voyageur to travel from Montreal to Missouri.[79] At River Raisin, he married Geneviève Marchand shortly after his arrival. When his wife passed away, in 1824, Joseph-Ambroise remarried to Monique Couture.[80] All his children married into French families of River Raisin.

Although most of the French newcomers to the Detroit River region at the turn of the nineteenth century were single men, French families also relocated to this area. In 1801, Joseph Bièque dit Lafleur (born in 1764) and Radegonde Desmarchais dit Parisien were married in Montreal's parish of Notre Dame.[81] Sometime between 1807 and 1812, they moved to the north shore of the Detroit River with their two children. Joseph's father had visited Detroit in 1751, as a voyageur.[82] It is not known whether or not Joseph also worked in the fur trade, but somehow he knew Detroit was an appealing destination. In 1817, Joseph and his family were renting a farm in the Côte des Pous. This property belonged to Louis Loignon (born in 1763 or 1765).[83] Little is known about Loignon's family history, except that he was born near Quebec City. The Voyageur Contracts Database does not include any entry pertaining to him. He was in Detroit before the War of 1812, for he is listed as a member of Captain Richard Smyth's Company of Twelve Months Volunteers Calvary when the conflict began.[84] Two years later, at Saint Anne's church, Loignon married Marie-Louise Drouillard, who was from River Raisin.[85]

In 1822, Joseph Picard (age twenty-six) and Marie-Louise Robert (age twenty) were married in the parish of Saint Philippe, in Lower Canada.[86] Fifteen years later, in 1837, with their seven children, they settled on the south shore of the Detroit River. There is no evidence that Joseph had visited the Detroit River region prior to relocating there with his family. It seems that neither his father nor his uncles had worked in the fur trade.[87] In 1839, the Picards moved across the border, to the recently created state of Michigan. Four of their sons, Joseph Jr, Louis, Norbert, and François, were married to French women at Saint Anne's church between 1845 and 1862. Their only daughter, Eulalie, married a man named Charles Parent at Saint Anne's church in 1850.[88]

THE WAR OF 1812

The United States declared war on Britain on 18 June 1812, and very quickly the Detroit River region was transformed into a battleground. On paper, nearly seven hundred French men of Michigan Territory were enrolled in the Wayne County militia companies during the conflict while more than three hundred other French men who resided across the Detroit River, in Upper Canada, served in the militia companies of Essex and Kent Counties. Regarding the south shore of the Detroit River, historian Dennis Carter-Edwards writes the following: "From surviving pay lists, it appears that approximately half the First Essex and nearly all of the Second Essex were composed of French Canadians [and that this] produced some concern among the senior officers who remained apprehensive concerning their loyalty and their overriding commitment to their farms and crops."[89] Indeed, on both sides of the border, most French men were reluctant to fight, not only because many of them had relatives and/or friends living across the Detroit River, but also because of their farm duties. On the north shore, only the few French families who had quickly developed connections with local American authorities in the 1790s, like the Navarres, showed some eagerness to fight for the Republic. Across the border, in Upper Canada, except for a few prominent families who had been pro-British for decades, such as the Bâbys, most of the local French settlers did not feel any hatred for the United States.

François Navarre (1763–1826), who in 1785 had acquired a tract of land along the River Raisin from the Potawatomi, as discussed in chapter 3, was appointed justice of the peace and squire for the

District of Sargent (River Raisin) by American authorities in 1796, and captain of the local militia the following year.⁹⁰ In 1805, after the creation of Michigan Territory, the American militia in the Detroit River region was reorganized into two regiments, called First Regiment (River Rouge, Detroit River, Lake St Clair) and Second Regiment (River Raisin). This time, François was appointed to the position of lieutenant colonel of the Second Regiment. During the War of 1812, at least twenty-three men from the Navarre family were enrolled in Michigan Territory's militia (at the time, virtually all the Navarres lived either in the Côte des Pous or at River Raisin, and apparently no Navarre resided on the south shore of the Detroit River).⁹¹ However, the actual involvement of this militia in the battles that took place on the Detroit frontier (Battle of Brownstown, Battle of Frenchtown, Siege of Fort Meigs, Battle of Lake Erie, Battle of the Thames, etc.) is difficult to assess. After British general Isaac Brock and Shawnee chief Tecumseh captured Fort Detroit on 16 August 1812, the Michigan Territory militia men were placed on parole. Any efforts to resist this takeover would have put these men in a dangerous position because, as historian Ralph Naveaux explains, this would have made "them illegal combatants, depriving them of any protection under the generally accepted rules of war."⁹² The Michigan Territory militia remained in this hazardous position until the American victory at the Battle of Lake Erie on 10 September 1813. During the year-long occupation of Fort Detroit by the British, a number of French men from Michigan Territory temporarily joined militia companies from Ohio and Kentucky, but their contributions were not always carefully recorded. Some Navarres did choose to resist by joining those Ohio and Kentucky militia companies or by working as scouts for General William Henry Harrison's Army of the Northwest. A descendant of François Navarre later described the participation of his ancestors in the War of 1812 as follows: "The sympathies of the Navarre families from Detroit to Presqu Isle were one hundred percent American. There were no less than 36 Navarres who fought with the Americans during this War. Peter was one of them. He did not officially enlist in the American army but offered his services as a scout to General Harrison for he knew the wilderness and water courses as well as he knew his hand. Because of his work as a scout the British put a price on his head!"⁹³

This Peter Navarre (1785–1874) had left the settlement of River Raisin in 1807 to build a fur trading post along the Maumee River, in northwest Ohio; later in his life, he gained much fame in the area for his participation as a scout in the War of 1812.[94] Peter was not a Métis but like most members of his extended family, and many of the French people of the Detroit River region, he had several friends among the local Aboriginal people, especially among the Potawatomi of the River Raisin and the Ottawa of the Maumee River.[95] During the War of 1812, he did not forget these friendships, but he and his family had their own priorities, one of which was continuing to strengthen their relations with American authorities.[96]

Jacques Bâby (1763–1833) was François Navarre's nemesis on the Upper Canada side of the border. In the early 1790s, the Bâbys lived within Fort Detroit, but in 1796 they relocated across the Detroit River, and soon settled in the newly established town of Sandwich. Between 1791 and 1796, British authorities, who still held Fort Detroit and controlled the north shore of the Detroit River, considered the whole area (including River Raisin) part of Upper Canada. The British authorities asked Jacques Bâby to organize a militia company at River Raisin. The government of Upper Canada had reasons to believe that some residents of River Raisin were pro-American. Therefore, it wanted to strengthen its influence over the locals.[97] In a letter dated 22 August 1794, lieutenant governor of Upper Canada John Graves Simcoe wrote to Fort Detroit commander Richard G. England to express his concerns about the feasibility of organizing a militia company in a place like River Raisin: "I have sent down some of the Militia Acts, but I once understood in conversation with Mr. Baby that it might be as well that the Canadians should as heretofore consider themselves as liable to the old Militia Ordinance."[98] The following day, England answered Simcoe as follows: "I think it right to apprise your Excellency that there is no kind of dependence to be placed in the French Militia, they have manifested upon every occasion a shameful and disgraceful backwardness and such a mutinous conduct as to oblige Colonel Baby to enter proceedings against them ... They are to a man stubborn and mutinous and their conduct so very improper as hitherto to prevent me from giving them arms."[99]

In the early 1790s, the Navarres and other families at River Raisin were clearly pro-American even though they were still living under British control. However, for many other families, owning property and residing at River Raisin had nothing to do with politics. The River Raisin settlement was not a place established for those French with pro-American feelings. It was simply another settlement of the Detroit

River region, with strong connections to the other settlements, including Petite Côte and Côte du Sud. When England used the words "backwardness," "stubborn," and "mutinous" to describe the residents of the River Raisin, he did not mean to say that they were different from the French who lived in the other settlements. To British authorities, most of the French of the Detroit River region, no matter where they lived, could not be relied upon when it came to fulfilling militia duties.[100] Still, the River Raisin settlement was more isolated than the others, located closer to the Ohio valley where Major General Anthony Wayne had recently defeated the Aboriginal resistance to American expansionism, at Fallen Timbers. Consequently, Bâby's task of organizing a militia company at River Raisin, without a doubt, became even more complicated. It probably did not help either that his counterpart, François Navarre, was already establishing connections with American authorities in the Ohio valley at the time, as discussed in chapter 5.

The stories of the Navarres and the Bâbys are not representative of the experiences of most French families of the Detroit River region at the turn of the nineteenth century. These two families had clearly chosen their camps years before the War of 1812 and, by design, they resided on only one side of the border. But for the overwhelming majority of the local French families, practical reasons more than anything else motived their decisions to settle either side. When a tract of land was put up for sale, its location did not really matter, and this reality did not change immediately after the creation of the international border in 1796. As a result, many families had members living all over the Detroit River region at the start of the War of 1812.

CROSS-BORDER MARRIAGES

Several cross-border marriages did take place within the French community of the Detroit River region after the War of 1812. The Goulet family is a good example. Born in Detroit in 1797, Louis Goulet was married twice. He was first married to Archange Tremblay at Saint Anne's church, in 1817. Archange was also from the north shore of the Detroit River. The couple first lived at Saginaw for a few years, before settling on a long and narrow tract of land in the côte of the Clinton River (established in the 1780s), near L'Anse Creuse, in present-day Mount Clemens, Michigan. When they moved back to the Detroit River region from Saginaw, Louis and Archange had one child. At Clinton River, they would have four more children. At least two of these children were baptized at Saint François de Sales church, established by Sulpician missionary Pierre Dejean along the Clinton River in 1824.[101] In 1833, Archange passed away. The following year, Louis married Gertrude Raymond dit Toulouse at Assumption church, where the couple's three children were baptized between 1834 and 1840. Interestingly, all of Louis's children from his first union married French individuals from the Michigan side of the border between 1843 and 1851, despite having presumably lived part of their youth on the Upper Canada side. As for Louis's children from his second marriage, two of them married but there is no information about the third one. His daughter Clémence married a resident of the south shore, Léo Lauzon, at Assumption church in 1850, while his daughter Archange married a man named Samuel Gagnon at Saint Anne's church in 1854.[102] Cross-border marriages such as these were not uncommon during the first decades of the nineteenth century, but as time went on they became less frequent.

The War of 1812 did not in itself disrupt cross-border marriages within the French community of the Detroit River region. However, the rich genealogical data available on the French families of the Detroit River region confirm that over time, after this event, these people increasingly married into nearby families, on the same side of the border, often within the same settlement. By the 1860s, cross-border marriages had become rare. The gradual division of the French community of the Detroit River region was not so much a result of the War of 1812, but a consequence of the development of strong economic and cultural connections between Detroit and the northeast of the United States after the completion of the Erie Canal, in 1825. In the 1830s, 1840s, and 1850s, the arrival to Detroit of thousands of American migrants from New England and New York completely altered the local demography. After the War of 1812, the vast majority of the French of the north shore of the Detroit River most likely did not hold any hard feelings towards their counterparts living across the border. But the Detroit River, officially an international border since 1796, was starting to have a significant impact on the regional economy by limiting "cross-river trade" and, to some degree, cross-river French cultural exchanges. Now, many French of the Michigan side, especially those at River Raisin, had more interactions with American migrants than with distant relatives in Essex and Kent Counties. The French community continued to grow on both sides of the border during the nineteenth century, but since the French people of the south shore were much more isolated from the effects of the urbanization of Detroit and the arrival of American and European newcomers, they were better able to preserve their culture.[103] On the one hand, the transformation of the Detroit River into an international border gradually divided the French community of present-day southwest Ontario and southeast Michigan. On the other hand, the border acted as a barrier preventing the vanishing of French culture on the south shore of the Detroit River, at least for a few generations.

When he visited Windsor in 1861, historian Edmé Rameau de Saint-Père seemed alarmed by the growing disconnection between the French people on either side of the border. Coming from France, Rameau de Saint-Père's purpose was not only to study the different French communities of North America, but also to promote French-Canadian nationalism. In Windsor, before a crowd of French people, he gave a talk that was more like a motivational speech rather than a summary of the French history of the region. During his speech, Rameau de Saint-Père referred to the Saint Jean Baptiste Society and encouraged his audience to establish their own chapter in Windsor. This society had been founded in Lower Canada by French-Canadian nationalist Ludger Duvernay on 24 June 1834.[104] Rameau de Saint-Père also urged members of his audience to reach out to their distant relatives across the border, all the way to River Raisin, to help save them from cultural assimilation. By sending some young people to visit these old settlements, he argued, it would revive the connections with the "homeland" (*la patrie*), that is, Lower Canada.[105] Unfortunately, it was too little too late for Rameau de Saint-Père's plan to have any success, especially regarding the French on the Michigan side of the border; cross-border marriages had become rare and the number of cross-border French cultural exchanges had been declining for decades.

CONCLUSION

Despite the creation of the border in 1796, the early attempts by local authorities to regulate cross-river trade, and the events of the War of 1812, the French community of the Detroit River region remained, over all, united in 1815. The region was still connected with the Saint Lawrence valley; many French people continued to arrive from there

Figure 7.3 Marentette homestead, perhaps dating to the 1780s, stood until 1917 on the north side of Riverside Drive, just east of Marentette Avenue, Windsor, Ontario.

and settled on either side of the Detroit River. But the rapid urbanization of Detroit throughout the following decades, especially after the completion of the Erie Canal in 1825, put a heavy strain on the unity of the French community. Fewer and fewer cross-border marriages were now celebrated and by the 1860s, the community had become divided into two separate French communities. On each respective side of the border, each French community continued to grow until the end of the nineteenth century. New French Catholic parishes were established on both sides of the border after 1815.[106] However, before long, the French became a minority group in the Detroit River region, especially on the American side of the border, and began to experience cultural assimilation.

Conclusion

In 1701, Cadillac founded Fort Pontchartrain along the north shore of the Detroit River. Between 1707 and 1710, he granted tracts of land near the fort to French settlers from the Saint Lawrence valley. However, due to the confusion regarding the boundaries of land, French colonial authorities at Quebec cancelled all of these grants in 1716. For almost two decades afterward, no settler at Detroit held any land title. This changed in 1734, with the establishment of a *seigneurie directe* at that location. On the positive side, until the fall of New France, the seigneurie directe allowed for the standardization of land granting and land organization along the Detroit River. During that period, French people from the Saint Lawrence valley, including many families, settled on land lots in the vicinity of Fort Pontchartrain. Aside from interacting with Aboriginal people on a more regular basis than where they had in the Saint Lawrence valley, their way of life did not differ much. On the negative side, it was easy for British authorities to deny the existence of a seigneurie directe after the fall of New France, especially in such an isolated place as the Detroit River region. However, the local French settlers had already developed a deep attachment to their lands, and they did not plan on leaving. Finding themselves in an awkward position regarding their property rights after the change in regime, especially after the 1763 Royal Proclamation and the creation of Indian Country, the Detroit French engaged in arguments about ownership of their lands with British authorities for three decades. It was not until the American Revolution obliged the British Crown to sign treaties of land cession with Aboriginal peoples in the Great Lakes (to accommodate the Loyalists) that the French settlers of the Detroit River region finally gained some recognition for their land titles. However, during the 1760s, 1770s, and 1780s, the French who claimed public property rights at Detroit were unsuccessful in getting any kind of acknowledgement. This led to the loss of a place like Hog Island (Belle Isle), which became private property before Britain surrendered Michigan to the United States in 1796. At the turn of the nineteenth century, both Britain and the United States finally resolved the question of land titles in the Detroit River region, on their respective sides of the border. This protected the French land organization (long and narrow strips of land) along the Detroit River and other nearby watercourses, at least for a few decades. However, with urbanization, especially on the American side of the border, the French farms and orchards progressively disappeared from the landscape during the nineteenth century.

In 1890, retired lawyer William C. Hoyt remembered that when he settled in Michigan, in the 1840s, Detroit's population was essentially French. He recalled that these people had ponies and carts that were continually "bobbing and moving all over the city" and that they also had windmills "scattered all along the river banks." However, Hoyt observed that now "these old French settlers have about all disappeared [as most of them] sleep in the Catholic cemeteries," but that "their names survive, though often pronounced with an English accent."[1] In the city of Detroit, the French population had been completely assimilated by the early twentieth century. Rapid urbanization and industrialization during the second half of the nineteenth century had contributed to the vanishing of French culture. The roots of this urbanization and industrialization process can be traced back to the fire of 11 June 1805, when almost all the buildings in the town of Detroit were destroyed. Detroit, which had only developed into a town by the 1780s, was still confined between the Côte du Nord-Est and the Côte des Pous when it burned. After the fire, Michigan Territory's Chief Justice Augustus Woodward envisioned laying out a large city instead of simply rebuilding the former town.[2] As Detroit lawyer and businessman Clarence M. Burton puts it, "the fire made it possible to enlarge the boundaries and rebuild on a larger scale, with wider streets and public squares and parks."[3] Also, with the completion of the Erie Canal in 1825, tens of thousands of American migrants from New England and New York began to move to the Midwest, and many of them settled in Detroit. These migrations directly contributed to marginalizing the French population on the American side of the Detroit River.

The French farmers who resided near the old town, in the Côte du Nord-Est and the Côte des Pous, did not suddenly have their properties expropriated. However, Congress supported the plan for the new city and pressured these landowners to sell their properties for its development. Yet, this process took longer to complete than anticipated, and several Anglo-American Detroiters blamed the French landowners who refused to sell their farms for delaying the expansion of the city. For instance, New York City resident and traveller Charles F. Hoffman (1806–1884) observed in 1835 that many French farms "now cross the main street of Detroit at right angles at the upper end of the town [and that their owners] persist in occupying them with their frail wooden tenements."[4] Regarding the south shore of the Detroit River, Detroit naturalist Bela Hubbard wrote that, still in the 1870s, "comparatively little change [had] taken place in the appearance and condition of many old French homesteads."[5] The more limited urbanization and industrialization of Windsor and Essex Counties certainly helped the local French to preserve their farms and, consequently, their culture for several more decades.

Besides leading to the disappearance of the French homesteads, industrialization and urbanization along the Detroit River also led to the vanishing of the orchards that the French had planted since the New France era. In 1949, Detroiter J. Bell Moran, a descendant of French settlers, wrote that "some of the ancient pear trees, frequently of remarkable size and now two centuries old, may still be seen on either side of the river."[6] Although these pear trees have by now disappeared from the landscape in Detroit, they have survived in Monroe County and across the border, in different parts of Essex County.

NOTES

ABBREVIATIONS

ANOM	Archives nationales d'outre-mer
AO	Archives of Ontario
BAnQ-M	Bibliothèque et Archives nationales du Québec, Montreal
BAnQ-Q	Bibliothèque et Archives nationales du Québec, Quebec
BHC	Burton Historical Collection
BHL	Bentley Historical Library
DAUM	Division de la gestion de documents et des archives de l'Université de Montréal
DCB	*Dictionary of Canadian Biography*
LAC	Library and Archives Canada
MCM	Monroe County Museum
PRDH	Programme de recherche en démographie historique
SHSB	Société historique de Saint-Boniface
UTA	University of Toledo Archives
WCL	William L. Clements Library

PREFACE

1 See the society's journal, *Michigan's Habitant Heritage*.
2 See Bénéteau, "Aspects de la tradition orale."

INTRODUCTION

1 For demographic data on the French population on the Canadian side (Essex County) in the mid-nineteenth century, see Clarke, *Ordinary People of Essex*; Ouellet, *Ontario français*, 363–424.

2 On French migrations from the Saint Lawrence valley to the Detroit River region during the New France era, see Gouger, "Peuplement colonisateur" and "Convois de colons." Many more French families settled in the Detroit River region during the British and American regimes than during the French regime. However, the context of their departure and their integration into the Detroit society still need to be better understood. My current project, funded by the Social Sciences and Humanities Research Council of Canada through an Insight Development Grant, focuses specifically on these post-French regime migrations. This project is entitled "Aller faire souche au-delà des limites de la vallée laurentienne: L'émigration de familles 'canadiennes' vers les Grands Lacs à l'ère préindustrielle (1760–1840)."
3 See, for example, Peterson, "Prelude to Red River"; Sleeper-Smith, *Indian Women and French Men*; Murphy, *Gathering of Rivers*.
4 Not all seigneuries particulières in the Saint Lawrence valley were owned by nobles or Roman Catholic orders. In the early eighteenth century, for instance, several were owned by merchants, local government officers, sailors, and ploughmen. Niort, "Aspects juridiques du régime seigneurial," 460.
5 Many nobles from France or the Saint Lawrence valley did visit Detroit or lived there during the French regime. However, French colonial authorities decided not to involve them in the development of agricultural settlements at that location. See Drolet, *Dictionnaire généalogique*.
6 Grenier, *Brève histoire*, 38. Annie Antoine writes, regarding French peasants in ancien régime France: "Qu'il soit locataire ou propriétaire, le paysan vit dans le cadre d'une seigneurie, il a donc le statut de tenancier." Antoine, "Les paysans en France," paragraph 14.
7 Englebert and Teasdale, *French and Indians in the Heart of North America*, xi–xxxiii.
8 Gagné, "Du lys naquit le trille." See also Dupuis et Savard, "Arpenté, défriché." Lucie Lecomte's master's thesis, completed at the University of Ottawa in 2002, is a notable exception. Her work examined the existence of four seigneuries particulières in present-day eastern Ontario during the French regime. Lecomte, "Seigneuries dans le territoire actuel de l'Ontario."
9 Cangany, *Frontier Seaport*. Cangany has more recently published a fascinating article on the French of the Detroit River region in which she looked at how the creation of the international border in 1796 affected their way of life. See Cangany, "'Inhabitants of both Sides of this Streight.'"

10 Hatter, *Citizens of Convenience.*
11 Gouger, "Peuplement colonisateur" and "Convois de colons."
12 Gitlin, *Bourgeois Frontier.*
13 Marrero, "Edge of the West." See also Marrero, "Founding Families." Other recent works have also examined the Aboriginal presence in colonial Detroit. On the topic of slavery, see Rushforth, *Bonds of Alliance.* On the Ottawa-Huron relations in the Detroit River region, see Sturtevant, "'Inseparable Companions.'" On French and Aboriginal material culture at Detroit during the New France era, see Kent, *Ft. Pontchartrain.*

CHAPTER ONE

1 See White, *Middle Ground*; McDonnell, *Masters of Empire.*
2 See Havard, *Empire et Métissages.*
3 Morin, "'Manger avec la même micoine,'" 99.
4 Morin, *L'usurpation de la souveraineté autochtone*, 73.
5 R. Cole Harris asserts that "settlement west of the Ile de Montréal was restricted by Canadian governors and intendants who would not grant seigneuries [particulières] along either the upper St. Lawrence or the Ottawa River, two of the principal routes of the fur trade." Harris, *Seigneurial System*, 10. In fact, in 1674 René Robert Cavelier, Sieur de La Salle, was granted a seigneurie particulière at Fort Frontenac, located in present-day downtown Kingston, Ontario. Fort Frontenac had been established the year before by Governor General Louis de Buade, Comte de Frontenac et de Palluau. Following the establishment of this fief, a few dozen French families settled on lands in the vicinity of the fort. Roy, ed., *Inventaire des concessions*, 3: 157; Roy, "Le fort Frontenac ou Catarakoui sous le régime français," 53–4; Havard, *Empire et Métissages*, 87, 627. On the few seigneuries particulières established in present-day eastern Ontario during the French regime, see Lecomte, "Seigneuries dans le territoire actuel de l'Ontario."
6 Regarding the fact that Aboriginal peoples in New France often welcomed the French because of the presents they received from the Crown, which helped to build alliances, Havard and Vidal write: "S'ils ne sont pas favorables à la colonisation de peuplement, ils ne sont pas satisfaits non plus de l'absence d'enracinement des Français, qui nuit à l'affermissement de l'alliance militaire et à la distribution régulière des présents." Havard and Vidal, *Histoire de l'Amérique française*, 315.
7 This inscription reads as follows: "Nous icy soubsignez, certifions avoir veu afficher sur les terres du lac nommé d'Érié les armes du Roy

de France au pied d'une croix, avec cette inscription: 'L'an de salut 1669, Clément IX estant assis dans la chaire de saint Pierre, Louis XIV régnant en France, Monsieur de Courcelles estant gouverneur de la Nouvelle France et Monsieur Talon y estant intendant pour le Roy, sont arrivez en ce lieu deux missionnaires du Séminaire de Montréal, accompagnez de sept autres François, qui les premiers de tous les peuples Européans ont hyverné en ce lac, dont ils ont pris possession au nom de leur Roy, comme d'une terre non occupée, par apposition de ses armes, qu'ils y ont attachées au pied de cette croix. En foy de quoy nous avons signé le présent certificat. François Dollier, prestre du diocèse de Nantes, en Bretagne; De Gallinée, diacre du diocèse de Rennes, en Bretagne." Margry, ed., *Découvertes et établissements*, 1: 166.

8 Ibid., 545–70.
9 ANOM, Colonies, C11A, vol. 8, fol. 53–53v, Lettre de Denonville à Dulhut, 6 June 1686; ANOM, Colonies, vol. 8, fol. 51–52, Lettre de Denonville à La Durantaye, 6 June 1686; ANOM, Colonies, C11A, vol. 8, fol. 161–164v, Lettre de Denonville au ministre, 11 November 1686. The first two letters have been transcribed in Margry, ed., *Découvertes et établissements*, 5: 22–5.
10 *Michigan Pioneer Collections*, 8: 413–14, 421; d'Eschambault, "La vie aventureuse de Daniel Greysolon, sieur Dulhut," 334; Lajeunesse, ed., *Windsor Border Region*, xxxvi.
11 ANOM, Colonies, C11A, vol. 8, fol. 161–164v, Lettre de Denonville au ministre, 11 November 1686; ANOM, Colonies, C11A, vol. 11, fol. 275, Remarques sur ce qui paraît important pour la conservation de la Nouvelle-France, 1691; ANOM, Colonies, C11A, vol. 12, fol. 152, Mémoire sur la nécessité d'établir un poste solide au Détroit, 1692. This Fort Saint Joseph should not be confused with another Fort Saint Joseph also built by the French in Michigan. This second fort, built in 1691, was located in the southwestern part of the state, in present-day Niles.
12 Hayne, "Louis-Armand de Lom d'Arce de Lahontan, Baron de Lahontan," in *DCB*.
13 "Déclarons à tous, à qui il appartiendra, estre venu sur le bord de la rivière Saint-Denys, située à trois lieues du lac Érié dans le destroit desdits lacs Erié et Huron ... [pour] réitérer la prise de possession desdits postes, faite par M. de La Salle." ANOM, C11A, vol. 9, fol. 206–206v, Nouvelle prise de possession des terres des environs du Détroit des lacs Erié et Huron, par le sieur de La Durantaye, 7 June 1687. This document has been transcribed in Margry, ed., *Découvertes et*

établissements, 5: 31–3. However, Margry changed the title of the document for "Morel de la Durantaye renouvelle la prise de possession des terres des environs du détroit des lacs Érié et Huron faite précédemment par Cavelier de La Salle." On the French planting of symbols such as crosses, as symbols of possession, see Seed, *Ceremonies of Possession*.

14 Cleland, *Rites of Conquest,* 114–15. See also Sheppard, "Proof that No Indians Lived in Permanent Villages."
15 ANOM, Colonies, C11A, vol. 9, fol. 61, Lettre de Denonville au ministre, 25 August 1687. On the coureurs de bois, see Havard, *Histoire des coureurs de bois*.
16 ANOM, Colonies, C11E, vol. 15, fol. 204, Mémoire adressé au Ministre et Secrétaire d'État à la marine Rouillé, récapitulant la carrière de Lamothe Cadillac, 1750. On the regions of Quebec and Montreal, Morin writes: "Ainsi, la fondation de Québec, en 1608 et celle de Montréal, en 1642 ont lieu dans un territoire où les Autochtones n'ont pas d'habitations permanentes … Pendant le Régime français, la majeure partie du territoire est recouverte de forêts et les nouvelles exploitations agricoles ne nuisent pas aux activités de chasse des Autochtones." Morin, "'Manger avec la même micoine,'" 98.
17 Margry, ed., *Découvertes et établissements*," 5: 292.
18 Ibid., 294. In the 1670s, for this very reason these same Ottawa had welcomed the establishment of French traders at the Catholic mission of Saint Ignace, near where Fort de Buade was built in 1683. Many of them converted to Catholicism. However, as Gregory E. Dowd asserted, the Ottawa who settled in the Detroit River region at the beginning of the eighteenth century were not converts and they did not relocate to be close to missionaries. Dowd, *War under Heaven*, 21, 26.
19 *Michigan Pioneer Collections*, 7: 149–50.
20 See Desbarats, "Cost of Early Canada's Native Alliances," 613–14.
21 ANOM, Colonies, C11A, vol. 87, fol. 191v, Journal de La Galissonière et Hocquart concernant ce qui s'est passé d'intéressant dans la colonie de novembre 1747 à octobre 1748.
22 Skinner, *Upper Country*, 158–61. The bay of Sandusky is located on the shore of Lake Erie, about 160 kilometres southeast of Detroit. Since the beginning of the eighteenth century many Huron of Detroit regularly wintered there.
23 ANOM, Colonies, C11A, vol. 87, fol. 17, Mémoire de Canada de 1747 par Beaucours, gouverneur de Montréal, 1747. See also Saint-Pierre, *Histoire des Canadiens du Michigan*, 132; *Michigan Pioneer*

Collections, 34: 337; Burton, *City of Detroit*, 2: 872. Aboriginal attacks against Detroit occurred periodically since the founding of Fort Pontchartrain. For instance, intrigues involving Miamis led to the killing of three French settlers and some cows when Cadillac commanded Detroit. Havard, *Empire et Métissages*, 470.

24 Gouger, "Convois de colons," 49.
25 Delâge, "Principaux paradigmes de l'histoire amérindienne," 59; Havard and Vidal, *Histoire de l'Amérique française*, 285.
26 Havard, "'Les forcer à devenir cytoyens,'" 1011. See also Havard, *Empire et Métissages*, 774.
27 Morin, "'Manger avec la même micoine,'" 98. In the Saint Lawrence valley, most of the domiciliés were Catholic converts living in one of the Jesuit or Sulpician reductions. Delâge, "Iroquois chrétiens des réductions, partie 1," 59–70; Jetten, *Enclaves amérindiennes*.
28 ANOM, Colonies, C11A, vol. 43, fol. 303–304, Résumé d'une lettre de Vaudreuil et Bégon touchant les prétentions et demandes de Lamothe Cadillac par rapport aux terres et établissements de Détroit, 4 November 1721.
29 Surtees, "Indian Land Cessions," 3–4.
30 Weyhing, "'Gascon Exaggerations.'"
31 On the important roles played by the Pontchartrain family in Versailles during Louis XIV's reign, see Chapman, *Private Ambition and Political Alliances*.
32 On the French companies that existed and that were present in the New World before 1626, see Dewar, "Assertions of Imperial Sovereignty," 24–157.
33 Here the term "owned" refers to a European, not an Aboriginal perspective.
34 Niort, "Aspects juridiques du régime seigneurial," 456.
35 Ibid., 454–5.
36 See Blaufarb, *Great Demarcation*, 16–18.
37 Niort, "Aspects juridiques du régime seigneurial," 456.
38 Regarding the territories in New France between the 1620s and 1660s, Helen Dewar describes the relation between the Company of One Hundred Associates and the king of France in similar terms. For example, she explains that the company was the "seigneur and semi-sovereign of New France" yet it "was required to acknowledge the suzerainty of the king." Dewar, "Assertions of Imperial Sovereignty," 207–8.
39 Niort, "Aspects juridiques du régime seigneurial," 457.

40 Blaufarb, *Great Demarcation*, 29.
41 Quoted in ibid., 19.
42 Ibid.
43 Goldsmith, *Lordship in France*, 14. Emphasis in the original.
44 Blaufarb, *Great Demarcation*, 30.
45 The French-Canadian Heritage Society of Michigan erected a plaque on the waterfront of downtown Detroit to commemorate Cadillac's landing. It is located south of Jefferson Avenue, in Hart Plaza. It lists the names of all the men who accompanied Cadillac in 1701.
46 ANOM, Colonies, C11A, vol. 21, fol. 129–131v, Lettre des directeurs de la Compagnie de la Colonie au ministre, 26 April 1703; ANOM, Colonies, C11A, vol. 21, fol. 170–171v, Extrait de l'acte de l'assemblée générale de la Compagnie de la Colonie tenue le 4 novembre 1703; ANOM, Colonies, C11A, vol. 21, fol. 288–289v, Résumé d'un mémoire de Riverin avec commentaires de Champigny, 1703.
47 ANOM, Colonies, C11A, vol. 21, fol. 207v, Lettre de Martin de Lino au ministre, 15 November 1703; ANOM, Colonies, C11E, vol. 14, fol. 166, Mémoire de Denis Riverin intitulé "Réflexions sur l'état présent de l'établissement du Détroit en Canada," 29 April 1704; ANOM, Colonies, C11E, vol. 14, fol. 192, Lettre du ministre Pontchartrain à Lamothe Cadillac à propos du Détroit, 14 June 1704; ANOM, Colonies, C11A, vol. 22, fol. 113–115v, Lettre des directeurs de la Compagnie de la Colonie au ministre, 7 August 1704; LAC, G3, vol. 2051, Notariat du Canada, 28 September 1705.
48 Gouger, "Peuplement colonisateur de Détroit," 75. For an article on medicine in French colonial Detroit, see Anderson, "Medicine at Fort Detroit."
49 Moreau-DesHarnais, "Land Conceded by Cadillac."
50 BAnQ-M, Fonds Juridiction royale de Montréal, cote TL4,S1,D1007, Acte sous seing privé d'une concession au Détroit par Antoine de Lamothe, commandant, à Pierre Estève dit Lajeunesse, 10 March 1707.
51 Translated by and transcribed in Moreau-DesHarnais and Sheppard, *Détroit du Lac Érié*, 93.
52 On the concept of "military-entrepreneurs" in New France, see Weyhing, "'Gascon Exaggerations.'"
53 For example, see Lettre de Lamothe Cadillac à Jérôme Pontchartrain, 31 August 1703, in Margry, ed., *Découvertes et établissements*, 5: 308.
54 Grenier, *Brève histoire*, 36.
55 Cabourdin and Viard, *Lexique historique*, 184–5.

56 "Sa Majesté vous permet de concéder des terres au Détroit comme vous trouverez bon et convenable au bien de la nouvelle colonie." ANOM, Colonies, C11A, vol. 125, fol. 320v, Lettre du ministre Pontchartrain à Lamothe Cadillac concernant le poste de Détroit, 14 June 1704.

57 BAnQ-M, Fonds Juridiction royale de Montréal, cote TL4,S1,D1007, Acte sous seing privé d'une concession au Détroit par Antoine de Lamothe, commandant, à Pierre Estève dit Lajeunesse, 10 March 1707.

58 "[Chaque roturier] sera pareillement tenu de venir moudre aux moulins que nous avons, ou aurons cy apres en payant pour le droit de mouture," in BAnQ-M, Fonds Juridiction royale de Montréal, cote TL4,S1,D1007. In France as well as in the Saint Lawrence valley, a seigneur particulier owned the mill of his seigneurie particulière, which was named the "lord's mill" (*Moulin banal*), and this entitled him to charge taxes called "banalité du Moulin" or "droit de mouture" for its use. Trudel, *Débuts du régime seigneurial*, 191.

59 There was a notary at Detroit during Cadillac's command, but he did not hold the title of "royal notary." For more information on this notary, see Sommerville, "Étienne Véron de Grandmesnil."

60 MM. de Vaudreuil et Raudot au ministre, 15 November 1707, in Roy, ed., *Rapport de l'archiviste, 1939-1940*, 391.

61 "Sa Majesté se fera rendre compte par le dit sieur de Lamotte des raisons qu'il a pour vendre [concéder?] les terrains qui sont enfermez dans le fort du Destroit et aux environs." Ibid., 408.

62 "Les officiers qui sont avec lui demandent des concessions en titre de hausse, moyenne et basse justice … qu'on érige l'établissement du Détroit en sa faveur." ANOM, Colonies, C11A, vol. 24, fol. 201-202, Résumé d'une lettre de Lamothe Cadillac concernant Détroit, 1706.

63 ANOM, Colonies, C11E, vol. 15, fol. 20, Ministre de la marine a Cadillac, 1708.

64 ANOM, Colonies, C11A, vol. 29, fol. 26-77v, Rapport de Clairambault d'Aigremont au ministre concernant sa mission d'inspection dans les postes avancés, 14 November 1708.

65 Translated and transcribed by Moreau-DesHarnais and Sheppard, *Détroit du Lac Érié*, 97.

66 BHC, Cadillac Papers, Extrait des demandes du Sieur de la Mothe Cadillac au sujet de ses prétentions sur le fort du Détroit en Canada (avec recommandations du Conseil de la Marine), 1718.

67 ANOM, Colonies, C11A, vol., 41, fol. 317v, Délibération du Conseil de la Marine, 14 June 1720.

68 BHC, Cadillac Papers, Lettre du Secrétaire d'État à la Marine, Paris, 19 May 1722.
69 "Il espère que Sa Majesté voudra bien lui accorder la concession de tout le Détroit à titre de haute, moyenne et basse justice." BHC, Cadillac Papers, Lettre du Secrétaire d'État à la Marine, Paris, 19 May 1722.
70 ANOM, Colonies, Recensements et documents divers, vol. 462, fol. 165–165v, Analyse d'une lettre de Beauharnois et Hocquart du 6 octobre 1734 sur l'état des concessions (fiefs et censives) accordées depuis 1731 (lac Champlain et Détroit).

CHAPTER TWO

1 "Cet establissement se fera avec plus de force lorsque les habitans releverons du Roy que de seigneurs particuliers." ANOM, Colonies, C11A, vol. 43, fol. 311, Résumé d'une lettre de Vaudreuil et Bégon touchant les prétentions et demandes de Lamothe Cadillac par rapport aux terres et établissements de Détroit, 4 November 1721. See also *Michigan Pioneer Collections*, 33: 701.
2 According to a royal edict dated 6 July 1711, in the Saint Lawrence valley, the king allowed himself to take back any seigneurie particulière still not improved one year after it had been granted and to reincorporate it into his domain. Assemblée législative du Canada, *Édits et ordonnances royaux*, 1: 325. In the present-day province of Quebec, many locations were considered to be part of the Domaine du Roi during the French regime. For instance, the shores of Lake Saint Jean (north of Quebec City) or the Côte Nord (northeast of Quebec City) were described as the Domaine du Roi. Roy, "Cartographie et l'arpentage," 37; ibid., "Les postes du roi," 187. A small territory in the government of Trois-Rivières that did not belong to any seigneur particulier was also referred to as Domaine du Roi. Guy Cabourdin and Georges Viard describe the Royal Domain as "un ensemble de propriétés et de droits appartenant en propre au roi en tant que propriété et seigneur direct." Abel Poitrineau also emphasizes this seigneurial relationship between the king and his domain by stating that "le Domaine [était] constitué par un vaste et complexe ensemble de propriétés et de droits incorporels appartenant en propre au Roi en toute propriété et directe seigneurie." James L. Goldsmith similarly writes that "the royal domain included all of the lordships which belonged directly to the king." Cabourdin and Viard, *Lexique*

historique, 110; Poitrineau, "Domaine," 485; Goldsmith, *Lordship in France*, 72. In Canada, British authorities also used the term "immediate seigneur" to describe the relationship between the king and his royal domain in New France. *Extract of the Proceedings of a Committee of the Whole Council*, 9; Committee of the House of Assembly of Lower Canada, *Seventh Report*, 272.

3 Poisson, "Notaires," 1099. See also Roy, ed., *Rapport de l'Archiviste*, 1921–1922, 2.

4 "Le notaire royal est nommé par le roi, ou par un représentant du roi commis à cet effet, pour instrumenter dans un territoire qui, en principe, est soumis directement à l'autorité royale. Le notaire seigneurial ne diffère guère du notaire royal, sauf qu'il est nommé par le seigneur pour instrumenter à l'intérieur des limites de la seigneurie. De là, la juridiction plus étendue du notaire royal, qui peut exercer dans tout le gouvernement où il est appointé." Vachon, "Inventaire critique," 423–4.

5 LAC, Fonds des Ordonnances des intendants de la Nouvelle-France, Commission de notaire au Détroit pour le sieur Rocbert Navarre, 22 May 1734; BAnQ-Q, Fonds Intendants, cote E1,S1,P2639, Commission de notaire au Détroit par l'intendant Hocquart pour le sieur Rocbert Navarre, 22 May 1734; BHC, Robert Navarre Papers, Commission de notaire au Détroit pour le sieur Rocbert Navarre, 22 May 1734.

6 Burton Historical Library Staff, "Robert Navarre," in *DCB*.

7 ANOM, Colonies, C11A, vol. 65, fol. 58, Lettre de Beauharnois et Hocquart au ministre, 5 October 1736.

8 "Recevoir les droits seigneuriaux qui sont dus ou qui le seront par la suite au Domaine de Sa Majesté accuse [réception] des cens et rentes, lots et ventes pour les terres concedées par Sa Majesté aux habitants du poste du Detroit." LAC, Fonds des Ordonnances des intendants de la Nouvelle-France, Mémoire pour servir d'instructions au sieur Navarre, receveur du Domaine au Détroit, 16 August 1736; BAnQ-Q, Fonds Intendants, cote E1,S1,P2851, Mémoire de l'intendant Hocquart pour servir d'instructions au sieur Navarre, receveur du Domaine au Détroit, 16 August 1736.

9 ANOM, Colonies, B, vol. 65, fol. 403, Le président du conseil de la marine à MM. de Beauharnois et Hocquart, 7 April 1737.

10 LAC, Fonds des Ordonnances des intendants de la Nouvelle-France, Mémoire pour servir d'instructions au sieur Navarre, receveur du Domaine au Détroit, 16 August 1736; BAnQ-Q, Fonds Intendants,

cote E1,S1,P2851, Mémoire de l'intendant Hocquart pour servir d'instructions au sieur Navarre, receveur du Domaine au Détroit, 16 August 1736.

11 LAC, Fonds des Ordonnances des intendants de la Nouvelle-France, Commission de subdélégué de l'intendant au Détroit du lac Erié au sieur Navarre, notaire royal au dit lieu, 9 June 1743; BAnQ-Q, Fonds Intendants, cote E1,S1,P3499, Commission de subdélégué de l'intendant au Détroit du lac Érié par l'intendant Hocquart au sieur Navarre, notaire royal audit lieu, 9 June 1743; BHC, Robert Navarre Papers, Commission de subdélégué de monsieur l'intendant au détroit du lac Érié pour le sieur Navarre au dit lieu, 9 June 1743. Navarre maintained his position when François Bigot was appointed intendant of New France in 1748, but was replaced in 1752. He was reappointed to this very position two years later, before being replaced again in 1759, this time for good. BAnQ-Q, Fonds Intendants, cote E1,S1,P3877, Commission de subdélégué de l'intendant au Détroit par l'intendant Bigot au sieur Navarre pour en ladite qualité connaître en première instance de toutes affaires personnelles entre les Français domiciliés audit lieu de Détroit, et les voyageurs, 1 April 1749; BAnQ-Q, Fonds Intendants, cote E1,S1,P4087, Mémoire de l'intendant Bigot pour servir d'instruction au sieur Landrièvre, écrivain principal de la Marine, nommé pour faire les fonctions de commissaire et de subdélégué de l'intendant au Détroit, 4 May 1752; BAnQ-Q, Fonds Intendants, cote E1,S1,P4164, Commission de subdélégué de l'intendant au Détroit par l'intendant Bigot pour le sieur Navarre, notaire royal, à la place du sieur Landrièvre, écrivain principal de la Marine, faisant fonction de commissaire, rappelé à Québec, 23 May 1754; BAnQ-Q, Fonds Intendants, cote E1,S1,P4283, Commission de subdélégué de l'intendant au Détroit par l'intendant Bigot pour le sieur Bazagier, écrivain ordinaire de la Marine, faisant les fonctions de commissaire audit lieu, à la place du sieur Navarre qui s'est retiré, 17 February 1759.

12 Roy, ed., *Rapport de l'Archiviste, 1920–1921*, 48. After 1734, French authorities had considered appointing a permanent commander to Detroit but this idea was never implemented. ANOM, Colonies, C11A, vol. 69, fol. 145–145v, Lettre de Beauharnois au ministre concernant le poste de Détroit, 18 October 1737; Gouger, "Convois de colons," 50.

13 Farmer, *History of Detroit and Michigan*, 19.

14 "Depuis lors en 1727, M. St-Ours-Deschaillons nouveau commandant du Poste avait délivré de nouveaux permis de cultiver entre les dits lots

et le Fort, mais tout cela ne constituait que des établissements précaires et sans régularité ... Les habitants s'en plaignaient, plusieurs étaient arrêtés dans leur dessein d'établir des cultures. Enfin, M. de Boishebert qui commandait le Fort en 1730, transmit leurs réclamations au gouverneur général de Québec et le 16 juin 1734, il régularisa les titres de propriété des divers occupants et accorda plusieurs concessions nouvelles." Rameau de Saint-Père, *Notes historiques*, 22–3.

15 ANOM, Colonies, C11A, vol. 58, fol. 227v, Résumé de lettres de Beauharnois et Hocquart avec commentaires, 1732.

16 "Les concessions qu'ils ont faites sons en faveur des autres habitans du Detroit qui ont commencé des deffrichements ou qui ont continué d'avancer ceux qui estaient abandonnés et qui avaient été successivement distribués par les commandants du poste sans autre titre ny formalité." ANOM, Colonies, Recensements et documents divers, vol. 462, fol. 164v, Analyse d'une lettre de Beauharnois et Hocquart du 6 octobre 1734 sur l'état des concessions (fiefs et censives) accordées depuis 1731 (lac Champlain et Détroit).

17 "Ils n'avoient osé entreprendre des défrichements et establir des terres au lieu parce qu'ils n'avoient aucun titre qui pû leur en assurer la proprieté." BAnQ-Q, Fonds Intendants, cote E1,S3,P268, Acte de concession par Charles de Boische, Marquis de Beauharnois, et Gilles Hocquart, gouverneur et intendant de la Nouvelle-France, au sieur Chauvin, 16 June 1734. See also LAC, Notaires de Détroit, MG 18, 15, tome 1, fol. 58.

18 BAnQ-Q, Fonds Intendants, cote E1,S3,P268, Acte de concession par Charles de Boische, Marquis de Beauharnois, et Gilles Hocquart, gouverneur et intendant de la Nouvelle-France, au sieur Chauvin, 16 June 1734.

19 Harris, *Seigneurial System*, 69.

20 Ibid., 64–5. The word "sol" later became "sou," which means one cent, however the actual value of a sol could vary. A livre equalled about 20 sols, although its actual value could vary. One minot equals about one bushel.

21 Ibid., 75; Trudel, *Débuts du régime seigneurial au Canada*, 188.

22 WCL, Thomas Gage Papers, American Series, Taxes Relating to the King's Rights at Detroit, 13 May 1766.

23 BAnQ-Q, Fonds Intendants, cote E1,S3,P268, Acte de concession par Charles de Boische, Marquis de Beauharnois, et Gilles Hocquart, gouverneur et intendant de la Nouvelle-France, au sieur Chauvin, 16 June 1734.

24 See "Un document inédit sur M. de Lamothe Cadillac." In a memoir on the career of Cadillac dated 1750, it is mentioned that Cadillac's windmill was demolished by Alphonse de Tonty, Baron de Paludy. ANOM, Colonies, C11E, vol. 15, fol. 206, Mémoire adressé au Ministre et Secrétaire d'État à la marine Rouillé, récapitulant la carrière de Lamothe Cadillac, 1750.

25 Deschênes, *Quand le vent faisait tourner les moulins*, 227–8.

26 It was almost certainly the mill built for Charles Campau on May's Creek. Burton, *City of Detroit*, 1: 530. See also Hubbard, *Memorials*, 135. May's Creek was located near the Huron village. Like the Savoyard River, it was filled in during the nineteenth century. Throughout most of the eighteenth century, May's Creek was known as Cabacier's Creek. Radike, *Detroit*, 5.

27 ANOM, Colonies, C11A, vol. 56, fol. 80v, Lettre de Maurepas à Beauharnois et Hocquart, 8 May 1731.

28 Harris, *Seigneurial System*, 72.

29 BAnQ-Q, Fonds Intendants, cote E1,S3,P268, Acte de concession par Charles de Boische, Marquis de Beauharnois, et Gilles Hocquart, gouverneur et intendant de la Nouvelle-France, au sieur Chauvin, 16 June 1734.

30 ANOM, Colonies, Recensements et documents divers, vol. 462, fol. 164–164v, Analyse d'une lettre de Beauharnois et Hocquart du 6 octobre 1734 sur l'état des concessions (fiefs et censives) accordées depuis 1731 (lac Champlain et Détroit).

31 ANOM, Colonies, Fonds des Ordonnances des intendants de la Nouvelle-France, Mémoire pour servir d'instructions au sieur Navarre, receveur du Domaine au Détroit, 16 August 1736; BAnQ-Q, Fonds Intendants, cote E1,S1,P2851, Mémoire de l'intendant Hocquart pour servir d'instructions au sieur Navarre, receveur du Domaine au Détroit, 16 August 1736.

32 Harris, *Seigneurial System*, 70. See also Trudel, *Débuts du régime seigneurial au Canada*, 4.

33 Still, Cadillac had initially included a hunting tax in the land titles he granted. See BAnQ-Q, Collection Centre d'archives de Québec, cote P1000,S3,D2734, Concession de terre par Antoine Lamothe Cadillac à Jacob de Marsac, 10 March 1707.

34 Thirteen of these grants were once more confirmed the following year. BAnQ-Q, Fonds Conseil Souverain, cote TP1,S28,P18227, Arrêt qui ordonne d'enregistrer le brevet de ratification des concessions faites aux nommés Chauvin, Tily, Pierre Estève dit Lajeunesse, Bineau,

Meloche, Gilbert dit Sanspeur, Jacques Campeau père, Moran, François Lauzon, Labutte, Ladéroute, Chesne, Saint-Aubin père et Saint-Aubin fils au fort Pontchartrain de Détroit, 26 September 1735.

35 Harris, *Seigneurial System*, 119.

36 Of the land titles granted at Detroit in 1734, the one of Pierre Estève dit Lajeunesse had already been granted to him by Cadillac in 1707. But since it had been cancelled in 1716, its new deed revalidated it. Estève actually gained much from the confirmation of his title because forty square arpents were added at the back of his old tract, which initially measured two arpents wide by only twenty arpents deep. BAnQ-M, Fonds Juridiction royale de Montréal, cote TL4,S1,D1007, Acte sous seing privé d'une concession au Détroit par Antoine de Lamothe, commandant, à Pierre Estève dit Lajeunesse, 10 March 1707. BAnQ-Q, Fonds Intendants, cote E1,S3,P270, Acte de concession par Charles de Boische, Marquis de Beauharnois, et Gilles Hocquart, gouverneur et intendant de la Nouvelle-France, à Pierre Estève dit Lajeunesse, 3 July 1734.

37 See BAnQ-Q, Fonds Intendants.

38 BAnQ-Q, Fonds Intendants, cote E1,S3,P359, Acte de concession par Charles de Boische, Marquis de Beauharnois, et Gilles Hocquart, gouverneur et intendant de la Nouvelle-France, à Jean Chapoton, 18 June 1743; BAnQ-Q, Fonds Intendants, cote E1,S3,P269, Acte de concession par Charles de Boische, Marquis de Beauharnois, et Gilles Hocquart, gouverneur et intendant de la Nouvelle-France, au nommé Philis, 1 July 1734.

39 BAnQ-Q, Fonds Intendants, cote E1,S3,P370, Acte de concession par Charles de Boische, Marquis de Beauharnois, et Gilles Hocquart, gouverneur et intendant de la Nouvelle-France, à Robert Navarre, 1 May 1747.

40 BAnQ-Q, Fonds Intendants, cote E1,S3,P372, Acte de concession par Charles de Boische, Marquis de Beauharnois, et Gilles Hocquart, gouverneur et intendant de la Nouvelle-France, à Eustache Gamelin, 1 May 1747. The Huron village located immediately next to Fort Pontchartrain, on that side, had moved several years earlier.

41 "Les habitations commencent du village des Pouté8atamis et viennent jusqu'à celles du fort elles recommencent à … du fort et continuent jusqu'à la presqu'isle." Roy, ed., *Rapport de l'Archiviste*, 1926–1927, 345. Chaussegros de Léry had been assigned to escort French families being transported from Montreal to Detroit by canoes in the context of a new effort by France to strengthen the Detroit settlement. BAnQ-Q,

Fonds Famille Chaussegros de Léry, cote P386,D291, Instructions de Rolland-Michel Barrin, Chevalier, Marquis de La Galissonière au sieur Chaussegros qui se rend au Détroit dans le convoi de M. de Sabrevois, 26 May 1749; BAnQ-Q, Fonds Famille Chaussegros de Léry, cote P386,D292, Ordre de Rolland-Michel Barrin, Chevalier, Marquis de La Galissonière au sieur Chaussegros de Léry, 26 May 1749. This colonization effort is analyzed further in the following pages. The "presqu'isle" described by Léry was actually called "la petite Presqu'Isle" by the locals. BHC, Robert Navarre Papers, Par devant Navarre notaire royal, 22 May 1776. In the Saint Lawrence valley of the early eighteenth century, the word "habitations" referred to farms situated in rural areas and the residents of habitations were identified as "habitants." Fillion, "Évolution du mot habitant," 400–1.

42 Munro, *The Seignorial System*, 81–2; Deffontaines, *Le rang*; Derruau, "À l'origine du 'rang' canadien," 39; Harris, *Seigneurial System*, 12; Courville, "Origine du rang au Québec," 208.

43 ANOM, Colonies, C11A, vol. 89, fol. 194, Lettre de Pierre-Jacques Payen de Noyan, commandant de Détroit, au ministre, 6 August 1740.

44 ANOM, Colonies, C11A, vol. 118, fol. 332, Mémoire sur le convoi du Détroit, 1749.

45 ANOM, Colonies, C11A, vol. 95, fol. 16, Règlement de La Galissonière et Varin portant sur les faveurs à accorder aux habitants qui sont allés s'établir à Détroit, 24 May 1749. See also Gouger, "Convois de colons," 51–2.

46 ANOM, Colonies, C11A, vol. 95, fol. 8–14, Règlement de La Jonquière et Bigot pour les gens qui iront s'établir à Détroit au printemps, 2 January 1750; ANOM, Colonies, C11A, vol. 95, fol. 18–20, Règlement de La Jonquière et Bigot au sujet des habitants qui iront s'établir sur des terres à Détroit, 2 January 1750; BAnQ-Q, Fonds Intendants, cote E1,S1,P3958, Ordonnance du gouverneur de la Jonquière et de l'intendant Bigot qui règle et fait connaître les avantages dont jouiront les habitants qui iront s'établir au Détroit, 2 January 1750; ANOM, Colonies, C11A, vol. 95, fol. 17–17v, Lettre de Bigot aux capitaines des côtes au sujet du règlement concernant les habitants qui iront s'établir à Détroit au printemps, 6 January 1750; BAnQ-Q, Fonds Intendants, cote E1,S1,P3959, Ordonnance du gouverneur de la Jonquière et de l'intendant Bigot qui règle et fait connaître les avantages dont jouiront les habitants qui iront s'établir au Détroit, 20 January 1750; Lajeunesse, "Canadian Shore of the Detroit River," 123; Lajeunesse, ed., *Windsor Border Region*, lii–lx; Gouger,

"Peuplement colonisateur de Détroit," 103–17; Gouger, "Convois de colons," 47–57; Burton, *City of Detroit*, 1: 488.

47 Harris, *Seigneurial System*, 121. Louise Dechêne also underlines this reality: "Les habitants ne groupent pas leurs maisons dans les bourgs parce qu'ils mettraient trop de temps à se rendre sur leur habitation, travailler aux champs, faire les foins, couper du bois, soigner les bêtes soir et matin." Dechêne, *Habitants et marchands*, 263.

48 Salone, *Colonisation de la Nouvelle-France*, 191; Harris, *Seigneurial System*, 172. See also Trudel, "Le village," 397–406.

49 ANOM, Colonies, C11A, vol. 10, fol. 330, Remarques sur ce qui paraît important au service du roi pour la conservation de la Nouvelle-France, 1689. In 1691, this exact same statement was also used in a second memorial. ANOM, Colonies, C11A, vol. 11, fol. 273, Remarques sur ce qui paraît important pour la conservation de la Nouvelle-France, 1691.

50 "Il est impossible que l'on mette les nouveaux habitans en village." ANOM, Colonies, Amérique septentrionale, vol. 9, fol. 4, Mémoire sur le projet d'un établissement commercial sur les terres qui bordent le Détroit sous la protection du fort français construit à cet endroit, 22 October 1749.

51 Governor General Jacques-Pierre de Taffanel, Marquis de la Jonquière, and Intendant François Bigot (1748–60) addressed this issue in 1750: "A l'egard du Règlement que M. Le comte de la Galissoniere forma l'année derniere pour etablir les habitans en village, nous en avons connaissance et nous nous sommes concertés pour pouvoir le mettre en exécution; mais la chose n'est pas possible, les habitans en corops nous ayant fait des representations contraires a ce projet, fondées sur ce qu'estant tous réunis dans un village leurs terres seroient en abandon et exposées au pillage des sauvages; que n'estant point à portée de les travailler la culture en seroit negligée; qu'ils doivent avoir une attention continuelle a ce que les oiseaux et bestes fauves ne mangent point leur recolte et qu'au surplus ils ne pouroient point elever des bestiaux, à moins de les laisser dans les prairies ou les sauvages seroient toujours en estat de s'en rendre maitres, n'estant pas possible de les ramener journellement au village." ANOM, Colonies, C11A, vol. 95, fol. 4v–5, Lettre de La Jonquière et Bigot concernant le poste de Détroit, 1750. See also ANOM, Colonies, C11A, vol. 96, fol. 231, Feuille au net ou résumé de lettres de La Jonquière et Bigot (année 1749) concernant le poste de Détroit, April 1750.

52 For more information about architecture in the Saint Lawrence valley in the seventeenth and eighteenth centuries, see Deffontaines, "Évolution du type d'habitation rurale."
53 Harris, *Seigneurial System*, 100. For a study on the côtes located on the island of Montreal during the seventeenth and eighteenth centuries, see Beauregard, "Géographie historique des côtes de l'île de Montréal."
54 Harris, *Seigneurial System*, 176.
55 Today, Grosse Pointe is divided into five suburban communities of Detroit which all bear the name "Grosse Pointe": Grosse Pointe Park, Grosse Pointe, Grosse Pointe Farms, Grosse Pointe Shores, and Grosse Pointe Woods.
56 According to a note added along with the copy of Charles Chesne's deed preserved in the BHC he would have been granted a tract of land in the "Côte du Nord-Ouest" in 1734. However, a close look at the document reveals that it is actually dated 1750. See BHC, Chene Family Papers. The Côte du Nord-Ouest is sometimes referred to as the "Côte du Sud-Ouest" in some sources.
57 United States Indian Claims Commission, *Indians of Ohio*, 413. In 1771, the Potawatomi deeded their abandoned village to the oldest son of Robert Navarre, Robert "Robiche" Navarre Jr. BHC, Robert Navarre Papers, Don d'une terre par les Chefs des tribus de la nation des Poutéouatamis à Robiche, 26 May 1771; Palmer, *Early Days in Detroit*, 607. This episode is analyzed in more detail in chapter 3.
58 Bénéteau, *Trois siècles de vie française*, 69.
59 The Huron mission of Detroit was known as "L'Assomption" at least since 1741, when it was located on the north shore of the Detroit River, before being located on BoBlo Island from 1742 to 1748. It was moved again to the south shore in 1748. Thwaites, ed., *Jesuit Relations*, 69: 53. Between 1765 and 1770, as a result of the failure by Pontiac to bring down the British troops positioned within Fort Detroit, but also perhaps because of the expansion of the French presence in the Detroit River region, this Ottawa village was progressively abandoned and deeded to both British and French settlers. BHC, Labadie Family Papers, Don d'une terre par Pontiak à George Croghan, 22 January 1770; Burton, *City of Detroit*, 1: 168; Lytwyn and Jacobs, "'For Good Will and Affection,'" 16. This episode is also analyzed in chapter 3.
60 Hamilton, ed., *Papers of Sir William Johnson*, 13: 256.

Notes to pages 35–40

61 See Roy, ed., *Inventaire des concessions en fief et seigneurie*, vols. 1–5.
62 Hamelin, "Rang, côte et concession," 524.
63 Harris, *Seigneurial System*, 123.
64 Hamelin, "Rang, côte et concession," 525.
65 "Nous commandant pour le Roy au Detroit, avons accordé a Guillaume Bernard acquereur de la terre concedée au titre des autres par la continuation de celle d'autant de profondeur et largeur et sur les mêmes allignements et aux mêmes charges, servitudes, droits et cens et rentes énoncés au titre de concession cy devant, dont le premier terme de païement echeoira au onze novembre prochain, et a condition qu'il sera laissé au bout des quarente premiers arpents une distance de trente six pieds de large pour servir de chemin public a lavenir aux habitants des profondeurs." BHC, Bellestre Family Papers, Octroi d'une terre à Guillaume Bernard par Piquoté de Belestre, 12 April 1759.
66 ANOM, Colonies, Recensements et documents divers, vol. 461, fol. 31, Dénombrement des habitants du Détroit, September 1750.
67 Cartier, "Québec 1608–2008," 135.
68 Salone, *Colonisation de la Nouvelle-France*, 122.
69 Séguin, "Le cheval," 236.
70 WCL, Thomas Gage Papers, American Series, Memorial by Robert Navarre, Detroit, 17 December 1770.
71 The French-Canadian Heritage Society of Michigan, based in Mount Clemens, has conducted massive genealogical research over the last three decades and has published numerous books and articles on specific French-Canadian families who settled in the Detroit River region during the eighteenth century. For more information on the activities of the French-Canadian Heritage Society of Michigan, see http://habitantheritage.org/.
72 ANOM, Colonies, Amérique septentrionale, vol. 9, fol. 2, Mémoire sur le projet d'un établissement commercial sur les terres qui bordent le Détroit sous la protection du fort français construit à cet endroit, 22 October 1749.
73 Bougainville, *Mémoire*, 566.

CHAPTER THREE

1 Marriott, *Plan of a Code of Laws*, 73. The French population of the Detroit River region actually amounted to approximately 1,200 people in 1774.

2 WCL, Michigan Collection, vol. 1: 1759–1799, Intelligence from Detroit, 12 December 1776.
3 Courville, "Espace, territoire et culture," 424.
4 Wampach, "Deux siècles de croissance agricole," 183.
5 The French of the Detroit River region were not the only French community of North America to go through years of uncertainties regarding their land titles after the British conquest. Several Acadian communities that had developed in present-day northern New Brunswick and eastern Quebec at the end of the eighteenth century, as a result of the Acadian Deportation, experienced similar difficulties. See Blais, "Pérégrinations et conquête du sol."
6 LAC, Amherst Papers, Correspondence between Commander-in-Chief and Officers at Detroit, W.O. 34, vol. 49, fol. 51, Capt. Donald Campbell to Gen. Jeffery Amherst, 10 March 1761.
7 LAC, Amherst Papers, Correspondence between Commander-in-Chief and Officers at Detroit, W.O. 34, vol. 49, fol. 439, Gén. Jeffery Amherst aux habitants du Détroit, 12 April 1761.
8 Sosin, *Whitehall and Wilderness*, 37.
9 Ibid., 138; Marshall, "Imperial Policy," 155.
10 Sosin, *Whitehall and Wilderness*, 164.
11 Ibid., 32, 51.
12 Ibid., "French Settlements," 190–1.
13 Sosin, *Whitehall and Wilderness*, 32.
14 Ibid., "French Settlements," 191.
15 Ibid., 192.
16 George III, *Proclamation*.
17 LAC, Indian Affairs Records, RG 10, vol. 1846/IT251, fol. 1–6, Surrender by the Ottawa & Chippewas of Detroit of a certain parcel of land on south side of Detroit River, also Bois Blanc Island, 15 May 1786.
18 LAC, Amherst Papers, Correspondence between Commander-in-Chief and Officers at Detroit, W.O. 34, vol. 49, fol. 165, Capt. Donald Campbell to Gen. Jeffery Amherst, 20 April 1762.
19 LAC, Amherst Papers, Correspondence between Commander-in-Chief and Officers at Detroit, W.O. 34, vol. 49, fol. 589, Gen. Jeffery Amherst to Capt. Donald Campbell, 20 June 1762.
20 LAC, Colonies General, Original Correspondence, Board of Trade, 1766–1768, MG11, C.O. 323, vol. 24, part 2, fol. 651,The petition of Lieutenant George McDougall, n.d.
21 WCL, Thomas Gage Papers, American Series, Gen. Thomas Gage to Lt. Edward Abbott, 2 October 1764.

22 WCL, Thomas Gage Papers, American Series, Gen. Thomas Gage to Lt. Edward Abbott, 2 October 1764.
23 Ibid.
24 WCL, Thomas Gage Papers, American Series, Lt. Deterecht Brehm to Lt. John Campbell, 31 October 1765.
25 WCL, Thomas Gage Papers, American Series, Gen. Thomas Gage to Lt. John Campbell, 1 March 1766.
26 Sosin, *Whitehall and Wilderness*, 25.
27 LAC, Amherst Papers, Correspondence between Commander-in-Chief and Officers at Detroit, W.O. 34, vol. 49, fol. 33, Capt. Donald Campbell to Gen. Jeffery Amherst, 23 January 1761.
28 WCL, Thomas Gage Papers, American Series, Gen. Thomas Gage to Lt. John Campbell, 20 April 1765.
29 WCL, Thomas Gage Papers, American Series, Lt. John Campbell to Gen. Thomas Gage, 27 April 1765.
30 WCL, Thomas Gage Papers, American Series, Gen. Thomas Gage to Lt. John Campbell, 5 October 1765.
31 WCL, Thomas Gage Papers, American Series, Lt. John Campbell to Gen. Thomas Gage, 10 April 1766.
32 WCL, Thomas Gage Papers, American Series, Gen. Thomas Gage to Capt. George Turnbull, 22 February 1768.
33 The names of these men are listed in two contracts, both dated 31 May 1766. The first listed the following men: Robert Navarre (grantee of 1747), Jacques Baudry dit Desbuttes dit St-Martin (grantee of 1750), Claude Campau (grantee of 1736), Joseph Cabassier (already owned a tract of land in 1754), Zacharie Cicotte (grantee of 1750), Claude Landry dit St-André (grantee of 1750), Martin Lavoie (no information), Étienne Livernois (settled at Detroit before 1760), Pierre Labadie Sr and Jr (Labadie Sr already owned a tract of land in 1754), Alexis Bienvenu dit Delisle (grantee of 1750), Laurent Eustache Gamelin (grantee of 1747), Charles Chêne (grantee of 1734), Charles Denis Courtois (settled at Detroit after 1760), Jean-Baptiste Cuillerier dit Beaubien (already owned a tract of land in 1754), Claude Jacques Thomas Gouin (already owned a tract of land in 1754), François Meloche (already owned a tract of land in 1754; his father was a grantee of 1734), Noël Casse dit St-Aubin (his father and three of his brothers were grantees of the 1730s), Jean Louis Bineau dit Lajeunesse (grantee of 1750), Julien Fréton dit Nantais (grantee of 1759), and Gabriel Casse dit St-Aubin (grantee of 1734). The second contract notably listed the following men: Jean Baptiste Guillet dit Tourangeau

(grantee of 1751 or 1752; settled on his land between 1758 and 1762), Charles Lamarre (no information), Joseph Guignard dit St-Étienne (heir of Pierre Guignard dit Saint-Pierre who settled on the south shore in the early 1750s), Jean Baptiste Lebeau (grantee of 1749), Jeanne Belleperche, widow of Joseph Pilet (grantee of 1750), Pierre Meloche Jr (heir of Pierre Meloche Sr, grantee of 1734), Jean Baptiste Billiau dit L'espérance (grantee of 1750), Louis Villers dit St-Louis Jr (heir of Louis Villers dit St-Louis Sr, grantee of 1750), Louis Jadot (likely received his tract between 1754 and 1760), Céloron (no information), Louis François Suzor (unknown when he received his tract, likely between 1749 and 1760), Étienne Jacques (no information), François Lebeau (grantee of 1749), Rocheleau (no information), Michel Vaudry Jr (unknown when he received his tract, married at Detroit in 1768), Jean Baptiste Drouillard Jr (grantee of 1750), and Louis Bineau dit Lajeunesse (had likely purchased his tract in the late 1750s or early 1760s). See WCL, Thomas Gage Papers, American Series, Etat des farines que les personnes soussignées et nommées fourniront dans les magasins du Roy, 31 May 1766; WCL; WCL, Thomas Gage Papers, American Series, List of the Inhabitants Living on both Sides of Detroit River who have Engaged to furnish Provisions for the use of His Majesty's Troops at this Post Yearly, specifying the Quantity and at what rate, 31 May 1766; BAnQ-Q, Fonds Intendants; BHC, Edward V. Cicotte Papers; WCL, Thomas Gage Papers, American Series, Memorial by Robert Navarre, 17 December 1770; Denissen, *Genealogy of French Families*, 117, 286, 318, 494, 539, 563, 590, 820, 1113–14, 1175, 1234, 1250.

34 *Michigan Pioneer Collections*, 19: 601.

35 WCL, Thomas Gage Papers, American Series, Capt. George Turnbull to Gen. Thomas Gage, 28 August 1768.

36 WCL, Thomas Gage Papers, American Series, Gen. Thomas Gage to Lt. John Campbell, 28 February 1766.

37 "[Je] certifie qu'au tems du gouvernement français les commandants avoient le pouvoir de conceder des emplacements dans le fort ... Il en étoit de meme pour les terres à la campagne." WCL, Thomas Gage Papers, American Series, Mons. Navarre's account of the King's Rights at the Detroit, 31 May 1766.

38 WCL, Thomas Gage Papers, American Series, Capt. James Stevenson to Gen. Thomas Gage, 18 December 1770.

39 WCL, Thomas Gage Papers, American Series, Gen. Thomas Gage to Capt. James Stevenson, 8 April 1771.

40 BHC, John Askin Papers, Reçu au Détroit le 28 février 1773.
41 LAC, Notaires de Détroit, MG 18, I5, tome 2, fol. 415–422; WCL, Thomas Gage Papers, American Series, A List of Lands Granted by Mr. Bellestre on the River Rouge and Ecorce, Grants dated 1st of September 1760, not yet possessed, 22 October 1768.
42 LAC, Amherst Papers, Correspondence between Commander-in-Chief and Officers at Detroit, W.O. 34, vol. 49, fol. 165, Capt. Donald Campbell to General Jeffery Amherst, 20 April 1762.
43 WCL, Thomas Gage Papers, American Series, Capt. George Turnbull to Gen. Thomas Gage, 28 August 28, 1768.
44 WCL, Thomas Gage Papers, American Series, Capt. George Turnbull to Gen. Thomas Gage, 22 October 1768.
45 Heneker, *Seigniorial Regime*, 252. On 10 September 1760, a letter was also sent from Montreal to Robert Navarre. LAC, Amherst Papers, Correspondence between Commander-in-Chief and Officers at Detroit, W.O. 34, vol. 49, fol. 29–30, M. Sauveur à M. Navarre, ancien subdélégué de M. l'intendant au Détroit, 10 September 1760.
46 WCL, Thomas Gage Papers, American Series, Major T. Bruce to Gen. Thomas Gage, 16 June 1770.
47 WCL, Thomas Gage Papers, American Series, Capt. James Stevenson to Gen. Thomas Gage, 14 December 1770.
48 Ibid.
49 WCL, Thomas Gage Papers, American Series, Memorial by Robert Navarre, 17 December 1770.
50 WCL, Thomas Gage Papers, American Series, Gen. Thomas Gage to Capt. James Stevenson, 8 April 1771.
51 WCL, Thomas Gage Papers, American Series, Gen. Thomas Gage to Capt. James Stevenson, 15 May 1772.
52 Marshall, "Imperial Policy," 180.
53 The instruction read as follows: "All and every French Inhabitants in Our said Province, who are now possessed of Lands within the said Province, in Virtue of Grants or Concessions made before the signing of the Preliminary Articles of Peace on the third Day of November 1762; do, within such limited Time as you in your Discretion shall think fit, register the several Grants, or other Deeds or Titles, by which they hold or claim such Lands, in the Secretary's Office; which said Grants, Deeds or other Titles, shall be entered at large in the said Office, so that the particular Quantity of Land, it's Site and Extent, the Conditions upon which it is granted, either as to Rents, Services, or Cultivation, may appear fully and at length." Shortt and Doughty, eds., *Documents*, 141.

54 WCL, Thomas Gage Papers, American Series, Copy of Order Registering Deeds and Sales, 16 April 1768.
55 Born in France, Dejean had settled at Detroit in 1766, after having lived in the Saint Lawrence valley for about six years. His nomination obviously pleased the French community for several of its members together expressed their gratitude to Gage. WCL, Thomas Gage Papers, American Series, Capt. George Turnbull to Gen. Thomas Gage, 28 April 1767; Lajeunesse, ed., *Windsor Border Region*, 100; Burton Historical Library Staff, "Philippe Dejean," in *DCB*.
56 WCL, Thomas Gage Papers, American Series, Gen. Thomas Gage to Capt. George Turnbull, 6 May 1767. In this letter, as in many other letters written by British officials throughout the second half of the eighteenth century, the term "Canadian" refers to French people.
57 WCL, Thomas Gage Papers, American Series, Capt. George Turnbull to Gen. Thomas Gage, Detroit, 25 July 1767.
58 WCL, Thomas Gage Papers, American Series, Capt. James Stevenson to Gen. Thomas Gage, Detroit, 14 December 1770.
59 LAC, Colonies General, Original Correspondence, Board of Trade, 1766–1768, MG11, C.O. 323, vol. 24, part 2, fol. 653, Know all men by these presents that I Pontiack Chief of the Ottawa Nation, 3 September 1765.
60 LAC, Colonies General, Original Correspondence, Board of Trade, 1766–1768, MG11, C.O. 323, vol. 24, part 1, fol. 21, The King most Excellent Majesty in Council, 30 July 1766.
61 Lytwyn and Jacobs, "'For Good Will and Affection,'" 16.
62 Hough, ed., *Diary of the Siege of Detroit*, 116–17.
63 WCL, Thomas Gage Papers, American Series, Copy of Order, 14 June 1768.
64 The three descendants of grantees of the French regime were Jean Baptiste Cuillerier dit Beaubien, Charles Delisle, and Bonaventure Réaume. According to Christian Denissen, Jean Baptiste Cuillerier dit Beaubien's father, Jean Baptiste Sr, was granted a tract of land at Detroit in 1745. Charles Delisle was the son of Alexis Bienvenu dit Delisle, who received a tract of land in 1750 whereas Bonaventure Réaume was the son of Pierre Réaume, who obtained his in 1751. Among the other grantees of Aboriginal deeds listed in the document of 1770, Louis Labadie and François Basile Campau were the descendants of settlers of the French regime. Louis Labadie had moved to Detroit with his parents in the 1740s and François Basile Campau was one of the sons of Jean Baptiste Campau, second royal notary of Detroit from 1758 to 1760. WCL, Thomas Gage Papers, American

Series, A List of the Inhabitants Possessing Lands by Indian Deeds, Detroit, 18 December 1770; Denissen, *Genealogy of French Families*, 53–5, 201–7, 339, 616, 1031; BAnQ-Q, Fonds Intendants, Acte de concession par Jacques-Pierre de Taffanel, Marquis de la Jonquière, et François Bigot, gouverneur et intendant de la Nouvelle-France, à Alexis de l'Isle, habitant du détroit du lac Érié (Détroit), 1 April 1750–30 April 1750; LAC, Collection Nouvelle-France et Détroit, MG 18-I2, fol. 10, Concession de terre dans la région de Détroit à Pierre Réaume, 1751; Lajeunesse, ed., *Windsor Border Region*, 59.

65 The document listing the 1771 grants stated that the widow of Mr. Dumais received her deed from the Ottawa. However, she had actually obtained her grant from the Potawatomi. WCL, Thomas Gage Papers, American Series, List of the Inhabitants who have the Ottawa Indians Leave to Settle Lands but have no Deeds yet, which they are to receive in the spring 1771; BHC, Chene Family Papers, Nous les chefs des tribus de la nation des Poutouatamis ..., 6 January 1777.

66 These men were Alexis Campau, Godet dit Marantette, two of the Marsac brothers, François Meloche, Jean Baptiste Meloche, Simon Pierre Meloche, Pierre Réaume, and Jean Baptiste Réaume. Alexis Campau was the oldest son of Antoine Campau, grantee of 1750. The document of 1771 mentions a man named Godet dit Marantette without providing his first name. This man was either François Godet dit Marantette or Joseph Charles Godet dit Marantette. The first one was the uncle of Jacques Godet dit Marantette, who obtained a tract of land in 1750 whereas the second was Jacques's son. The two Marsacs listed were François, Jean Baptiste or Paul, whose father was François Marsac Sr, grantee of 1734. François Meloche, Jean Baptiste Meloche, and Simon Pierre Meloche were three brothers whose father, Pierre, had received a tract of land in 1734. Although this cannot be confirmed, Pierre Réaume was perhaps the son of Hyacinthe Réaume, grantee of 1750. Jean Baptiste Réaume was clearly the son of Hyacinthe Réaume. WCL, Thomas Gage Papers, American Series, List of the Inhabitants who have the Ottawa Indians Leave to Settle Lands but have no Deeds yet, which they are to receive in the spring 1771; Denissen, *Genealogy of French Families*, 199–202, 794, 801–2, 820–3, 1031–2; BAnQ-Q, Fonds Intendants, Acte de concession par Jacques-Pierre de Taffanel, Marquis de la Jonquière, et François Bigot, gouverneur et intendant de la Nouvelle-France, à Antoine Campeau, habitant du détroit du lac Érié (Détroit), 1 April 1750–30 April 1750; BAnQ-Q, Fonds Intendants, Acte de concession par Jacques-Pierre de Taffanel,

Marquis de la Jonquière, et François Bigot, gouverneur et intendant de la Nouvelle-France, à Jacques Godet, habitant du détroit du lac Érié (Détroit), 1 April 1750–30 April 1750; BAnQ-Q, Fonds Intendants, Acte de concession par Charles de Boische, Marquis de Beauharnois, et Gilles Hocquart, gouverneur et intendant de la Nouvelle-France, au sieur Marsac Desrochers père, habitant du fort Pontchartrain, 6 July 1734; BAnQ-Q, Fonds Intendants, Acte de concession par Charles de Boische, Marquis de Beauharnois, et Gilles Hocquart, gouverneur et intendant de la Nouvelle-France, à Pierre Meloche, habitant du fort Pontchartrain, 8 July 1734; BAnQ-Q, Fonds Intendants, Acte de concession par Jacques-Pierre de Taffanel, Marquis de la Jonquière, et François Bigot, gouverneur et intendant de la Nouvelle-France, à Hyacinthe Réaume, habitant du détroit du lac Érié (Détroit), 1 April 1750–30 April 1750.

67 These two men were Laurent Parent and Pierre Réaume dit Thémus. The father of Laurent Parent, Laurent Sr, had moved to Fort Pontchartrain in the early 1730s. The father of Pierre Réaume dit Thémus, Pierre Sr, had relocated from the region of Quebec to Detroit in 1722. Denissen, *Genealogy of French Families*, 926–7, 1031–2.

68 BHC, Robert Navarre Papers, Nous les chefs des tribus de la nation des Poutéouatamis …, 26 May 1771.

69 WCL, Thomas Gage Papers, American Series, Thomas Gage to Capt. James Stevenson, New York, 8 April 1771. This letter was translated into French. See BHC, John Askin Papers, Extrait d'une lettre de Son Excellence le general Gage a l'officier commandant au Detroit datte de l'envoye le 8 avril 1771.

70 WCL, Thomas Gage Papers, American Series, Capt. James Stevenson to Gen. Thomas Gage, Detroit, 25 June 1771.

71 LAC, Fonds Alexis Maisonville, MG19-F3, R7934-0-6-E; WCL, Thomas Gage Papers, American Series, A List of the Inhabitants Possessing Lands by Indian Deeds, Detroit, 18 December 1770; LAC, Notaires de Détroit, MG 18, I5, tome 5, fol. 100-101.

72 WCL, Thomas Gage Papers, American Series, Gen. Thomas Gage to Capt. James Stevenson, New York, 15 August 1771. In 1773, Maisonville travelled to Philadelphia for the same reason. There he met with British official George Morgan, to whom he gave a petition signed by other French settlers of the Detroit River region regarding their property rights over lands granted to them by Aboriginal people. Flick, ed., *Papers of Sir William Johnson*, 8: 929.

73 Shortt and Doughty, eds., *Documents*, 383.

74 Ibid., 390.
75 Ibid., 428.
76 For more information on the impact of the Royal Proclamation on Aboriginal lands in present-day Ontario, see Morin, "Concepts of Extinguishment."
77 Lajeunesse, ed., *Windsor Border Region*, 66, 269–70; Denissen, *Genealogy of French Families*, 1031; BAnQ-Q, Fonds Intendants, Acte de concession par Jacques-Pierre de Taffanel, Marquis de la Jonquière, et François Bigot, gouverneur et intendant de la Nouvelle-France, à Hyacinthe Réaume, habitant du détroit du lac Érié (Détroit), 1 April 1750–30 April 1750.
78 BHC, Chene Family Papers, Nous les chefs des tribus de la nation des Poutouatamis ..., 6 January 1777. Mrs. Dumais's maiden name was Marie Madeleine Chevalier. Her husband Dumais was killed by a Potawatomi in December of 1760. Both from the Saint Lawrence valley, Marie Madeleine Chevalier and Jacques Dumais had married at Michilimackinac in 1744 before settling at Detroit in the late 1750s. The tract of land that she received in the Côte des Pous in 1771 was perhaps a gift to compensate for the death of her husband. Denissen, *Genealogy of French Families*, 437.
79 Denissen, *Genealogy of French Families*, 274–5; BAnQ-Q, Fonds Intendants, Acte de concession par Jacques-Pierre de Taffanel, Marquis de la Jonquière, et François Bigot, gouverneur et intendant de la Nouvelle-France, à Charles Chesne, habitant du détroit du lac Érié (Détroit), 1 April 1750–30 April 1750.
80 BHC, John Askin Papers, Nous les chefs de la nation des Poutéouatamis ..., 26 July 1780; Denissen, *Genealogy of French Families*, 1120.
81 Knapp, *History of Maumee Valley*, 533; Lajeunesse, ed., *Windsor Border Region*, lxxix.
82 United States Indian Claims Commission, *Indians of Ohio*, 413. Gregory E. Dowd estimates that the Ottawa, Potawatomi, and Huron villages located along the Detroit River altogether included about two thousand people in 1760. With the departures of most of the Ottawa and Potawatomi for the Maumee River and the River Raisin, this number had certainly decreased by the 1780s. Dowd, *War under Heaven*, 61.
83 BHC, John Askin Papers, Nous les chefs de la nation outaouaise ..., 24 July 1780. See also Quaife, ed., *John Askin Papers*, 1: 172–744.
84 MCM, Bidlack Papers, fol. 15, 1780–1796: Written by Russell E. Bidlack and edited by Dennis M. Au.

85 BHC, Gabriel Godfroy Papers, Nous les chefs de la nation des Poutéouatamis ..., 28 July 1780.
86 Denissen, *Genealogy of French Families*, 534; WCL, Thomas Gage Papers, American Series, A List of Lands Granted by Mr. Bellestre on the River Rouge and Ecorce, Grants dated 1st of September 1760, not yet possessed, Detroit, 22 October 1768.
87 Denissen, *Genealogy of French Families*, 64–5; WCL, Thomas Gage Papers, American Series, A List of Lands Granted by Mr. Bellestre on the River Rouge and Ecorce, Grants dated 1st of September 1760, not yet possessed, Detroit, 22 October 1768. For other examples of Potawatomi land grants on the River Rouge in 1780, see LAC, Notaires de Détroit, MG 18, I5, tome 2, fol. 8–9, 14–15, 20–2, 29–40.
88 LAC, Indian Affairs Records, RG 10, vol. 2015, fol. 8060, Claim by C.F. Labadie to a piece of land at Stoney Point, mouth of the Thames River surrendered to his relatives by the Chippewas at Detroit, 1877; Denissen, *Genealogy of French Families*, 616–17. For other examples of Chippewa land grants along the Thames River, see LAC, Notaires de Détroit, MG 18, I5, tome 2, fol. 43-5.
89 MCM, Col. Francis Navarre Papers, Nous les principaux chefs du village des Poutéouatamis ..., 3 June 1785; WCL, Michigan Collection, volume 1: 1759–1799, Nous les principaux chefs du village des outéouatamis ..., 3 June 1785; BHC, Francis Navarre Papers, Certificate of George McDougall for the Entrance of Land Taxation by Francis Navarre, 13 November 1798.
90 BHC, Robert Navarre Papers, Nous les chefs des tribus de la nation des Poutéouatamis ..., 26 May 1771.
91 Russell, ed., *Michigan Censuses*, 89.
92 BHL, Navarre Family Papers, Récapitulation de divers petits comptes dus à la Société entre Messieurs François Navarre & Godfroy à la Rivière-aux-Raisins le 6 juin 1798.
93 Bond, *Quit-Rent System*, 25–6.
94 Shortt and Doughty, eds., *Documents*, 121.
95 Bond, *Quit-Rent System*, 387.
96 Ibid., 375–6.
97 On 22 August 1761, British official William Johnson wondered what type of rent the French settlers of the Detroit River region were required to pay during the French regime and he noted to himself that he should look into this question further. However, Johnson's questioning did not lead to any concrete effort on behalf of British

authorities to clarify the issue of private property taxation at Detroit. Hamilton, ed., *Papers of Sir William Johnson*, 13: 243.

98 WCL, Thomas Gage Papers, American Series, Gen. Thomas Gage to Lt. Col. John Campbell, 28 February 1766. Between 1760 and 1766, taxation at Detroit remained ambiguous. British commanders imposed different taxes on landowners but these taxes, which were not exactly quit-rents, were not consistently collected. See *Michigan Pioneer Collections,* 8: 465; Lajeunesse, ed., *Windsor Border Region*, lxx.

99 WCL, Thomas Gage Papers, American Series, Lt. Col. John Campbell to Gen. Thomas Gage, 31 May 1766.

100 Bond, *Quit-Rent System*, 29.

101 See LAC Notaires de Détroit, MG 18, I5, tome 2; BHC, John Askin Papers, Pardevant Thomas Williams notaire residant au Detroit ..., 2 May 1780; Quaife, ed., *John Askin Papers*, 1: 167, 181.

102 The implementation of English civil laws in the Saint Lawrence valley in 1764 led to the immediate vanishing of the title of "royal notary." It was replaced by "notary public." Vachon, "Inventaire critique des notaires royaux," 426.

103 LAC, MG23-GIII4, Quit Rent, Detroit no. 5, 1770–1784.

104 Holli, "French Detroit," 81. In Upper Canada, the quit-rents to the Crown were officially relinquished in 1796, which may explain Holli's belief that a quit-rent was paid until that year in the Detroit River region. Cruikshank, ed., *Correspondence of Lieutenant Governor John Graves Simcoe*, 4: 341.

105 Bond, *Quit-Rent System*, 380.

CHAPTER FOUR

1 For example, see Bouthors, *Sources du droit rural*; Wagnien, *Bois communaux*; Trapenard, *Pâturage communal*; Bloch, *Caractères originaux de l'histoire rurale française*. For more recent studies of public properties in France from the Middle Ages until today, see Charbonnier et al., eds., *Espaces collectifs dans les campagnes*.

2 Cabourdin and Viard, *Lexique historique*, 72.

3 Gruter, "Communaux," 370.

4 Trudel, *Débuts du régime seigneurial au Canada*, 115–16.

5 Roy, ed., *Inventaire des concessions en fief et seigneurie*, 1: 285.

6 Séguin, "Étude d'histoire économique," 428.

7 Harris, *Seigneurial System*, 71.

8 See Blais, "Représentation en Nouvelle-France."
9 ANOM, Colonies, C11A, vol. 33, fol. 223, Mémoire de Gédéon de Catalogne sur le Canada, 7 November 1712.
10 Bouchette, *Description topographique*, 202–3, 204, 210, 231, 248, 250.
11 De Koninck, et al., "Pâturages communaux," 319.
12 WCL, Thomas Gage Papers, American Series, Gen. Thomas Gage to Lt. John Campbell, 20 November 1764.
13 LAC, Colonies General, Original Correspondence, Board of Trade, 1766–1768, MG11, C.O. 323, vol. 24, part 2, fol. 651, The petition of Lieutenant George McDougall, n.d.
14 *Michigan Pioneer Collections*, 10: 235.
15 WCL, Thomas Gage Papers, American Series, Gen. Thomas Gage to Capt. George Turnbull, New York, 29 August 1768. See also *Michigan Pioneer Collections*, 10: 234.
16 Roy, ed., *Rapport de l'Archiviste*, 1926–1927, 344.
17 *Michigan Pioneer Collections*, 10: 237.
18 BANQ-Q, Fonds Intendants, Acte de concession par Charles Lemoine, Baron de Longueuil, et François Bigot, administrateur et intendant de la Nouvelle-France, au sieur Douville de Quindre de l'île aux Cochons située dans le lac Érié (Détroit) au-dessus du fort de Détroit, 12 June 1752.
19 *Michigan Pioneer Collections*, 10: 237.
20 DAUM, Collection Louis-François-Georges Baby, B1-145, mf770–77, Requête de Jacques Campeau, Eustache Gamelin …, 18 May 1769.
21 *Michigan Pioneer Collections*, 10: 237–8.
22 Ibid., 237.
23 DAUM, Collection Louis-François-Georges Baby, B1-146, mf771, Requête de Jacques Campeau, Pierre Réaume …, 24 May 1769.
24 See BHC, Cadillac Papers, box 2.
25 WCL, Thomas Gage Papers, American Series, Maj. T. Bruce to Gen. Thomas Gage, Detroit, 15 October 1769.
26 WCL, Thomas Gage Papers, American Series, Gen. Thomas Gage to Maj. T. Bruce, 6 April 1770.
27 WCL, Thomas Gage Papers, American Series, Extract of a Letter from the Right Honorable The Earl of Hills Borough, one of His Majesty's Principal Secretarys of State, to General Gage, 9 December 1769.
28 WCL, Thomas Gage Papers, American Series, Capt. James Stevenson to Gen. Thomas Gage, 12 March 1771.
29 WCL, Thomas Gage Papers, American Series, Capt. James Stevenson to Gen. Thomas Gage, 31 March 1771.

30 "Il n'y a personne de nous qui ne se ressente journellement dans ses troupeaux de la cession de cette commune." DAUM, Collection Louis-François-Georges Baby, B1-149, mf770, Requête de Jacques Campeau, A. Barthe, Pierre Réaume ..., 2 April 1771.
31 WCL, Thomas Gage Papers, American Series, Gen. Thomas Gage to Capt. James Stevenson, 17 June 1771.
32 "Les commandants français ordonnaient souvent de mettre certains chevaux ou autres animaux dans l'Isle aux cochons qui causaient du dommage et troublaient le public, mais cela ne prouve pas que les habitants eussent la propriété de cette isle." BHC, Campau Family Papers, Nous soussignés habitants du Detroit ..., 12 June 1772.
33 LAC, Haldimand Papers, MG21, vol. 21782, fol. 26, Lt.-Gov. Henry Hamilton to Lt.-Gov. Théophile-Hector de Cramahé, 12 August 1778. It is not clear whether Hamilton actually referred to the French or the British Crown.
34 Gates, *Land Policies of Upper Canada*, 11.
35 *Michigan Pioneer Collections*, 20: 189.
36 LAC, Upper Canada: Land Board Minutes and Records, RG 1, L. 4, vol. 2, Hesse District Records, 1765-1790, Letter by Haldimand, 1 October 1784.
37 Denissen, *Genealogy of French Families*, 204, 772.
38 *Michigan Pioneer Collections*, 20: 18, 262.
39 Burton, *Barnabas Campau*, 6; *Michigan Pioneer Collections*, 2: 588; Burton, *City of Detroit*, 1: 131, 452; Rodriguez and Featherstone, *Detroit's Belle Isle*, 13.
40 From the 1760s to the 1780s, besides Robert Navarre and Jean-Baptiste Campau, at least four other French notaries worked for several years at Detroit: Philippe Dejean, François Desruisseaux Bellecour, Gabriel Legrand, and Guillaume Monforton; British notary Thomas Williams also signed many legal documents in the French language.

CHAPTER FIVE

1 Surtees, "Indian Land Cessions," 1.
2 LAC, Indian Affairs Records, RG 10, vol. 1846/IT251, fol. 1-3, Surrender by the Ottawa & Chippewas of Detroit of a certain parcel of land on south side of Detroit River, also Bois Blanc Island, 15 May 1786.
3 *Michigan Pioneer Collections*, 8: 490-1; Fraser, ed., *Report of the Bureau of Archives*, 3: 31.

4 See LAC, Indian Affairs Records, RG 10, vol. 1840/IT002, fol. 1–4, Surrender of land by the Ottawa, Chippawa, Pot-to-wa-to-my, and Huron Indian Nations of Detroit, 15 May 1790; LAC, Indian Affairs Records, RG 10, vol. 1840/IT003, fol. 1–6, Grant from the Indians to the Crown – District of Hesse, 15 May 1790; LAC, Indian Affairs Records, RG 10, vol. 1840/IT004, fol. 1–6, Copy of Treaty No. 2, 15 May 1790.
5 LAC, Indian Affairs Records, RG 10, vol. 1843/IT102, fol. 1–2, An Agreement to surrender the Huron Reserve in the Township of Malden in the Western District, 13 July 1833; Fraser, ed., *Report of the Bureau of Archives*, 3: 9.
6 Lytwyn and Jacobs, "'For Good Will and Affection,'" 25.
7 Fraser, ed., *Report of the Bureau of Archives*, 3: lxx.
8 Ibid., cviii.
9 Douglas, *Uppermost Canada*, 7.
10 East Windsor, *City of East Windsor*, 44. Fred C. Hamil writes, "Kent County then consisted of the land north of the Thames River [and Fort] Detroit, which was connected to the rest of the county by a four-mile wide strip along the south shore of Lake St. Clair." Hamil, *Valley of the Lower Thames*, 20.
11 Lajeunesse, ed., *Windsor Border Region*, lxxxv.
12 Clarke, *Land, Power, and Economics*, 75.
13 Ibid.
14 Fraser, ed., *Report of the Bureau of Archives*, 3: lxx, cv.
15 MacDonald, "New Settlement on Lake Erie," 3.
16 Fraser, ed., *Report of the Bureau of Archives*, 3: 64. For more information on Patrick McNiff, see Quint, "Patrick McNiff."
17 Fraser, *Report of the Bureau of Archives*, 3: 116.
18 Ibid.
19 Ibid., xciv–xcv.
20 "Les soussignés ... ont presque tous des familles nombreuses et des enfants en état de s'établir et les metre (sic) en valeur, eh! quelle consolation d'avoir auprès de nous, nos familles, tout pour nous entraider mutuellement que pour leur donner de bons conseils, et les maintenir dans le bon ordre." Ibid., 120.
21 Ibid., 183; Lajeunesse, ed., *Windsor Border Region*, 178.
22 Lajeunesse, ed., *Windsor Border Region*, 179.
23 Ibid., 177.
24 Ibid., 181.

25 Fraser, ed., *Report of the Bureau of Archives*, 3: 179.
26 Ibid., 201.
27 Ibid., 253.
28 Gates, "The Heir and Devisee Commission," 25, 36.
29 Clarke, *Land, Power, and Economics*, 194–5.
30 See, for instance, LAC, RG I-L 5, vol. 43, fol. 61, Records of the Heir and Devisee Commission accumulated by the Executive Council, 1777–1854.
31 Cruikshank, ed., *Correspondence of Lieutenant Governor John Graves Simcoe*, 3: 230.
32 Ibid., 77.
33 "Des habitants et citoyens de la coste du Nordest de cette ville étant alarmés d'avoir vu il y a quelques jours un des arpenteurs de sa Majesté tirer la ligne d'entre le domaine de sa dite Majesté et leurs terres." Cruikshank, ed., *Correspondence of Lieutenant Governor John Graves Simcoe*, 3: 94.
34 "S'il falait [sic], que quelques changements se fissent ... cela causerait, un dérangement, et un dommage très considerable jusqua [sic] l'étendue de six lieux de front en remontant dans la dite Coste du Nordest." Ibid.
35 Ibid., 113.
36 Ibid.
37 It is known that François de Joncaire de Chabert held at least two Aboriginal deeds, and that both pertained to lands along the River Rouge. The first Aboriginal deed he acquired had initially been granted by the Potawatomi to Isidore Chêne on 6 January 1777. He obtained the second deed directly from the Potawatomi on 28 July 1780. Denissen, *Genealogy of French Families*, 237; Quaife, ed., *John Askin Papers*, 2: 113–14; BHC, Chene Family Papers, Nous les chefs de tribus de la nation des Poutouatamis ..., 6 January 1777; Lowrie, ed., *American State Papers*, 1: 279; MCM, Bidlack Papers, fol. 47–48, Russell E. Bidlack's Manuscript on Early Monroe.
38 French men from the Detroit River region fought along with Aboriginal people against American troops at the Battle of Fallen Timbers. However, their contribution was fairly minor. After the clash, British colonel R.G. England wrote to John Graves Simcoe, lieutenant-governor of Upper Canada, that he had sent about one hundred French men to help finish the construction of Fort Miami, near where the battle took place, but that they had "all deserted at the first alarm." For his part, British military officer William Campbell reported that

Colonel England had arrived at Fort Miami with French men, "but from the natural indolence and listlessness of some, and the timidity of others, who ran away when things were likely to become serious, they have not afforded that assistance which might have been expected." Some were apparently willing to fight against Wayne's troops, but Campbell recounted that most of these had actually "remained in the fort" during the battle. Prior to this event Jacques Bâby had notified Simcoe that the county of Kent, which then included the French settlements of the Detroit River region, consisted of nearly "seven hundred men fit to bear arms." Therefore, only a small fraction of these militia men had showed up at Fort Miami before the battle, and most of these men did not get involved. Cruikshank, ed., *Correspondence of Lieutenant Governor John Graves Simcoe*, 2: 93, 415, 418.

39 Carter, ed., *Territorial Papers*, 2: 534.
40 Horsman, "American Indian Policy," 47.
41 Lowrie, ed., *American State Papers*, 1: 266.
42 Burton, ed., "Documents Relating to Wayne County and Michigan Territory," 6–7.
43 Carter, ed., *Territorial Papers*, 3: 458.
44 See Hatter, "Transformation of the Detroit Land Market."
45 "Nous prions l'honorable Congré [sic] de faire une distinction au plus vite entre ceux qui ont obtenus des étendus de terre immence [sic] pour peut [sic] de chose des Sauvages un peut avant le dit traité de Grenville avec l'idée de prendre avantage des droits des états unis et de ces individus, nous, ayant obtenu légitiment des morceaux raisonnables de terre pour les cultiver." MCM, Jacques Navarre Papers, Requête des habitants canadiens et autres de la Rivière-aux-Raisins & dépendances au Congrès des États-Unis, 23 March 1799.
46 Lowrie, ed., *American State Papers*, 1: 281.
47 Carter, ed., *Territorial Papers*, 3: 103–4.
48 Ibid., 104.
49 Ibid.
50 Ibid.
51 Ibid.
52 Ibid., 105.
53 The district of Hamtramck was named after Jean-François Hamtramck. Born at Quebec in 1756, Hamtramck was later colonel in the United States troops. He was the second American commander of Fort Detroit (1796–97). On 22 October 1796, he purchased a tract of land from Jacques Campau in the Côte du Nord-Est. He died in

Detroit in 1803. Denissen, *Genealogy of French Families*, 571; Dunnigan, *Frontier Metropolis*, 103; WCL, Michigan Collection, vol. 2: 1800–1819, Jacques Campau Deed to Col. Hamtramck, 22 October 1796.

54 A property tax may have been collected earlier in Wayne County. In 1798, François Navarre paid such tax although it is not clear if taxes from other landowners were collected that year. BHC, Francis Navarre Papers, Sargent Township Territorial Tax, 1800; BHC, Francis Navarre Papers, Certificate of George McDougall for the Entrance of Land for Taxation by Francis Navarre, 13 November 1798.
55 *Michigan Pioneer Collections*, 8: 530–40.
56 On taxation in the first decades of the American regime in Michigan, see Farmer, *History of Detroit and Michigan*, 1: 149–60.
57 Lowrie, ed., *American State Papers*, 1: 266. See also Eldredge, *Past and Present of Macomb County*, 557.
58 Lowrie, ed., *American State Papers*, 1: 263; Gilpin, *The Territory of Michigan*, 6.
59 Adams, ed., *Writings of Albert Gallatin*, 1: 218.
60 Peters, ed., *Public Statutes at Large*, 2: 344–5.
61 BHC, Laferté Family Papers, Avis aux proprietaires des terres dans le comté de Wayne, 14 May 1805.
62 Greffenius, "Michigan Public Land Policy," 116–19.
63 Lowrie, ed., *American State Papers*, 1: 263. See also Farmer, *History of Detroit and Michigan*, 1: 21.
64 Lowrie, ed., *American State Papers*, 1: 305.
65 Carter, ed., *Territorial Papers*, 10: 77.
66 Ibid.
67 Ibid., 87–8.
68 Denissen, *Genealogy of French Families*, 30.
69 Gilpin, *Territory of Michigan*, 23.
70 BHC, Abbott Family Papers, Potawatomi Deed to James Abbott Sr, 28 July 1780; BHC, Abbott Family Papers, Chippewa Deed to James Abbott Sr, 16 September 1780.
71 Carter, ed., *Territorial Papers*, 10: 139–41.
72 Lowrie, ed., *American State Papers*, 1: 264.
73 Ibid., 592.
74 Carter, ed., *Territorial Papers*, 10: 220. See also BHC, Francis Navarre Papers, Le greffier du bureau des terres au Detroit …, 2 June 1808.
75 Carter, ed., *Territorial Papers*, 10: 96.

76 The ancestors of François Rivard had established roots in the Côte du Nord-Est during the French regime. There is written evidence that Rivard had lived on this property since at least 1800. Denissen, *Genealogy of French Families*, 1063–6; WCL, Thomas Gage Papers, American Series, Memorial by Robert Navarre, 17 December 1770; BHC, Rivard Family Papers, Pardevant les temoins soussignés residant en cette ville du Détroit territoire des Etats Unis nord-ouest de l'Ohio fur present François Rivard …, 1800.
77 Lowrie, ed., *American State Papers*, 1: 356.
78 Ibid., 446.
79 Ibid., 357–8.
80 Carter, ed., *Territorial Papers*, 10: 623.
81 WCL, Michigan Collection, vol. 2: 1800–1819, Charles Chovin and Susanne Chovin Contract of Sale, 7 July 1811; Denissen, *Genealogy of French Families*, 264–6.
82 BHC, Rivard Family Papers, Pardevant les temoins soussignés furent present Laurent Griffard et Marianne Griffard …, 29 August 1818.
83 For example, see, BHC, Campau Family Papers, Deed of a Farm in the U.S. Settlement of Detroit Received for Record, 26 July 1815. For more information on Aaron Greeley, see Quaife, "Aaron Greeley."
84 Lowrie, ed., *American State Papers*, 1: 305–557.
85 *Michigan Pioneer Collections*, 22: 433.
86 Ibid., 435.
87 Carter, ed., *Territorial Papers*, 10: 153.
88 Abijah Hull resigned a few months later, on 2 August 1808. Ibid., 221; *Michigan Pioneer Collections*, 37: 98; Cruikshank and Hunter, eds., *Correspondence of the Honourable Peter Russell*, 1: 189; Talman, ed., *Loyalist Narratives*, 89.
89 Lowrie, ed., *American State Papers*, 1: 269.
90 Ibid.
91 Ibid., 283.
92 Carter, ed., *Territorial Papers*, 10: 81.

CHAPTER SIX

1 Kerrigan, "Apples on the Border," 28.
2 Canniff, *Settlement of Upper Canada*, 588–9.
3 Martin, *Fruits du Québec*, 26. On the fact that Louis Hébert was the first actual settler, see Roy, ed., *Ville de Québec*, 1: 59–60.

4 Champlain, *Voyages de la Nouvelle France*, 68. On these apple trees, see also Sagard, *Grand voyage*, 54–5.
5 Boucher, *Histoire véritable*, 53.
6 Bacqueville de La Potherie, *Histoire de l'Amérique septentrionale*, 342–3.
7 Kalm, *Travels in North America*, 2: 242.
8 Anbury, *Journal d'un voyage*, 1: 65.
9 Lambert, *Travels through Canada*, 1: 90–1.
10 Gray, *Letters from Canada*, 150–1.
11 On the French orchards in the region of Montreal, see Dépatie, "Jardins et vergers."
12 Catalogne, "Mémoire," 266.
13 Harris, *Seigneurial System*, 154.
14 "Le païe des deux costez de ce beau Détroit est garny de belles campagnes découvertes, & l'on voit quantité de cerfs, de biches, de chevreüls, d'hours peu farouches & tres bons à manger, de Poules d'Inde, & de toute forte de gibier, des cignes en quantité ... Le reste du Détroit est couvert de forest, d'arbres fruitiers, comme noyers, chastaigniers, pruniers, pomiers, de vignes sauvages, & chargées de raisins, dont nous fismes quelque peu de vin, il y a des bois propres à bâtir, c'est l'endroit où les bestes fauves se plaisent le plus." Hennepin, *Description de la Louisiane*, 52. Chrestien Le Clercq, who was also on board the *Griffon*, later used similar words to describe his experience on the Detroit River: "Le païs de la plus belle situation: un sol temperé, estant Nord & Sud, bordé de vastes prairies, terminés par des côteaux pleins de vignes, d'arbres fruitiers, de bocages & de bois de haute futaye, le tout distribué d'espace, en forte que l'on croiroit que les anciens Romains, les Princes & les Grands en auroient fait autrefois autant de maisons de plaisance. Les terres par tout également fertiles." Le Clercq, *Premier établissement*, 147.
15 "Ce destroit a trente lieues de longueur et presque partout une lieue de largeur ... [il] est couvert de forests d'arbres fruitiers, comme noyers, chastaigners, pruniers, pommiers, et de bois propres à bastir." Margry, ed., *Découvertes et établissements*, 1: 445–6.
16 "Vous ne sauriez imaginer la beauté de ce détroit & de ce petit Lac [Sainte-Claire] par la quantité d'arbres fruitiers sauvages qu'on voit de toutes les espéces [sic] sur les bords." Ouellet, ed., *Lahontan*, 1: 70–1.
17 ANOM, Colonies, C11E, vol. 14, fol. 23–24, Description de la rivière du Détroit par Lamothe Cadillac, 5 October 1701, Correspondance

générale des limites et des postes. Margry, ed., *Découvertes et établissements,* 5: 192–4.

18 ANOM, Colonies, C11E, vol. 14, fol. 132–133v, Description du Détroit par Alphonse Tonty adressée au Ministre, 1702.

19 "Tous les officiers qui sont en garnison au detroit conviennent comme luy [Cadillac] qu'il n'y a pas un plus beau n'y meilleur païs et que tout le bien qu'on en dit en es veritable." ANOM, Colonies, C11A, vol. 24, fol. 205v, Résumé d'une lettre de La Forest avec commentaires, 20 August 1706.

20 Hoffman, *Winter in the West,* 1: 122.

21 MCM, French Pear Trees Papers, French Pear Trees: Excerpt from a Speech by Bela Hubbard, May 1872.

22 *Michigan Pioneer Collections,* 1: 355.

23 Jameson, *Winter Studies and Summer Rambles,* 315–16.

24 Moran, *Moran Family,* 54; BAnQ-Q, Fonds Intendants, cote E1,S3,P278, Acte de concession par Charles de Boische, Marquis de Beauharnois, et Gilles Hocquart, gouverneur et intendant de la Nouvelle-France, au nommé Moran, 11 July 1734; Denissen, *Genealogy of French Families,* 866–71.

25 "Je ne m'attacheray point à la qualité de la terre, pourvu qu'elle produise de bons grains et de bons fruits avec abondance." Margry, ed., *Découvertes et établissements,* 5: 233.

26 ANOM, Colonies, C11A, vol. 24, fol. 200–200v, Résumé d'une lettre de Lamothe Cadillac concernant Détroit, 1706.

27 LAC, Collection Nouvelle-France et Détroit, MG18-I2, Inventaire général des bâtiments, moulins, bestiaux, marchandises et ustensilles, meubles et immeubles et autres effets apartenant à Monsieur de Lamothe Cadillac, gouverneur de la Louisiane, laissés entre les mains du Sr Pierre Roy, habitant de Détroit (25 August 1711).

28 ANOM, Colonies, C11A, vol. 43, fol. 246–249v, Résumé d'une requête de Lamothe Cadillac et délibération du Conseil de Marine, 20 May 1721; ANOM, Colonies, C11A, vol. 124, fol. 200–206v, Extrait des demandes du sieur de Lamothe Cadillac au sujet de ses prétentions sur le fort du Détroit, ca. 1720; Délibération du Conseil de Marine, 14 June 1720, ANOM, Colonies, C11A, vol. 41, fol. 317–333v; Délibération du Conseil de Marine, July 1720, ANOM, Colonies, C11A, vol. 41, fol. 339–341; ANOM, Colonies, C11G, vol. 8, fol. 152–153, Brevet de concession à La Mothe Cadillac des terrains sur lesquels il a fait bâtir au Détroit et des terres qu'il a défrichées, 23 July

1720; ANOM, Colonies, C11A, vol. 43, fol. 291–313v, Résumé d'une lettre de Vaudreuil et Bégon touchant les prétentions et demandes de Lamothe Cadillac par rapport aux terres et établissements de Détroit, 4 November 1721.

29 ANOM, Colonies, C11E, vol. 15, fol. 196, Requête du fils aîné de Lamothe Cadillac au Ministre, February 1732; ANOM, Colonies, C11E, vol. 15, fol. 198, Nouvelle requête du fils aîné de Lamothe Cadillac au Ministre, 10 February 1733.

30 BHC, John Askin Papers, "Étant en outre compris en cette vente tout ce qui peut être [?] au dit vendeur pour raison des dites terres, fruits, fermes, et loyers meme des dits batiments et bestiaux." Au nom de Dieu soit lan mil sept cens trente huit ..., 28 August 1738.

31 Paré, *Catholic Church*, 182–90; Lajeunesse, "Armand de La Richardie," in DCB.

32 Toupin, ed., *Écrits de Pierre Potier*, 12.

33 ANOM, Colonies, Amérique septentrionale, vol. 9, fol. 4, Mémoire sur le projet d'un établissement commercial sur les terres qui bordent le Détroit sous la protection du fort français construit à cet endroit, 22 October 1749.

34 "A Montreal, le dit Sr de Lery prépara des noyaux, pépins et graines de toutes espèces pour en fournir le Détroit." Roy, ed., *Rapport de l'Archiviste, 1926-1927*, 335.

35 BHC, Edward V. Cicotte Papers, Jean Baptiste Cardinal ... ; WCL, Thomas Gage Papers, American Series, Memorial by Robert Navarre, Detroit, 17 December 1770; LAC, Notaires de Détroit, MG 18, 15, tome 1, fol. 92.

36 LAC, Notaires de Detroit, MG 18, 15, tome 1, fol. 88.

37 Denissen, *Genealogy of French Families*, 46.

38 Besides Navarre, these sons-in-law were Pierre Chêne dit Labutte, Jean Baptiste Cuillerier dit Beaubien, Pierre Laurent, and Jean Baptiste Réaume. Denissen, *Genealogy of French Families*, 53, 275, 307, 1031–2; BAnQ-Q, Fonds Intendants, cote E1,S3,P370, Acte de concession par Charles de Boische, Marquis de Beauharnois, et Gilles Hocquart, gouverneur et intendant de la Nouvelle-France, à Robert Navarre, 1 May 1747; BAnQ-Q, Fonds Intendants, cote E1,S3,P279, Acte de concession par Charles de Boische, Marquis de Beauharnois, et Gilles Hocquart, gouverneur et intendant de la Nouvelle-France, au nommé Labutte, 12 July 1734; BAnQ-Q, Fonds Intendants, cote E1,S3,P307, Acte de concession par Charles de Boische, Marquis de Beauharnois,

et Gilles Hocquart, gouverneur et intendant de la Nouvelle-France, à Pierre Cosme, 8 September 1736; BANQ-Q, Fonds Intendants, cote E1,S3,P393, Acte de concession par Jacques-Pierre de Taffanel, Marquis de la Jonquière, et François Bigot, gouverneur et intendant de la Nouvelle-France, à Hyacinthe Réaume, 1750.
39 BHC, Edward V. Cicotte Papers, François Godefroy dit St-Georges.
40 Jacques Campau was the son of 1734 grantee Jean Louis Campau. Denissen, *Genealogy of French Families*, 200–4; BANQ-Q, Fonds Intendants, cote E1,S3,P272, Acte de concession par Charles de Boische, Marquis de Beauharnois, et Gilles Hocquart, gouverneur et intendant de la Nouvelle-France, à Louis Campaux, 5 July 1734; BHC, Edward V. Cicotte Papers, François Prud'homme.
41 Denissen, *Genealogy of French Families*, 204.
42 LAC, Notaires de Détroit, MG 18, I5, tome 1, fol. 235.
43 "Tous les batiments qui sont actuellement sur l'étendue des dits trois arpents sans exception avec tous les grains et fruits ceux tenant déjà à leurs raciness ... avec les clotures." LAC, Notaires de Détroit, MG 18, I5, tome 1, fol. 188.
44 LAC, Notaires de Détroit, MG 18, I5, tome 1, fol. 575.
45 Ibid.
46 Denissen, *Genealogy of French Families*, 264, 696.
47 BANQ-Q, Fonds Intendants, cote E1,S3,P268, Acte de concession par Charles de Boische, Marquis de Beauharnois, et Gilles Hocquart, gouverneur et intendant de la Nouvelle-France, au sieur Chauvin, 16 June 1734; BANQ-Q, Fonds Intendants, cote E1,S3,P284, Acte de concession par Charles de Boische, Marquis de Beauharnois, et Gilles Hocquart, gouverneur et intendant de la Nouvelle-France, à François Lauzon, 17 July 1734.
48 "Se reserve néanmoins le dit sieur Jacques Godfroy sur les dits biens, le verger." LAC, Notaires de Détroit, MG 18, I5, tome 2, fol. 166.
49 Denissen, *Genealogy of French Families*, 534.
50 LAC, Notaires de Détroit, MG 18, I5, tome 3, fol. 297.
51 Denissen, *Genealogy of French Families*, 198–200; ANOM, Colonies, C11A, vol. 31, fol. 160, Recensement nominatif de Détroit, 1710; Burton, *City of Detroit*, 1: 486.
52 Russell, ed., *Michigan Censuses*, 72; Denissen, *Genealogy of French Families*, 662.
53 Eldredge, *Past and Present of Macomb County*, 560.
54 Denissen, *Genealogy of French Families*, 662–4.

55 "15 pomier qui sont plantez sur la ditte terre, 9 peche petit et gros, 1 petit cerisier." BHC, Campau Family Papers, Riviere Huron le 6me octobre 1808.
56 Russell, ed., *Michigan Censuses*, 73.
57 "S'oblige de livrer la dite maison & grange ainsi que le verger, clotures en general de la dite terre." BHC, Campau Family Papers, Par devant temoins fut present le sieur Joseph Campau …, 24 March 1810.
58 "Le dit Joseph Campau se reserve son verger entierement." BHC, Campau Family Papers, Par devant le dit Joseph Desnoyers …, 9 January 1812.
59 For example, see the deed for the land grant to Charles Chauvin. BAnQ-Q, Fonds Intendants, cote E1,S3,P268, Acte de concession par Charles de Boische, Marquis de Beauharnois, et Gilles Hocquart, gouverneur et intendant de la Nouvelle-France, au sieur Chauvin, 16 June 1734.
60 The great majority of land transactions in the Detroit River region between the 1760s and 1810s did specify the presence of fences on the property being sold, even in instances where the property had obviously been acquired through an Aboriginal deed. See LAC, Notaires de Détroit, MG 18, I5, tomes 1–6; BHC, Campau Family Papers.
61 Darnell, *A Journal Containing an Accurate and Interesting Account*, 34–5. On 16 January 1813, American military officer Elijah McClanehan also remarked that French farms at River Raisin were enclosed by fences: "The land was cleared and entirely open, except fencing and some buildings for near a mile on every side from the encampment." Brannan, ed., *Official Letters*, 131.
62 Moore, "Governor, Judge, and Priest," 5. Born at River Huron (where Mount Clemens, Michigan, stands today) in 1855, Charles Moore was the grandson of Laurent Maure. In the 1780s, Laurent Maure had moved from Quebec to Detroit with his brother Louis Maure Sr, and sold his property at River Huron (Clinton River) to merchant Joseph Campau in 1808, as discussed above. Denissen, *Genealogy of French Families*, 862–4.
63 Carter, ed., *Territorial Papers*, 11: 8; Burton, *City of Detroit*, 2: 1050.
64 "J'ai bu du cidre qui aussi est fait avec ces pommes qui m'a semble amer comme du fiel." ANOM, Colonies, C11A, vol. 29, fol. 65, Rapport de Clairambault d'Aigremont au ministre concernant sa mission d'inspection dans les postes avancés, 14 November 1708. See also *Michigan Pioneer Collections*, 33: 444.

65 BHC, Jean Baptiste Crête Papers, Livre de compte de Jean Bapiste Crête; BHC, Beaubien Family Papers, Livre de compte de Jean Baptiste Beaubien père.
66 *Michigan Pioneer Collections*, 27: 627; Moore, ed., *Gladwin Manuscripts*. Jacques Amable Peltier, who resided on his father's farm in the Côte du Nord-Est at the time of these events, told Charles C. Throwbridge in the 1820s that the day following the Battle of Bloody Run dead British soldiers were found "by the Canadians in the orchards and front yards at the different farms, and were there buried." *Michigan Pioneer Collections*, 8: 362.
67 WCL, Michigan Collection, vol. 1: 1759–1799, James MacDonald to Horatio Gages, 8 August 1763. See also Mante, *History of the Late War*, 488.
68 *Michigan Pioneer Collections*, 10: 267; Lajeunesse, ed., *Windsor Border Region*, 85.
69 Quaife, ed., *War on the Detroit*, 234, 256–7.
70 Talman, ed., *Loyalist Narratives*, 89.
71 *Report and Collections of the Wisconsin Historical Society*, 7: 213.
72 *Michigan Pioneer Collections*, 4: 93.
73 Watts, *This Remote Country*, 77.
74 Ibid., 37.
75 Hull, *Memoirs of the Campaign*, 76.
76 *Michigan Pioneer Collections*, 1: 352.
77 In 1809, regarding the Saint Lawrence valley Hugh Gray said that "the Canadian farmer is not sufficiently aware of the value of manures." In 1813, John Lambert described the French there as "miserable farmers," mainly because "they seldom or never manure their land." In 1849, James E. Alexander wrote that the French along the Saint Lawrence River probably no longer threw "the manure from their stables into the river, as they are said formerly to have done." Gray, *Letters from Canada*, 137; Lambert, *Travels through Canada*, 131; Alexander, *L'Acadie*, 56–7.
78 Regarding such negative remarks about the farming techniques of the French settlers in the Saint Lawrence valley, Allan Greer has reminded us that they are not necessarily reliable sources. Greer, *Peasant, Lord, and Merchant*, 209. On the fact that William Hull intentionally portrayed the French settlers in Michigan Territory as backward people, notably because he did not get along with them, see Gitlin, *Bourgeois Frontier*, 7–8.

79 In literature, these "Muskrat French" are sometimes distinguished from the "Railroad French," French Canadians who migrated from the province of Quebec to southwest Ontario and the American Midwest after the construction of the Grand Trunk Railway in the 1850s. See, for instance, Bénéteau and Halford, *Mots choisis*, 8–9.
80 *Michigan Pioneer Collections*, 1: 352.
81 Au, "The Muskrat French." See also DuLong, *French Canadians in Michigan*, 12.
82 Blowe, *View of the United States of America*, 692.
83 Major, "Héritage culinaire des Québécois."
84 Watts, *This Remote Country*, 4. It is probably no coincidence that Congress acknowledged hundreds of private property claims by the French of Michigan Territory when Thomas Jefferson (1801–09) was president of the United States. Tangi Villerbu observes that the French farmers of Vincennes, located halfway between the Detroit River region and the Illinois Country, who in the 1790s claimed to have private property rights for the individual tracts of land that they had cultivated for decades, defended values that corresponded to those of Jefferson: "Et, somme toute, ce que ces Français défendent n'est pas loin d'un idéal jeffersonien demeuré toujours théorique, celui d'un monde de fermiers propriétaires de leurs terres et y faisant vivre leur famille, modèle qui est source de toutes les vertus républicaines." Villerbu, "Pouvoir, religion et société," 208.
85 See Teasdale, "French of Orchard Country," 226–32.

CHAPTER SEVEN

1 Carter, ed., *Territorial Papers*, 10: 296–7.
2 Cowan, *Canadian Achievement*, 16.
3 Another French community divided by the British North America–United States border is that of the Acadian community of the Madawaska region, in the upper Saint John valley, where Quebec, New Brunswick, and Maine meet. This community had begun to develop in the late eighteenth century, but was split in half by the Webster-Ashburton Treaty of 1842. For more information on this community, see Craig, "Before Borderlands."
4 Only on the Michigan side, the non-Aboriginal population amounted to more than four thousand people on the eve of the War of 1812, most of which were French. Au, "'Best Troops in the World,'" 106.

5 http://royditdesjardinsbuchananancestor.weebly.com/family-of-helene-soulliere-paternal.html, 22 May 2017; Lajeunesse, ed., *Windsor Border Region*, 359.
6 "Deuxième régiment," 340. No Soullière was enrolled in a Michigan militia regiment during the War of 1812. Barnett and Rosentreter, ed., *Michigan's Early Military Forces*, 138–40.
7 Lowrie, ed., *American State Papers*, 1: 305–557.
8 Carter, ed., *Territorial Papers*, 10: 871.
9 For a detailed history of the Meloches in North America, see Meloche, *Meloche Legacy*.
10 WCL, Thomas Gage Papers, American Series, List of Lots in the Fort of Detroit, showing the several titles to the same, taken by Capt. Morris of the 17th Regiment in October 1765.
11 BANQ-Q, Fonds Intendants, cote E1,S3,P275, Acte de concession par Charles de Boische, Marquis de Beauharnois, et Gilles Hocquart, gouverneur et intendant de la Nouvelle-France, à Pierre Meloche, 8 July 1734.
12 Denissen, *Genealogy of French Families*, 820; Russell, ed., *Michigan Censuses*, 20, 22.
13 Lajeunesse, ed., *Windsor Border Region*, 358–9; *Michigan Pioneer Collections*, 8: 530–40.
14 AO, Series RG-40-5, Second Heir and Devisee Commission, microfilms 19, 23, 25, and 62.
15 Russell, ed., *Michigan Censuses*, 20–56.
16 Denissen, *Genealogy of French Families*, 295; Lajeunesse, ed., *Windsor Border Region*, 358.
17 Denissen, *Genealogy of French Families*, 295.
18 Lajeunesse, ed., *Windsor Border Region*, 358; Moreau-DesHarnais, "Burials from L'Assomption," 203.
19 Denissen, *Genealogy of French Families*, 296.
20 Lowrie, ed., *American State Papers*, 1: 435.
21 BANQ-Q, Fonds Intendants, cote E1,S3,P284, Acte de concession par Charles de Boische, Marquis de Beauharnois, et Gilles Hocquart, gouverneur et intendant de la Nouvelle-France, à François Lauzon, 17 July 1734.
22 Russell, ed., *Michigan Censuses*, 53.
23 Lajeunesse, ed., *Windsor Border Region*, 359; *Michigan Pioneer Collections*, 8: 539.
24 Burton, ed., "Documents Relating to Wayne County and Michigan Territory," 26.

25 Denissen, *Genealogy of French Families*, 697.
26 Ibid., 699.
27 Ibid., 89; Russell, ed., *Michigan Censuses*, 24, 51; Lajeunesse, ed., *Windsor Border Region*, 359.
28 AO, Series RG-40-5, Second Heir and Devisee Commission, microfilms 43 and 47.
29 Another Jean-Baptiste Paré also lived on a farm in the Côte du Sud in 1794. His family appears to have always lived on the south shore of the Detroit River between the 1770s and 1810s. Denissen, *Genealogy of French Families*, 922–3.
30 No Paré is listed in Wayne County's 1802 Return of the Taxable Property. *Michigan Pioneer Collections*, 8: 530–40.
31 Lowrie, ed., *American State Papers*, 1: 346.
32 Russell, ed., *Michigan Censuses*, 129–33.
33 In 1815, there were two French Catholic parishes on the American side of the border (Saint Anne's, Detroit, established in 1701; Saint Antoine, River Raisin, established in 1788), and one on the Canadian side (Assumption, between Petite Côte and Côte du Sud, established in 1767).
34 Denissen, *Genealogy of French Families*, 921–2.
35 Hatter, "Jay Charter," 697.
36 Ibid., 697.
37 Ibid., 698.
38 Gourlay, *Statistical Account of Upper Canada*, 278, 282.
39 Burton, *City of Detroit*, 1: 530.
40 Palmer, *Detroit in 1837*, 17.
41 Hubbard, *Memorials*, 135. In a 1932 article published in the newspaper *The Border Cities Star*, it is written that landowner Antoine Labadie had built a windmill around 1776 near the corners of Riverside Drive and Devonshire Road, in Windsor. It is also mentioned that this windmill "was not dismantled until 1874." MacPherson, "First Labadie, Father of 33, Here in 1769," *The Border City Star*, 10 December 1932.
42 "An Old Tower," *Detroit Free Press*, 22 February 1885.
43 Cangany, "'Inhabitants of both Sides of this Streight,'" 41.
44 Denissen, *Genealogy of French Families*, 790.
45 Lajeunesse, ed., *Windsor Border Region*, lxxii; Douglas, *Uppermost Canada*, 7. In the book *City of East Windsor*, published in 1929, it is mentioned that in 1792 "the Maisonville mill seems to have been situated about where the Walkerville Ferry dock is now, according to this

map and this conforms with popular belief." East Windsor, *City of East Windsor*, 44.
46 Maisonville is listed among the landowners in the Côte du Sud in 1796. See Lajeunesse, ed., *Windsor Border Region*, 359.
47 Cangany, "'The Inhabitants of both Sides of this Streight,'" 42.
48 Ibid., 49.
49 Ibid., 54.
50 Ibid., 57.
51 Englebert, "Merchant Representatives," 63–4. Englebert coined the term "French river world."
52 Ibid., 65. Emphasis added. On the continuity of the fur trade beyond 1803, see St-Onge, "Blue Beads, Vermilion, and Scalpers," and "Persistence of Travel and Trade"; Podruchny, *Making the Voyageur World*.
53 One notable exception is historian Yves Frenette, who currently holds the Canada Research Chair in Migrations, Transfers and Francophone Communities at Université de Saint-Boniface, Manitoba. It is also the topic of one of my current projects, entitled "Aller faire souche au-delà des limites de la vallée laurentienne: L'émigration de familles 'canadiennes' vers les Grands Lacs à l'ère préindustrielle (1760–1840)." This project is funded by the Social Sciences and Humanities Research Council of Canada through an Insight Development Grant. The following pages are based on preliminary findings of this project. I would like to thank my research assistants Jason Lavin, John-Michael Markovic, and Shane Miller for helping to develop charts on French migrations from the Saint Lawrence valley to the Detroit River region between 1760 and 1840.
54 Following the 1848 California Gold Rush, many French Canadians left the Saint Lawrence valley for the Pacific coast. See, for example, Boucher, "Les Québécois au 'pays des rêves.'"
55 Yves Frenette writes: "Beaucoup de jeunes hommes n'avaient d'autre possibilité que de devenir ouvriers agricoles. Ils passaient d'une localité à l'autre, à la recherche de travail, n'ayant même pas l'espoir d'un héritage paternel avec lequel ils pourraient acheter une terre. Dans leur cas, il y eut rupture de la reproduction familiale ... Malheureusement, dans l'état actuel des connaissances, on ne peut faire la part des causes de départ, que ce fût l'endettement, le chômage, la reproduction familiale, le désir d'aventure ou une combinaison de ces facteurs. On sait seulement que le cycle familial jouait un rôle important. Ainsi, les couples déménageaient dans les nouvelles zones de colonisation au

moment de fonder une famille." Frenette, "L'histoire sociale de l'Amérique française," 129–31.
56 For information on the French Canadians who migrated to the Midwest between the 1840s and 1920s, see McQuillan, "French-Canadian Communities."
57 Podruchny, *Making the Voyageur World*, 287. On the French voyageurs who settled down in the settlement of Sainte Geneviève, in the Illinois Country, see Constantin, "Canots, terres et fourrures." See also Blouin, "Entre frères et cousins," 102. Instead of joining already existing agricultural settlements of the Great Lakes, like those of the Detroit River region, other voyageurs established new ones. For example, some settled down in present-day Penetanguishene, Ontario. In this case, many of these voyageurs had both Aboriginal and French ancestry. See Marchand, "La colonisation de Penetanguishene." In Quebec, seigneurialism was abolished only in 1854.
58 SHSB, Voyageur Contracts Database, "Joseph Jubinville, contract date: 17910411."
59 PRDH, #92777, "Joseph-Marie Jubinville, paroisse de Saint-Michel."
60 SHSB, Voyageur Contracts Database, "Jean-Baptiste Jubinville, contract date: 18040410."
61 PRDH, #309283, "Jean-Baptiste Jubinville, paroisse de Saint-Michel"; Denissen, *Genealogy of French Families*, 601.
62 Denissen, *Genealogy of French Families*, 601.
63 Ibid., 601.
64 Sheppard, "Essex County, Ontario Militia Rolls," 174; ibid., "Michigan Militia Members, Part 2," 105; Barnett and Rosentreter, ed., *Michigan's Early Military Forces*, 114.
65 Sheppard, "Essex County Militia Rolls," 176; ibid., "Michigan Militia Members, Part 2," 105. François Jubinville had no son named "François." No other "François Jubinville" was living in the Detroit River region at the time.
66 SHSB, Voyageur Contracts Database, "Gabriel Ménard, contract date: 17990814."
67 Denissen, *Genealogy of French Families*, 830, 1035.
68 Sheppard, "Michigan Militia Members, Part 2," 102.
69 Denissen, *Genealogy of French Families*, 830.
70 François-Luc Montreuil was the father of the Luc Montreuil mentioned earlier. Denissen, *Genealogy of French Families*, 854.
71 Ibid.
72 SHSB, Voyageur Contracts Database, "François-Luc Montreuil, contract date: 18010411."

73 Ibid., contract date: 18050412.
74 Ibid., "Jean-Marie Sédilot dit Montreuil, contract date: 17540610"; PRDH, #667109, "François-Luc Montreuil."
75 SHSB, Voyageur Contracts Database, "Jean-Marie Montreuil, contract dates: 17950321, 18010207, 18040125, 18100420."
76 Ibid., "Louis Montreuil, contract dates: 18000301, 18020514, 18040511, 18070219, 18130430."
77 Denissen, *Genealogy of French Families*, 855.
78 AO, Series RG-40-5, Second Heir and Devisee Commission, microfilm 50; Denissen, *Genealogy of French Families*, 854.
79 SHSB, Voyageur Contracts Database, "Joseph-Ambroise Généreux fils, contract date: 18110221."
80 Denissen, *Genealogy of French Families*, 518.
81 Ibid., 653; PRDH, #577322, "Joseph Beique Lafleur."
82 PRDH, #315775, "Joseph Beique"; SHSB, Voyageur Contracts Database, "Joseph Beique (dit Lafleur), contract date: 17510601."
83 According to Christian Denissen, Louis Loignon was born in 1765. However, records found through the PRDH state that he was born in 1763. Denissen, *Genealogy of French Families*, 653; PRDH, #202031, "Louis Loignon,"
84 Sheppard, "Michigan Militia Members, Part 2," 105.
85 Denissen, *Genealogy of French Families*, 758.
86 PRDH, #663060, "Joseph Picard."
87 For genealogical information about Joseph's father and uncles, see PRDH, #67622, "Famille de Alexis Picard et Marie Angélique Rouleau"; PRDH, #76564, "Famille de Alexis Picard et Catherine Lanctot." None of them have entries in the Voyageur Contracts Database.
88 Denissen, *Genealogy of French Families*, 973.
89 Carter-Edwards, "War of 1812," 31.
90 BHC, Francis Navarre Papers, Lettre de Pierre Audrain à François Navarre, Détroit, 10 October 1796; BHC, Francis Navarre Papers, Lettre de John Dodemead à François Navarre, 27 September 1797.
91 Barnett and Rosentreter, ed., *Michigan's Early Military Forces*, 128–9.
92 Naveaux, *Invaded on All Sides*, 73. See also "Proclamation by Isaac Brock, Esquire, Major General commanding His Majesty's forces in the Province of Upper Canada," in Burton, *City of Detroit*, 2: 1019.
93 UTA, Navarre-Williams Family Papers, Research and Speak Notes.
94 *Transactions*; MCM, Newspapers Clippings Files, Henry Howe, "Peter Navarre Is Prominent among Early Settlers"; Michaels and Hage, *Peter Navarre*.

95 A man named Pierre Navarre is one example of a member of the Navarre family who married an Aboriginal woman. In 1820, after having been hired by the American Fur Company at the age of thirty, Pierre built a small trading post along the Saint Joseph River in present-day South Bend, Indiana. Born on the farm of his father in the Côte des Pous, Pierre was the younger brother of François and Jacques Navarre, who obtained from the Potawatomi a tract of land at River Raisin in 1785. In South Bend, Pierre married a Potawatomi woman named Angélique Kichoueckouay with whom he had three sons and three daughters. Their children were baptized by French Catholic missionaries who periodically visited the area. When the United States removed most Potawatomi of the Saint Joseph valley to present-day Kansas in the fall of 1838, Pierre followed his wife's band. However, he later moved back to South Bend, apparently by himself, and died there in 1864. In the 1860s, his son Antoine, along with two other French-Potawatomi Métis who also lived in Kansas, Joseph N. Bourassa and B.H. Bertrand, petitioned the United States government regarding unpaid compensations for territorial dispossession which they signed as "delegates of the Pottowatomie Nation." Pierre was seemingly the only member of his extended family who moved permanently outside of the Detroit River region in the first half of the nineteenth century, and the only male who married an Aboriginal woman. Howard, *History of St. Joseph County*, 130–1; McKee, ed., "Trail of Death," 135; Bourassa, Bertrand, and Navarre, *Appeal of the Pottawatomie Nation*, 4; Kansas State Historical Society, "Surprise!"; Denissen, *Genealogy of French Families*, 110, 156–7, 888.

96 On the growing disconnection between the destinies of the French of the Detroit River region and their Aboriginal neighbours in the last decades of the eighteenth century, see Teasdale, "Des destinées distinctes" and "Old Friends and New Foes." Nathan Elliot Marvin observed a similar phenomenon regarding the French of Vincennes, in present-day southern Indiana. See Marvin, "'A Thousand Prejudices.'"

97 Besides trying to organize a militia company at River Raisin, the Upper Canada government also appointed a Catholic priest to the parish of that settlement, Saint Antoine's, to counter American influence. See Tucker, "From Fallen Timbers."

98 John Graves Simcoe to R.G. England, 22 August 1794, in Cruikshank, ed., *Correspondence of Lieutenant Governor John Graves Simcoe*, 2: 410.

99 R.G. England to John Graves Simcoe, 23 August 1794, in ibid., 2: 414.

100 On 30 August 1794, Simcoe wrote that "the Canadian Militia [of the Detroit River region] for the greater part have shewn themselves not to be depended upon." From J.G. Simcoe to Henry Dundas, Upper Canada, Navy Hall, 30 August 1794, in ibid., 3: 20.
101 Teasdale, "Débuts de l'Église catholique américaine," 50. Pierre Dejean was from France.
102 Denissen, *Genealogy of French Families*, 544–5.
103 On the founding of the city of Windsor along the south shore of the Detroit River in the 1830s, see Brode, *River & the Land*.
104 Lebel, "Ludger Duvernay," in DCB.
105 "Cette société si elle était une fois fortement établie ici, pourrait se ramifier alors de l'autre côté de la rivière, si vous êtes des patriotes zèlés, quelque uns d'entre vous pourraient aller dans ces paroisses françaises qui doivent vous être doublement chères, car non seulement ce sont des Canadiens Français, mais la plupart sortent des mêmes familles que vous, ces familles s'étant doublées de l'un et l'autre côté du Détroit; et là en établissant la même société et les mêmes fêtes, ranimer parmi eux l'esprit et le sentiment national avec plus d'énergie et plus de ressort ... Quoi de plus facile, pour quelques-uns de vos jeunes gens, d'aller quelquefois passer un jour de fête dans les paroisses américaines; là ils causeront avec les gens, les rassembleront, réveilleront chez eux la voix du sang et de la patrie, ils pourront les amener à se réunir comme vous, à se grouper comme vous, à se serrer tous ensembles, de telle sorte que vous vous souteniez en toute circonstance pour vous conserver, pour vous étendre, et pour vous défendre contre tous ceux qui vous seront hostiles sur un bord ou sur l'autre du Détroit." Rameau de Saint-Père, *Notes historiques*, 63–4.
106 On the Canadian side of the border, in Essex and Kent Counties, the following French Catholic parishes were established after 1815: Saint Jean Baptiste (Amherstburg, 1827), Saint Simon and Saint Jude (Belle River, 1842), Immaculée Conception (Paint Court, 1851). Société franco-ontarienne d'histoire et de généalogie régionale Windsor-Essex, *Le Sud-Ouest ontarien*, xvi.

CONCLUSION

1 Hoyt, "The French of Detroit," 42–3. In 1898, Edgar E. Brandon discussed the survival of French culture at River Raisin (Monroe, Michigan) as follows: "At the present day all can speak English, and

those who live in the towns and villages [of southeast Michigan] speak it without French accent. Many of the older men and women can not read or write any language, but almost all under thirty years of age can read and write English. But notwithstanding this, and the fact that the colony has been surrounded by an English-speaking population for a century, French still remains in most of the families the language of the home. It is the language of the church, and is commonly employed in business and social intercourse. There has been not much intermarriage between the two races." Brandon, "French Colony in Michigan," 244.
2 Reps, "Planning in the Wilderness."
3 Burton, *City of Detroit*, 1: 309.
4 Hoffman, *Winter in the West*, 1: 121.
5 *Michigan Pioneer Collections*, 1: 358; Hubbard, *Memorials*, 133.
6 Moran, *Moran Family*, 16. J. Bell Moran was the descendant of Jean Moran, who received a tract of land on the north shore of the Detroit River in 1734. BAnQ-Q, Fonds Intendants, cote E1,S3,P278, Acte de concession par Charles de Boische, Marquis de Beauharnois, et Gilles Hocquart, gouverneur et intendant de la Nouvelle-France, au nommé Moran, 11 July 1734; Denissen, *Genealogy of French Families*, 866–71.

BIBLIOGRAPHY

ARCHIVAL SOURCES

Archives of Ontario (AO)
Series RG-40-5, Second Heir and Devisee Commission

Archives nationales d'outre-mer, Aix-en-Provence, France (ANOM)
Amérique septentrionale
Fonds des Ordonnances des intendants de la Nouvelle-France
Recensements et documents divers
Série B, Lettres envoyées
Série C11A, Correspondance générale, Canada
Série C11E, Des limites et des postes
Série C11G, Canada et divers

Bentley Historical Library, University of Michigan (BHL)
Navarre Family Papers

Bibliothèque et Archives nationales du Québec, Montreal (BAnQ-M)
Fonds Juridiction royale de Montréal

Bibliothèque et Archives nationales du Québec, Quebec (BAnQ-Q)
Collection Centre d'archives de Québec
Fonds Conseil Souverain
Fonds Famille Chaussegros de Léry
Fonds Intendants

Burton Historical Collection, Detroit Public Library, Michigan (BHC)
Abbott Family Papers
Beaubien Family Papers
Bellestre Family Papers
Cadillac Papers
Campau Family Papers
Chene Family Papers
Edward V. Cicotte Papers
Francis Navarre Papers
Gabriel Godfroy Papers
John Askin Papers
Joseph Campau Papers
Labadie Family Papers
Laferté Family Papers
Rivard Family Papers
Robert Navarre Papers

Division de la gestion de documents et des archives de l'Université de Montréal (DAUM)
Collection Louis-François-Georges Baby

Library and Archives Canada, Ottawa (LAC)
Amherst Papers
Collection Nouvelle-France et Détroit
Colonies General, Original Correspondence, Board of Trade
Fonds Alexis Maisonville
Fonds Notaires de Détroit
Fonds des Ordonnances des intendants de la Nouvelle-France Haldimand Papers
RG 10, Indian Affairs Records
Upper Canada, Land Board Minutes and Records

Monroe County Museum, Monroe, Michigan (MCM)
Bidlack Papers
Colonel Francis Navarre Papers
French Pear Trees Papers
Jacques Navarre Papers
Newspapers Clippings Files

Programme de recherche en démographie historique, Université de Montréal (PRDH)

Société historique de Saint-Boniface, Saint Boniface, Manitoba (SHSB)
Voyageur Contracts Database

University of Toledo Archives, Toledo, Ohio (UTA)
Navarre-Williams Family Papers

William L. Clements Library, University of Michigan (WCL)
Michigan Collection
Thomas Gage Papers, American Series

OTHER SOURCES

Adams, Henry, ed. *The Writings of Albert Gallatin.* Vol. 1. Philadelphia: J.B. Lippincott, 1879.

Alexander, James Edward. *L'Acadie; or, Seven Years' Exploration in British America.* London: H. Colburn, 1849.

Anbury, Thomas. *Journal d'un voyage fait dans l'intérieur de l'Amérique septentrionale.* Vol. 1. 2nd ed. Translated from English by M. Noël. Paris: La Villette Libraire, 1793.

Anderson, Fanny J. "Medicine at Fort Detroit in the Colony of New France, 1701–1760." *Journal of the History of Medicine and Allied Sciences* 1, no. 2 (1946): 208–28.

Antoine, Annie. "Les paysans en France de la fin du Moyen Âge à la Révolution: Propriétaires? tenanciers? locataires?" In *Ruralité française et britannique, XIIIe–XXe siècles*, edited by Nadine Vivier, 153–66. Rennes: Presses universitaires de Rennes, 2005.

Assemblée législative du Canada. *Édits et ordonnances royaux, déclarations et arrêts du conseil d'État du roi concernant le Canada.* Vol. 1. Quebec: E.R. Fréchette, 1854.

Au, Dennis M. "'Best Troops in the World': The Michigan Territorial Militia in the Detroit River Theater During the War of 1812." In *Select Papers from the 1991 and 1992 George Rogers Clark Trans-Appalachian Frontier History Conferences*, edited by Robert J. Holden, 105–27. Vincennes, Indiana: Vincennes University, 1994.

– "The Muskrat French: The Survival of French Canadian Folklife on the American Side of Le Détroit." In *Passages: Three Centuries of Francophone Presence at Le Détroit*, edited by Marcel Bénéteau. Windsor: University of Windsor, 2003.

Bacqueville de La Potherie, Claude-Charles. *Histoire de l'Amérique septentrionale contenant le voyage du Fort de Nelson, dans la Baie d'Hudson à l'extrémité de l'Amérique, le premier établissement des*

Français dans ce vaste pays, la prise dudit Fort de Nelson, la description du fleuve de Saint-Laurent, le gouvernement de Québec, des Trois-Rivières & de Montréal, depuis 1534 jusqu'à 1701. Paris: Chez Jean-Luc Nion et François Didot, 1722.

Barnett, Le Roy, and Roger Rosentreter, eds. *Michigan's Early Military Forces*. Detroit: Wayne State University Press, 2003.

Beauregard, Ludger. "Géographie historique des côtes de l'île de Montréal." *Cahiers de géographie du Québec* 28, nos. 73–4 (1984): 47–62.

Bénéteau, Marcel. "Aspects de la tradition orale comme marqueurs d'identité culturelle: Le vocabulaire et la chanson traditionnelle des francophones du Détroit." PhD diss., Université Laval, 2001.

– *Trois siècles de vie française au pays de Cadillac*. Windsor: Sivori, 2002.

Bénéteau, Marcel, and Peter W. Halford. *Mots choisis: Trois cents ans de francophonie au Détroit du Lac Érié*. Ottawa: Presses de l'Université d'Ottawa, 2008.

Blais, Christian. "Pérégrinations et conquête du sol (1755–1836): L'implantation acadienne sur la rive nord de la Baie-des-Chaleurs." *Acadiensis* 35, no. 1 (2005): 3–23.

– "La représentation en Nouvelle-France." *Bulletin d'histoire politique* 18, no. 1 (2009): 51–75.

Blaufarb, Rafe. *The Great Demarcation: The French Revolution and the Invention of Modern Property*. New York: Oxford University Press, 2016.

Bloch, Marc. *Les caractères originaux de l'histoire rurale française*. Vol. 1. 2nd ed. Paris: Armand Colin, 1964.

Blouin, Sonia. "Entre frères et cousins: L'expérience familiale des voyageurs de la seigneurie de Rivière-du-Loup dans le commerce des fourrures." MA thesis, Université d'Ottawa, 2003.

Blowe, Daniel. *A Geographical, Historical, Commercial, and Agricultural View of the United States of America; Forming a Complete Emigrant's Directory through Every Part of the Republic*. London: Edwards & Knibb, 1820.

Bluche, François, ed. *Dictionnaire du Grand Siècle*. Paris: Fayard, 1990.

Bond, Beverley W., Jr. *The Quit-Rent System in the American Colonies*. New Haven: Yale University Press, 1919.

Boucher, Marc T. "Les Québécois au 'pays des rêves': Nouveaux enjeux, nouvelles tendances en Californie." In *Franco-Amérique*, edited by Dean Louder and Éric Waddell. Sillery, QC: Septentrion, 2008.

Boucher, Pierre (Sieur de Boucherville). *Histoire véritable et naturelle des moeurs & productions du pays de la Nouvelle France, vulgairement dite le Canada*. Paris: Chez Florentin Lambert, 1664.

Bouchette, Joseph. *Description topographique de la Province du Bas Canada avec des remarques sur le Haut Canada sur les relations des deux provinces avec les États-Unis d'Amérique*. London: W. Faden, 1815.

Bougainville, Comte Louis Antoine de. *Mémoire de Bougainville sur l'état de la Nouvelle-France à l'époque de la guerre de Sept ans, 1757*. N.p., 1790.

Bourassa, Joseph N., B.H. Bertrand, and Antoine Navarre. *Appeal of the Pottawatomie Nation of Indians to the Congress of the United States*. Washington, DC: s.n., 18?.

Bouthors, Alexandre. *Les sources du droit rural cherchées dans l'histoire des communaux et des communes*. Paris: A. Durand Libraire, 1865.

Brandon, Edgar E. "A French Colony in Michigan." *Modern Language Notes* 13, no. 4 (1898): 242–8.

Brannan, John, ed. *Official Letters of the Military and Naval Officers of the United States during the War with Great Britain in the Years 1812, 13, 14, & 15, with some Additional Letters and Documents Elucidating the History of That Period*. Washington, DC: Way & Gideon, 1823.

Brode, Patrick. *The River & the Land: A History of Windsor to 1900*. Windsor, ON: Biblioasis, 2014.

Burton, Clarence M. *Barnabas Campau and His Descendants*. Detroit, 1916.

– *The City of Detroit, Michigan, 1701–1922*. Vols. 1–2. Detroit: S.J. Clarke, 1922.

– ed. "Documents Relating to the Erection of Wayne County and Michigan Territory." *Historical Publications of Wayne County, Michigan* 1–2 (1922): 1–39.

Burton Historical Library Staff. "Robert Navarre." In *Dictionary of Canadian Biography*. Vol. 4. University of Toronto/Université Laval, 2003, http://www.biographi.ca/en/bio/navarre_robert_4E.html.

– "Philippe Dejean." In *Dictionary of Canadian Biography*. Vol. 5. University of Toronto/Université Laval, 2003–, http://www.biographi.ca/en/bio/dejean_philippe_5E.html.

Cabourdin, Guy, and Georges Viard. *Lexique historique de la France d'Ancien régime*. Paris: Armand Colin, 1978.

Cangany, Catherine. *Frontier Seaport: Detroit's Transformation into an Atlantic Entrepôt*. Chicago: University of Chicago Press, 2014.

– "'The Inhabitants of both Sides of this Streight constitute a french Colony': The Detroit River and the Politics of International Milling, 1796–1837." In *Une Amérique française, 1760–1860: Dynamiques du corridor créole*, edited by Guillaume Teasdale and Tangi Villerbu. Paris: Les Indes Savantes, 2015.

Canniff, William. *The Settlement of Upper Canada, with Special Reference to the Bay of Quinte*. 2nd ed. Belleville, ON: Mika Silk Screening Limited, 1971.

Carter, Clarence E., ed. *The Territorial Papers of the United States*. Vols. 3, 7, 10, & 11. Washington, DC: United States Government Printing Office, 1934–1943.

Carter-Edwards, Dennis. "The War of 1812 along the Detroit Frontier: A Canadian Perspective." *Michigan Historical Review* 13, no. 2 (1987): 25–50.

Cartier, Gwenaël. "Québec 1608–2008: 400 ans de statistiques démographiques tirées des recensements." *Cahiers québécois de démographie* 37, no. 1 (2008): 131–61.

Catalogne, Gédéon de. "Mémoire de Gédéon de Catalogne sur les plans des seigneuries et habitations des gouvernement de Québec, des Trois-Rivières et Montréal." *Bulletin des recherches historiques* 21, no. 9 (1915): 257–69.

Champlain, Samuel de. *Les voyages de la Nouvelle France occidentale, dicte Canada faits par le Sr. de Champlain Sainctongeois, capitaine pour le Roy en la Marine du Ponant, & toutes les descouvertes qu'il a faites en ce pais depuis l'an 1603, jusques en l'an 1629, où se voit comme ce pays a esté descouvert par les François sous l'authorité de nos Roys très-Chrestiens, jusques au règne de Sa Majesté à présent régnante Louis XIII de France & de Navarre*. Paris: Chez Louis Sevestre, 1632.

Chapman, Sara E. *Private Ambition and Political Alliances: The Phélypeaux de Pontchartrain Family and Louis XIV's Government, 1650–1715*. Rochester, NY: University of Rochester Press, 2004.

Charbonnier, Pierre et al., eds. *Les espaces collectifs dans les campagnes, XIe–XXIe siècle*. Clermont-Ferrand: Presses universitaires Blaise-Pascal, 2007.

Clarke, John. *Land, Power, and Economics on the Frontier of Upper Canada*. Montreal & Kingston: McGill-Queen's University Press, 2001.

– *The Ordinary People of Essex: Environment, Culture, and Economy on the Frontier of Upper Canada*. Montreal & Kington: McGill-Queen's University Press, 2010.

– "James Baby." In *Dictionary of Canadian Biography*. Vol. 6. University of Toronto/Université Laval, 2003–, http://www.biographi.ca/en/bio/baby_james_6E.html.

Cleland, Charles E. *Rites of Conquest: The History and Culture of Michigan's Native Americans*. Ann Arbor: University of Michigan Press, 1992.

Committee of the House of Assembly of Lower Canada. *Seventh Report of the Committee of the House of Assembly on that Part of the Speech of His Excellency the Governor in Chief which Relates to the Settlement of the Crown Lands with the Minutes of Evidence taken Before the Committee.* Quebec City: Neilson & Cowan, 1824.

Constantin, Jennifer. "Canots, terres et fourrures en Haute-Louisiane: Les voyageurs de Sainte-Geneviève convertis à la sédentarité (1763–1803)." MA thesis, Université d'Ottawa, 2011.

Courville, Serge. "Contribution à l'étude de l'origine du rang au Québec: La politique spatiale des Cent-Associés." *Cahiers de géographie du Québec* 25, no. 65 (1981): 197–235.

– "Espace, territoire et culture en Nouvelle-France: Une vision géographique." *Revue d'histoire de l'Amérique française* 37, no. 3 (1983): 417–29.

Cowan, Hugh. *Canadian Achievement in the Province of Ontario.* Vol. 1: *The Detroit River District.* Windsor, ON: The Algonquin Historical Society of Canada, 1929.

Craig, Béatrice. "Before Borderlands: Yankees, British and the St. John Valley French." In *New England and the Maritime Provinces: Connections and Comparisons*, edited by Page Range. Montreal & Kingston: McGill-Queen's University Press, 2005.

– "Le Madawaska, 1785–1870." In *La francophonie nord-américaine*, edited by Yves Frenette, Étienne Rivard, and Marc St-Hilaire. Quebec: Presses de l'Université Laval, 2012.

Cruikshank, Ernest A., ed. *The Correspondence of Lieutenant Governor John Graves Simcoe, with Allied Documents Relating to His Administration of the Government of Upper Canada.* 4 vols. Toronto: Ontario Historical Society, 1921–1926.

Cruikshank Ernest, and Andrew F. Hunter, eds. *The Correspondence of the Honourable Peter Russell: with Allied Documents Relating to his Administration of the Government of Upper Canada during the Official Term of Lieut.-Governor J. G. Simcoe, while on Leave of Absence.* Vol. 1. Toronto: Ontario Historical Society, 1932.

Darnell, Elias. *A Journal Containing an Accurate and Interesting Account of the Hardships, Sufferings, Battles, Defeat, and Captivity of those Heroic Kentucky Volunteers and Regulars.* Philadelphia: Lippincott, Grambo and Co., 1854.

Dechêne, Louise. *Habitants et marchands de Montréal au XVIIe siècle.* 2nd ed. Montreal: Boréal, 1988.

Deffontaines, Pierre. "Évolution du type d'habitation rurale au Canada français." *Cahiers de géographie du Québec* 11, no. 24 (1967): 497–522.

- *Le rang, type de peuplement rural du Canada français.* Quebec: Presses de l'Université Laval, 1953.
De Koninck, Rodolphe, Anne-Marie Turcot, and Andrée G. Zubrzycki. "Les pâturages communaux du lac Saint-Pierre: De leur histoire et de leur actualité." *Cahiers de géographie du Québec* 17, no. 41 (1973): 317–29.
Delâge, Denys. "Les Iroquois chrétiens des réductions, 1667–1770. Partie 1: Migration et rapports avec les Français." *Recherches amérindiennes au Québec* 21, nos. 1–2 (1991): 59–70.
- "Les principaux paradigmes de l'histoire amérindienne et l'étude de l'alliance franco-amérindienne aux XVIIe et XVIIIe siècles." *Revue internationale d'études canadiennes* 12 (1995): 51–67.
Denissen, Christian. *Genealogy of the French Families of the Detroit River Region, 1701–1936.* 2 vols. 2nd ed. Detroit: Detroit Society for Genealogical Research, 1987.
Dépatie, Sylvie. "Jardins et vergers à Montréal au XVIIIe siècle." In *Vingt ans après Habitants et marchands: Lectures de l'histoire des XVIIe et XVIIIe siècles canadiens*, edited by Sylvie Dépatie et al. Montreal & Kingston: McGill-Queen's University Press, 1998.
Derruau, Max. "À l'origine du 'rang' canadien." *Cahiers de géographie du Québec* 1, no. 1 (1956): 39–47.
Desbarats, Catherine. "The Cost of Early Canada's Native Alliances: Reality and Rhetoric of Scarcity." *William and Mary Quarterly* 52, no. 4 (1995): 609–30.
- "Following *The Middle Ground*." *William and Mary Quarterly* 63, no. 1 (2006): 81–96.
d'Eschambault, Antoine. "La vie aventureuse de Daniel Greysolon, sieur Dulhut." *Revue d'histoire de l'Amérique française* 5, no. 3 (1951): 320–39.
Deschênes, Gilles. *Quand le vent faisait tourner les moulins: Trois siècles de meunerie banale et marchande au Québec.* Sillery, QC: Septentrion, 2009.
"Deuxième régiment de la malice du comté d'Essex, bordereau de paye du 2 au 24 juillet 1812." Transcribed by Benjamin Sulte. *Bulletin des recherches historiques* 10, no. 11 (1904): 337–41.
Dewar, Helen Mary. "'Y establir nostre auctorité': Assertions of Imperial Sovereignty through Proprietorships and Chartered Companies in New France." PhD diss., University of Toronto, 2012.
"Un document inédit sur M. de Lamothe Cadillac: Inventaire général des bâtiments, moulins, bestiaux, marchandises et ustensiles, meubles et

immeubles et autres effaits apartenant à Monsieur de Lamothe Cadillac, gouverneur de la Louisiane, laissés entre les mains du Sr. Pierre Roy, habitant de Détroit (25 aoust 1711)." *Bulletin des recherches historiques* 24, no. 1 (1918): 19–29.

Douglas, R. Alan. *Uppermost Canada: The Western District and the Detroit Frontier, 1800–1850*. Detroit: Wayne State University Press, 2001.

Dowd, Gregory E. *War under Heaven: Pontiac, the Indian Nations, and the British Empire*. Baltimore: Johns Hopkins University Press, 2002.

DuLong, John P. *French Canadians in Michigan*. East Lansing: Michigan State University Press, 2001.

Dunnigan, Brian L. *Frontier Metropolis: Picturing Early Detroit, 1701–1838*. Detroit: Wayne State University Press, 2001.

Dupuis, Serge, and Stéphane Savard. "Arpenté, défriché, mais pas encore entièrement labouré: Le champ de l'historiographie franco-ontarienne en bref." *Bulletin d'histoire politique* 24, no. 2 (2016): 10–32.

East Windsor. *The City of East Windsor*. East Windsor, ON, 1929.

Eldredge, Robert F. *Past and Present of Macomb County, Michigan*. Chicago: S.J. Clarke, 1905.

Englebert, Robert. "Merchant Representatives and the French River World, 1763–1803." *Michigan Historical Review* 34, no. 1 (2008): 63–82.

Englebert, Robert, and Guillaume Teasdale. "Introduction." In *French and Indians in the Heart of North America, 1630–1815*, edited by Robert Englebert and Guillaume Teasdale, xi. East Lansing: Michigan State University Press, 2013.

Extract of the Proceedings of a Committee of the Whole Council: Under the Following Order of Reference Relative to a Conversion of the Present Tenures in the Province of Quebec into that of Free and Common Socage. Quebec City: Samuel Neilson, 1790.

Farmer, Silas. *The History of Detroit and Michigan or the Metropolis Illustrated: A Chronological Cyclopaedia of the Past and Present*. 2 Vols. Detroit: Silas Farmer & Co., 1884 and 1889.

Fillion, Konrad. "Essai sur l'évolution du mot habitant (XVIIe–XVIIIe siècles)." *Revue d'histoire de l'Amérique française* 24, no. 3 (1970): 375–401.

Flick, Alexander C., ed. *The Papers of Sir William Johnson*. Vols. 5–6. Albany: The University of the State of New York, 1927–1928.

Fraser, Alexander, ed. *Report of the Bureau of Archives for the Province of Ontario*. Vols. 3, 6, 13 &14. Toronto: A.T. Wilgress, 1905–1918.

French-Canadian Heritage Society of Michigan. *Michigan's Habitant Heritage*.

Frenette, Yves. "L'histoire sociale de l'Amérique française de 1763 à 1914: État des lieux." *Cahiers Charlevoix* 11 (2016): 115–55.

Gagné, Joseph. "Du lys naquit le trille: Survol historiographique de l'Ontario sous le Régime français et perspectives de recherche." *Revue du Nouvel-Ontario* 41 (2016): 33–58.

Gates, Lillian F. "The Heir and Devisee Commission of Upper Canada, 1797–1805." *Canadian Historical Review* 38, no. 1 (1957): 21–36.

– *Land Policies of Upper Canada*. Toronto: University of Toronto Press, 1968.

George III. *By the King, a Proclamation Whereas We Have Taken into our Royal Consideration the Extensive and Valuable Acquisitions in America*. London: Printed by Mark Baskett, Printer to the King's most Excellent Majesty; and by the Assigns of Robert Baskett, 1763.

Gilpin, Alec R. *The Territory of Michigan, 1805–1837*. East Lansing: Michigan State University Press, 1970.

Gitlin, Jay. *The Bourgeois Frontier: French Towns, French Traders, and American Expansion*. New Haven, CT: Yale University Press, 2010.

Goldsmith, James L. *Lordship in France, 1500–1789*. New York: Peter Lang, 2005.

Gouger, Lina. "Les convois de colons de 1749–1750: Impulsion gouvernementale décisive pour le développement de la région de Windsor." In *Passages: Three Centuries of Francophone Presence at Le Détroit*, edited by Marcel Bénéteau. Windsor, ON: University of Windsor, 2003.

– "Le peuplement colonisateur de Détroit, 1701–1765." PhD diss., Université Laval, 2002.

Gourlay, Robert. *Statistical Account of Upper Canada Compiled with a View to a Grand System of Immigration*. London: Simpkin & Marshall, 1822.

Gray, Hugh. *Letters from Canada Written during a Residence there in 1806, 1807 and 1808, Showing the Present State of Canada, its Productions, Trade, Commercial and Political Importance*. London: Longman, 1809.

Greer, Allan. *Peasant, Lord, and Merchant: Rural Society in Three Quebec Parishes, 1740–1840*. Toronto: University of Toronto Press, 1985.

Greffenius, Ruben J.E. "Development of Michigan Public Land Policy." PhD diss., University of Michigan, 1968.

Grenier, Benoît. *Brève histoire du système seigneurial*. Montreal: Boréal, 2012.

Gruter, Édouard. "Communaux." In *Dictionnaire du Grand Siècle*, edited by François Bluche. Paris: Fayard, 1990.

Hamelin, Louis Edmond. "Rang, côte et concession au sens de 'peuplement aligné' au Québec depuis le XVIIe siècle." *Revue d'histoire de l'Amérique française* 42, no. 4 (1989): 519–43.

Hamil, Fred C. *The Valley of the Lower Thames, 1640–1850*. Toronto: University of Toronto Press, 1951.

Hamilton, Milton W., ed. *The Papers of Sir William Johnson*. Vol. 12. Albany: The University of the State of New York, 1957.

Hammes, Raymond H. "Land Transactions in Illinois Prior to the Sale of Public Domain." *Journal of the Illinois State Historical Society* 77, no. 2 (1984): 101–14.

Harris, R. Cole. *The Seigneurial System in Early Canada*. 2nd ed. Montreal & Kingston: McGill-Queen's University Press, 1984.

Hatter, Lawrence B. A. *Citizens of Convenience: The Imperial Origins of American Nationhood on the US-Canada Border*. Charlottesville: University of Virginia Press, 2017.

– "The Jay Charter: Rethinking the American National State in the West, 1796–1819." *Diplomatic History* 37, no. 4 (2013): 693–726.

– "The Transformation of the Detroit Land Market and the Formation of the Anglo-American Border, 1783–1796." *Michigan Historical Review* 34, no. 1 (2008): 83–99.

Havard, Gilles. *Empire et Métissages: Indiens et Français dans le Pays d'en Haut, 1660–1715*. Sillery, QC and Paris: Septentrion and Presses de l'Université de Paris-Sorbonne, 2003.

– "'Les forcer à devenir cytoyens': État, sauvages et citoyenneté en Nouvelle-France (XVIIe –XVIIIe siècle)." *Annales: Histoire, sciences sociales* 64, no. 5 (2009): 985–1018.

– *Histoire des coureurs de bois: Amérique du Nord, 1600–1840*. Paris: Les Indes Savantes, 2016.

Havard, Gilles, and Cécile Vidal. *Histoire de l'Amérique française*. 2nd ed. Paris: Flammarion, 2006.

Hayne, David M. "Louis-Armand de Lom d'Arce de Lahontan, Baron de Lahontan." In *Dictionary of Canadian Biography*. Vol. 2. University of Toronto/Université Laval, 2003–, http://www.biographi.ca/en/bio/lom_d_arce_de_lahontan_louis_armand_de_2E.html.

Heneker, Dorothy A. *The Seigniorial Regime in Canada*. Quebec City: Government of the Province of Quebec, 1926.

Hennepin, Louis. *Description de la Louisiane nouvellement découverte au sud'ouest de la Nouvelle-France, par ordre du Roy, avec la carte du pays, les moeurs et la manière de vivre des sauvages, dédié à Sa Majesté*. Paris: Chez la veuve Sébastien Huré, 1683.

Hoffman, Charles F. *Winter in the West*. Vol. 1. New York: Harper & Brothers, 1835.

Holli, Melvin G. "French Detroit: The Clash of Feudal and Yankee Values." In *The Ethnic Frontier: Essays in the History of Group Survival in Chicago and the Midwest*, edited by Melvin G. Holli and Peter d'Alroy Jones. Grand Rapids, MI: William B. Eerdmans, 1977.

Horsman, Reginald. "American Indian Policy in the Old Northwest, 1783–1812." *William and Mary Quarterly* 18, no. 1 (1961): 35–53.

Hough, Franklin B., ed. *Diary of the Siege of Detroit in the War with Pontiac, also a Narrative of the Principal Events of the Siege, by Major Robert Rogers; a Plan for Conducting Indian Affairs, by Colonel Bradstreet; and other Authentic Documents, Never Printed Before*. Albany: J. Munsell, 1860.

Howard, Timothy E. *A History of St. Joseph County, Indiana*. Vol. 1. Chicago: The Lewis Publishing Co., 1907.

Hoyt, William. "The French of Detroit in My Day." In *Chronography or Notable Events in the History of the Northwest Territory and Wayne County*, edited by Fred Carlisle. Detroit: O.S. Gulley, Bornman, 1890.

Hubbard, Bela. *Memorials of a Half-Century*. New York: G.P. Putman's Sons, 1887.

Hull, William. *Memoirs of the Campaign of the North Western Army of the United States, AD 1812, in a Series of Letters Addressed to the Citizens of the United States with an Appendix containing a Brief Sketch of the Revolutionary Services of the Author*. Boston: True & Greene, 1824.

Irving, L. Homfray, ed. *Officers of the British Forces in Canada during the War of 1812–15*. Welland, ON: Welland Tribune Print, 1908.

Jameson, Anna. *Winter Studies and Summer Rambles in Canada*. London: Saunders & Otley, 1838.

Jetten, Marc. *Enclaves amérindiennes: Les "réductions" du Canada, 1637–1701*. Sillery, QC: Septentrion, 1994.

Kalm, Pehr. *Travels in North America; Containing Its Natural History, and a Circumstantial Account of Its Plantations and Agriculture in General, with the Civil, Ecclesiastical and Commercial State of the Country, the Manners of the Inhabitants, and Several Curious and Important Remarks on Various Subjects*. Translated into English by John Reinhold Forster. Vol. 2. London: T. Lowndes, 1773.

Kansas State Historical Society. "Surprise! This Was Written in 1876." *Kansas Historical Quarterly* 21 (1954–55): 487–91.

Kent, Timothy J. *Ft. Pontchartrain at Detroit: A Guide to the Daily Lives of Fur Trade and Military Personnel, Settlers, and Missionaries at French Posts*. 2 Vols. Ossineke, MI: Silver Fox Enterprises, 2001.

Kerrigan, William. "Apples on the Border: Orchards and the Contest for the Great Lakes." *Michigan Historical Review* 34, no. 1 (2008): 25–41.

Knapp, Horace S. *History of the Maumee Valley: Commencing with its Occupation by the French in 1680; to which is Added Sketches of Some of its Moral and Material Resources as they Exist in 1872*. Toledo, OH: Blade Mammoth, 1872.

Lajeunesse, Ernest J. "Armand de La Richardie." In *Dictionary of Canadian Biography*. Vol. 3. University of Toronto/Université Laval, 2003, http://www.biographi.ca/en/bio/la_richardie_armand_de_3E.html.

– "The First Four Years of the Settlement on the Canadian Shore of the Detroit River." *Ontario History* 47 (1955): 122–31.

– ed. *The Windsor Border Region: Canada's Southernmost Frontier: A Collection of Documents*. Toronto: University of Toronto Press for the Champlain Society, 1960.

Lambert, John. *Travels through Canada, and the United States of North America, in the Years 1806, 1807, & 1808 to which are Added, Biographical Notices and Anecdotes of some of the Leading Characters in the United States*. Vol. 1. London: C. Cradock and W. Joy, 1813.

Lebel, Jean-Marie. "Ludger Duvernay." In *Dictionary of Canadian Biography*. Vol. 8. University of Toronto/Université Laval, 2003–, http://www.biographi.ca/en/bio/duvernay_ludger_8E.html.

Le Clercq, Chrestien. *Premier établissement de la foy dans la Nouvelle France contenant la publication de l'évangile, l'histoire des colonies françaises, & les fameuses découvertes depuis le fleuve de Saint Laurent, la Loüisiane & le fleuve Colbert jusqu'au Golphe Mexique*. Paris: Chez Amable Auroy, 1691.

Lecomte, Lucie. "Les seigneuries dans le territoire actuel de l'Ontario." MA thesis, Université d'Ottawa, 2002.

Lowrie, Walter, ed. *American State Papers: Documents, Legislative and Executive, of the Congress of the United States, from the First Session of the First to the Third Session of the Thirteenth Congress, Inclusive: Commencing March 3, 1789, and Ending March 3, 1815*. Vol. 1. Washington, DC: Published by Gales and Seaton, 1832.

Lytwyn, Victor, and Dean Jacobs. "'For Good Will and Affection': The Detroit Indian Deeds and British Land Policy, 1760–1827." *Ontario History* 92, no. 1 (2000): 9–29.

MacDonald, George F. "The New Settlement on Lake Erie." In *Read at a Meeting of the Essex Historical Society, Windsor, Ontario, 25th April, 1918*. Amherstburg: Echo Printing, 1918.

McDonnell, Michael. *Masters of Empire: Great Lakes Indians and the Making of America*. New York: Hill and Wang, 2015.

McKee, Irving, ed. "The Trail of Death: Letters of Benjamin Marie Petit." *Indiana Historical Society Publications* 14, no. 1 (1941): 1–141.

McQuillan, D. Aidan. "French-Canadian Communities in the American Upper Midwest during the Nineteenth Century." *Cahiers de géographie du Québec* 23, no. 58 (1979): 53–72.

Major, Éric. "L'héritage culinaire des Québécois: Un legs de l'ancienne et de la Nouvelle-France." *Le Devoir*, 23 August 2008.

Mante, Thomas. *The History of the Late War in North America*. London: Printed for W. Strahan, 1772.

Marchand, Micheline. "La colonisation de Penetanguishene par les voyageurs (1825–1871)." MA thesis, Université Laurentienne, 1988.

Margry, Pierre, ed. *Découvertes et établissements des Français dans l'Ouest et dans le Sud de l'Amérique septentrionale: Mémoires et documents originaux*. Vols. 1 and 5. Paris: Maisonneuve frères & C.H. Leclerc éditeurs, 1879 and 1887.

Marrero, Karen Lynn. "Founding Families: Power and Authority of Mixed French and Native Lineages in Eighteenth-Century Detroit." PhD diss., Yale University, 2011.

– "On the Edge of the West: The Roots and Routes of Detroit's Urban Eighteenth Century." In *Frontier Cities: Encounters at the Crossroads of Empire*, edited by Jay Gitlin, Barbara Berglund, and Adam Arenson. Philadelphia: University of Pennsylvania Press, 2013.

Marriott, Sir James. *Plan of a Code of Laws for the Province of Quebec*. London, 1774.

Marshall, Peter. "Imperial Policy and the Government of Detroit: Projects and Problems, 1760–1774." *Journal of Imperial and Commonwealth History* 2, no. 2 (1974): 153–89.

Martin, Paul-Louis. *Les fruits du Québec: Histoire et traditions des douceurs de la table*. Sillery, QC: Septentrion, 2002.

Marvin, Nathan Elliot. "'A Thousand Prejudices': French *Habitants* and Catholic Missionaries in the Making of the Old Northwest, 1795–1805." In *Une Amérique française, 1760–1860: Dynamiques du corridor créole*, edited by Guillaume Teasdale and Tangi Villerbu. Paris: Les Indes Savantes, 2015.

Meloche, James Lawrence Joseph. *The Meloche Legacy: A Meloche Family History Dating Back to the Year 1575*. N.p.: L'Association des Familles Meloche, 2001.

Michaels, Larry, and Robyn Hage. *Peter Navarre: War of 1812 Scout*. Toledo, OH: Bihl House, 2002.

Michigan Pioneer and Historical Collections. Vols. 1, 2, 4, 7, 8, 10, 19, 20, 22, 33, 34, 37. Lansing: State Printers, 1876–1929.

Moore, Charles. *Governor, Judge, and Priest: Detroit, 1805–1815. A Paper Read Before the Witenagemote on Friday Evening, October 2, 1891*. New York: De Vinne, 1891: 5–24.

Moore, Charles, ed. *The Gladwin Manuscripts*. Lansing: Robert Smith, 1897.

Moran, J. Bell. *The Moran Family: 200 Years in Detroit*. Detroit: Alved of Detroit, 1949.

Moreau-DesHarnais, Gail. "Burials from L'Assomption-de-la-Pointe-de-Montréal-du-Detroit, 12 July 1800–27 December 1805: Part 4." *Michigan's Habitant Heritage* 33, no. 4 (October 2012): 197–207.

– "Land Conceded by Cadillac Outside of the Fort." http://habitantheritage.org/

Moreau-DesHarnais, Gail, and Diane Wolford Sheppard. *Le Détroit du Lac Érié, 1701–1710*. Vol. 1. Royal Oak, MI: French-Canadian Heritage Society of Michigan, 2016.

Morin, Jean-Pierre. "Concepts of Extinguishment in the Upper Canada Land Surrender Treaties." In *Aboriginal Policy Research*. Vol. 7: *A History of Treaties and Policies*, edited by Jerry P. White, Erik Anderson, Jean-Pierre Morin, and Dan Beavon. Toronto: Thompson Educational, 2010.

Morin, Michel. "'Manger avec la même micoine dans la même gamelle': À propos des traités conclus avec les Amérindiens au Québec, 1665–1760." *Revue générale de droit* 33, no. 1 (2003): 93–129.

– *L'usurpation de la souveraineté autochtone: Le cas des peuples de la Nouvelle-France et des colonies anglaises de l'Amérique du Nord*. Montreal: Boréal, 1997.

Munro, William B. *The Seignorial System in Canada: A Study in French Colonial Policy*. Cambridge, MA: Harvard University Press, 1907.

Murphy, Lucy Eldersveld. *A Gathering of Rivers: Indians, Métis, and Mining in the Western Great Lakes, 1737–1832*. Lincoln: University of Nebraska Press, 2000.

Naveaux, Ralph. *Invaded on all Sides: The Story of Michigan's Greatest Battlefield Scene of the Engagements at Frenchtown and the River Raisin in the War of 1812*. Marceline, MO: Walsworth, 2008.

Neal, Frederick. *The Township of Sandwich (Past and Present)*. Windsor, ON: The Record Printing, 1909.

Niort, Jean-François. "Aspects juridiques du régime seigneurial en Nouvelle-France." *Revue générale de droit* 32, no. 3 (2002): 443–526.

Ouellet, Fernand, ed. *Lahontan: Œuvres complètes*. Vol. 1. Montreal: Presses de l'Université de Montréal, 1990.

– *L'Ontario français dans le Canada français avant 1911: Contribution à l'histoire sociale*. Sudbury, ON: Prise de Parole, 2005.

Palmer, Friend. *Early Days in Detroit*. Detroit: Hunt & June, 1906.

Palmer, Thomas W. *Detroit in 1837: Recollections of Thomas W. Palmer*. Detroit: Burton Abstract & Title Company, 1954. First published Detroit, 1922.

Paré, George. *The Catholic Church in Detroit, 1701–1888*. Detroit: The Gabriel Richard Press, 1951.

Peters, Richard, ed. *The Public Statutes at Large of the United States of America, from the Organization of the Government in 1789, to March 3, 1845*. Vol. 2. Boston: Charles C. Little & James Brown, 1850.

Peterson, Jacqueline. "Prelude to Red River: A Social Portrait of the Great Lakes Métis." *Ethnohistory* 25, no. 1 (1978): 41–67.

Podruchny, Carolyn. *Making the Voyageur World: Travelers and Traders in the North American Fur Trade*. Toronto: University of Toronto Press, 2006.

Poisson, Jean-Paul. "Notaires." In *Dictionnaire du Grand Siècle*, edited by François Bluche. Paris: Fayard, 1990.

Poitrineau, Abel. "Domaine." In *Dictionnaire du Grand Siècle*, edited by François Bluche. Paris: Fayard, 1990.

Quaife, Milo M. "Detroit Biographies: Aaron Greeley." *Burton Historical Collection Leaflet* 5, no. 4 (1927): 49–57.

– *War on the Detroit: The Chronicles of Thomas Verchères de Boucherville and the Capitulation by an Ohio Volunteer*. Chicago: The Lakeside Press, 1940.

Quaife, Milo, M., ed. *The John Askin Papers*. 2 Vols. Detroit: Detroit Library Commission, 1928 & 1931.

Quint, Jonathan. "Patrick McNiff and the 'Aristocratic Element' of Detroit." MA paper, University of Windsor, 2016.

Radike, Floyd. *Detroit: A French Village on the Frontier*. Detroit: Wayne State University Press, 1951.

Rameau de Saint-Père, Edmé. *Notes historiques sur la colonie canadienne du Détroit: Lecture prononcée par Mr. Rameau à Windsor sur le*

Détroit, comté d'Essex, C.W. le Lundi 1er avril 1861. Montreal: J.B. Rolland & fils, Libraires-éditeurs, 1861.

Reps, John W. "Planning in the Wilderness: Detroit, 1805–1830." *Town Planning Review* 25, no. 4 (1955): 240–50.

Rodriguez, Michael, and Thomas Featherstone. *Detroit's Belle Isle.* Mt Pleasant, SC: Arcadia Publishing, 2003.

Roy, Antoine. "Le fort Frontenac ou Catarakoui sous le régime français." *Report of the Annual Meeting of the Canadian Historical Association* 29, no. 1 (1950): 51–7.

Roy, J.-Edmond. "La cartographie et l'arpentage sous le régime français (Partie 2)." *Bulletin des recherches historiques* 1, no. 3 (1895): 33–40.

– "Les postes du Roi." *Bulletin des recherches historiques* 2, no. 12 (1896): 187–8.

Roy, Pierre-Georges, ed. *Inventaire des concessions en fief et seigneurie fois et hommages et aveux et dénombrements conservés aux Archives de la province de Québec.* Vols. 1–5. Beauceville, QC: L'Éclaireur, 1927–1929.

– *Rapport de l'Archiviste de la province de Québec pour l'année 1920–1921.* Quebec: Ls-A. Proulx, 1921.

– *Rapport de l'Archiviste de la province de Québec pour l'année 1921–1922.* Quebec: Ls-A. Proulx, 1922.

– *Rapport de l'Archiviste de la province de Québec pour l'année 1926–1927.* Quebec: Ls-A. Proulx, 1927.

– *Rapport de l'archiviste de la province de Québec pour 1939–1940.* Quebec: Rédempti Paradis, 1940.

Roy, Pierre-Georges. *La ville de Québec sous le Régime français.* Vol. 1. Quebec: Rédempti Paradis, 1930.

Report and Collections of the Wisconsin Historical Society. Vol. 7. Madison: E.B. Bolens, 1876.

Rushforth, Brett. *Bonds of Alliance: Indigenous and Atlantic Slaveries in New France.* Chapel Hill: University of North Carolina Press, 2014.

Russell, Donna V., ed. *Michigan Censuses, 1710–1830: Under the French, British, and Americans.* Detroit: Detroit Society for Genealogical Research, 1982.

Sagard, Gabriel. *Le grand voyage du pays des Hurons situé en l'Amérique vers la mer douce, ès derniers confins de la Nouvelle France, dite Canada, où il est amplement traité de tout ce qui est du pays, des moeurs & coutumes & du naturel des Sauvages, de leur gouvernement & façons de faire, avec un dictionnaire de la langue huronne, pour la commodité de ceux qui ont à voyager dans le pays & n'ont l'intelligence d'icelle langue*. Paris: Chez Denys Moreau, 1632.

Saint-Pierre, Télesphore. *Histoire des Canadiens du Michigan et du comté d'Essex, Ontario*. 2nd ed. Sillery, QC: Septentrion, 2000.

Salone, Émile. *La colonisation de la Nouvelle-France: Étude sur les origines de la nation canadienne française*. Paris: E. Guilmoto éditeur, 1905.

Seed, Patricia. *Ceremonies of Possession in Europe's Conquest of the New World, 1492–1640*. Cambridge: Cambridge University Press, 1995.

Séguin, Robert-Lionel. "Le cheval et ses implications historiques dans l'Amérique française." *Revue d'histoire de l'Amérique française* 5, no. 2 (1951): 227–51.

– "Étude d'histoire économique: Les bêtes à cornes et leurs implications historiques en Amérique française." *Revue d'histoire de l'Amérique française* 7, no. 4 (1954): 538–57.

Sheppard, Diane Wolford. "Essex County, Ontario Militia Rolls for the Period 25 July to 24 August 1812." *Michigan's Habitant Heritage* 33, no. 3 (2012): 170–80.

– "Michigan Militia Members Serving in the War of 1812, Part 2." *Michigan's Habitant Heritage* 34, no. 2 (2013): 99–106.

– "Proof That No Indians Lived in Permanent Villages on Either Side of the Detroit River When Antoine de Lamothe, *Sieur* de Cadillac, Founded Fort Pontchartrain on 24 July 1701." The French-Canadian Heritage Society of Michigan, http://www.habitantheritage.org/yahoo_site_admin/assets/docs/Proof_No_Indians_Prior_to_Founding_in_1701_-_Final.317132128.pdf (accessed 5 December 2017).

Shortt, Adam, and Arthur G. Doughty, ed. *Documents Relating to the Constitutional History of Canada, 1759–1791*. Ottawa: S.E. Dawson, 1907.

Skinner, Claiborne A. *The Upper Country: French Enterprise in the Colonial Great Lakes*. Baltimore: Johns Hopkins University Press, 2008.

Sleeper-Smith, Susan. *Indian Women and French Men: Rethinking Cultural Encounter in the Western Great Lakes*. Amherst: University of Massachusetts Press, 2001.

Société franco-ontarienne d'histoire et de généalogie régionale Windsor-Essex. *Le Sud-Ouest ontarien à la recherche de nos ancêtres*. Windsor, ON: Société franco-ontarienne d'histoire et de généalogie régionale Windsor-Essex, 2001.

Sommerville, Suzanne Boivin. "Étienne Véron de Grandmesnil, Father and Son: An Example of Misinterpreted Evidence." *Michigan's Habitant Heritage* 22, no. 2 (2001): 72–80.

Sosin, Jack M. "The French Settlements in British Policy, 1760–1774." *Canadian Historical Review* 39, no. 3 (1958): 185–208.
- *Whitehall and the Wilderness: The Middle West in British Colonial Policy, 1760–1775.* Lincoln: University of Nebraska Press, 1961.
St-Onge, Nicole. "Blue Beads, Vermilion, and Scalpers: The Social Economy of the 1810–1812 Astorian Overland Expedition's French Canadian Voyageurs." In Englebert and Teasdale, eds., *French and Indians in the Heart of North America*, 183–216.
- "The Persistence of Travel and Trade: St. Lawrence River Valley French Engagés and the American Fur Company, 1818–1840." *Michigan Historical Review* 34, no. 2 (2008): 17–37.
Sturtevant, Andrew. "'Inseparable Companions' and Irreconcilable Enemies: The Hurons and Odawas of French Détroit, 1701–38." *Ethnohistory* 60, no. 2 (2013): 219–44.
Surtees, Robert J. "Indian Land Cessions in Ontario, 1763–1862: The Evolution of a System." PhD diss., Carleton University, 1982.
Talman, James J., ed. *Loyalist Narratives from Upper Canada.* Toronto: The Champlain Society, 1946.
Teasdale, Guillaume. "Les débuts de l'Église catholique américaine et le monde atlantique français: Le cas de l'ancienne colonie française de Détroit." *Histoire & Missions chrétiennes* 17 (2011): 35–58.
- "Des destinées distinctes: Les Français de la région de la rivière Détroit et leurs voisins amérindiens, 1763–1815." *Recherches amérindiennes au Québec* 39, nos. 1–2 (2009): 23–45.
- "The French of Orchard Country: Territory, Landscape, and Ethnicity in the Detroit River Region, 1680s–1810s." PhD diss., York University, 2010.
- "Old Friends and New Foes: French Settlers and Indians in the Detroit River Border Region." *Michigan Historical Review* 38, no. 2 (2012): 35–62.
Thwaites, Reuben Gold, ed. *The Jesuit Relations and Allied Documents.* Vol. 69. Cleveland: The Burrows Brothers, 1899.
Toupin, Robert, ed. *Les Écrits de Pierre Potier.* Ottawa: Presses de l'Université d'Ottawa, 1996.
Transactions at the Annual Meeting of the Maumee Valley Pioneer and Historical Association. Toledo, OH: Blade Printing & Paper, 1877.
Trapenard, Camille. *Le pâturage communal en Haute-Auvergne (XVIIe–XVIIIe siècles).* Paris: L. Larose & L. Tenin, 1904.
Trudeau, Jean-Baptiste. *Voyage sur le Haut-Missouri, 1794–1796.* Sillery, QC: Septentrion, 2006.

Trudel, Marcel. *Les débuts du régime seigneurial au Canada*. Montreal: Fides, 1974.
– "Le village en étoile, innovation des Jésuites et non de Talon." *Revue d'histoire de l'Amérique française* 44, no. 3 (1991): 397–406.
Tucker, Patrick M. "From Fallen Timbers to the British Evacuation of Detroit, 1794–1796: The Roman Catholic Priest Who Was a British Agent." *Michigan Historical Review* 37, no. 1 (2011): 40–76.
United States Indian Claims Commission. *Indians of Ohio, Indiana, Illinois, Southern Michigan, and Southern Wisconsin*. New York: Garland, 1974.
Vachon, André. "Inventaire critique des notaires royaux des gouvernements de Québec, Montréal et Trois-Rivières (1663–1764)." *Revue d'histoire de l'Amérique française* 9, no. 3 (1955): 423–38.
Villerbu, Tangi. "Pouvoir, religion et société en des temps indécis: Vincennes, 1763–1795." *Revue d'histoire de l'Amérique française* 62, no. 2 (2008): 185–214.
Wagnien, R. *Bois communaux: Examen, critique et défense des droits des habitants de la ville de Lormes*. Nevers, France: I.-M. Fay, Imprimeur de la Préfecture et de l'Évêché, 1861.
Wampach, Jean-Pierre. "Deux siècles de croissance agricole au Québec, 1760–1985." *Recherches sociographiques* 29, nos. 2–3 (1988): 181–99.
Watts, Edward. *In this Remote Country: French Colonial Culture in the Anglo-American Imagination, 1780–1860*. Chapel Hill: University of North Carolina Press, 2006.
Weyhing, Richard. "'Gascon Exaggerations': The Rise of Antoine Laumet dit de Lamothe, Sieur de Cadillac, the Foundation of Colonial Detroit, and the Origins of the Fox Wars." In Englebert and Teasdale, eds., *French and Indians in the Heart of North America*, 77–112.
White, Richard. *The Middle Ground: Indians, Empires, and Republics in the Great Lakes Region, 1650–1815*. New York: Cambridge University Press, 1991.

Index

Abbott, Edward (British military officer and 1765 Ottawa deed recipient), 44, 52
Abbott, James, Jr (Michigan private claims commissioner), 89, 93
Allard, Jacques, 91, 93
Amherst, Jeffery (British commander-in-chief in North America), 41–5, 48
Amherstburg, 3, 115, 121, 189n106
Anderdon Reserve, 74, 77
Anthon, Christian (1765 Ottawa deed recipient), 52–3
Askiby (Potawatomi chief), 57
Askin, John, 55
Assumption mission (L'Assomption) 35, 157n59
Assumption parish or church, 79, 118–20, 127–9, 134, 184n33
Audrain, Peter (Michigan private claims commissioner), 88–9, 93

Bâby, François, x
Bâby, Jacques (son of Jacques Bâby dit Dupéron), 78, 132–3, 173n38

barns, 12, 32, 105, 107

Barrin de La Galissonière, Roland-Michel (Roland-Michel Barrin de La Galissonière, Marquis de La Galissonière, governor general of New France), 12, 32
Barthe, André Charles, 68
Bassett, Henry (British commander of Fort Detroit), 47
Bates, Frederick (Michigan private claims commissioner), 88, 95
Baudry dit Desbuttes dit St-Martin, Jacques (1750 grantee), 160n33
Beaubien, Jean Baptiste (merchant), 108, 181n65
Beauharnois de la Boische, Charles de (Marquis de Beauharnois, governor general of New France), 26, 28, 30
Bégon de la Picardière, Michel (intendant of New France), 13, 25–6, 28
Belleperche, Jacques, 118–19
Belleperche, Jeanne, 161n33
Bergeron, Simon, 37

Bernard, Guillaume, 36–7
Bernier, Charles, 79
Bienvenu dit Delisle, Alexis (1750 grantee), 160n33, 163n64
Bièque dit Lafleur, Joseph, 129
Billiau dit L'espérance, Jean Baptiste (1750 grantee), 161n33
Bineau dit Lajeunesse, Jean Louis (1750 grantee), 160n33
Bois Blanc Island (Boblo Island), 73, 103, 157n59
Bondy, Joseph, Sr, 79
border, x, xiv, 3, 6, 95, 109, 114–21, 123, 125, 128, 129–30, 132–6, 138–9, 142n9, 182n3, 184n33, 189n106
Bouchette, Joseph (surveyor), 62
Bougainville, Louis-Antoine de (military officer), 37
Boyer, Antoine, 105
Boyer, Pierre, 105
Bradstreet, John (British commander of Fort Detroit), 42
Bréhant de Galinée, René de (Sulpician missionary), 10
Brehm, Deterecht (British military officer), 44–5
Bruce, Thomas (British commander of Fort Detroit), 47–8, 68

Cadillac. *See* Laumet de Lamothe Cadillac, Antoine
Caldwell, William (British military officer), 76
Callière, Louis-Hector de (governor general of New France), 11
Campau, Antoine (1750 grantee), 164n66
Campau, Barnabé, 70

Campau, Claude (1736 grantee), 160n33
Campau, Geneviève, 127
Campau, Jean Louis (1734 grantee), 46, 105, 107
Campau, Joseph (merchant), 7, 89, 106–7, 116–19, 180n62
Campau, Marguerite, 106
Campau, Michel (1707 grantee), 106
Campau, Thérèse, 118
Campbell, Donald (British commander of Fort Detroit), 41, 43–5, 48, 63
Campbell, John (British commander of Fort Detroit), 44–6, 58, 63
Carleton, Guy (First Baron Dorchester and governor of the Province of Quebec), 54, 64, 67–8, 73–4, 81
Cass, Lewis (governor of Michigan Territory), 110
Casse dit St-Aubin, Gabriel (1734 grantee), 160n33
Catalogne, Gédéon de (military engineer), 62, 100
Cavelier, de La Salle, René Robert (Sieur de La Salle), 10, 26, 100, 143n5
Chaboillez, Louis (Montreal notary), 127–8
Chapoton, Antoine Alexis, 105
Chapoton, Jean (surgeon), 31
Chapoton, Jean Baptiste, 67–8
Chaussegros de Léry, Gaspard-Joseph, Jr (military engineer), 32, 34–5, 37–8, 64, 103, 105, 154n41

Chauvin, Charles (1734 grantee), 28–9, 46, 93, 105
Chêne, Charles (1734 grantee), 54, 154n34, 157n56, 160n33, 166n79
Chêne, Isidore (1777 Potawatomi deed recipient), 54, 172n37
Chêne dit Labutte, Pierre (1765 Ottawa deed recipient), 52, 154n34, 178n38
Chevalier, Marie Madeleine, 166n78
Chevalier de Longueuil. *See* Le Moyne de Longueuil, Paul-Joseph
Chippewa: in Detroit River region, 11–12; land deed, 55, 63, 65, 67; man's death, 81; treaty, 73–4, 89
Cicotte, Zacharie (1750 grantee), 160n33
Clairambault d'Aigremont, François (naval commissary in Canada), 21, 23, 108
Cloutier, Charles, 117
Company of One Hundred Associates, 14, 17, 62, 146n38
Côte des Pous: and District of Hamtramck, 85; and farm rental, 129; and François de Joncaire de Chabert, 83; as future Huron village, 103; land tract, 37, 44, 47, 54, 57, 91, 166n78; and the Navarres, 131, 188n95; orchards, 103, 105–6; settlement, 35; and urban Detroit, 138–9
Côte du Nord-Est: and District of Hamtramck, 85; and François Rivard, 175n76; and Jacques Amable Peltier, 181n66; land tract, 37, 44, 91, 117–19, 173n53; as oldest côte, 34–5; orchards, 103–7, 109–10; residents, 81–2; and Treaty of Greenville, 83; and urban Detroit, 138–9
Côte du Nord-Ouest 34, 157n56. *See also* Côte des Pous
Côte du Sud, 35, 75, 133, 184n33; and Alexis Maisonville, 123, 185n46; land tract, 37; orchards, 103, 107; residents, 76, 78, 81, 117–19, 128–9, 184n29; windmills, 120. *See also* L'Assomption
Couture, Monique, 129
Cramahé, Théophile-Hector (lieutenant-governor of the Province of Quebec), 69
Crête, Jean Baptiste (merchant), 108

Dagneau Douville de Quindre, Louis-Césaire, 64
Darnell, Elias, 108
Dauphin de La Forest, François (military officer), 100
Dearborn, 3
Dearborn, Henry (US secretary of the Department of War), 85
Dehêtres, Gonzague (1750 grantee), 37
Dehêtres, Hyacinthe (1750 grantee), 37
Dehêtres, Louis, 37
Dejean, Philippe (Detroit notary), 50, 59, 64, 67, 69, 105, 163n55, 170n40
Dejean, Pierre (Sulpician missionary), 134, 189n101

de Joncaire de Chabert, François (Potawatomi deeds recipient), 83, 172n37
de La Richardie, Armand (Jesuit missionary), 103
Delisle, Charles, 163n64
Deniau, Cherubin (Recollet missionary), 102
De Peyster, Arent Schuyler (British commander of Fort Detroit), 46
Deschamps de Boishébert, Henri-Louis (commander of Fort Pontchartrain), 27
Deschatelet, Joseph, 91
Descomps dit Labadie, Antoine Louis (1781 Chippewa deed recipient), 55
Desmarchais dit Parisien, Radegonde, 129
Desnoyers, Joseph, 107
Desnoyers, Pierre, 37
Desruisseaux Bellecour, François (Detroit notary), 170n40
Detroit Land Board (British), 73–6, 78, 80–2, 96
Dollier de Casson, François (Sulpician missionary), 10
Drouillard, Jean Baptiste, Jr (1750 grantee), 161n33
Drouillard, Marie-Louise, 129
Dubois, Berthelot de Beaucours Josué (governor of Montreal), 12
Dubuisson, Jacques-Charles Renaud (acting commander of Fort Pontchartrain), 23
Dufour, Catherine, 127
Dulhut, Daniel Greysolon (trader), 10
Dumais, Jacques, 164n65, 166n78

Dumoulin, Charles (French jurist), 17
Durocher, Martin, 106

England, Richard G. (British commander of Fort Detroit), 132–3, 172n38, 173n38
Erie Canal, 134, 136, 138
Estève dit Lajeunesse, Angélique, 118
Estève dit Lajeunesse, Pierre (1707 grantee), 154n36

Fafard, Jean (1750 grantee), 37
farmers, 7, 37, 41, 45–6, 53, 61, 101, 139
farms, 40, 55, 64, 76, 97–8, 103, 113, 180n6; and families, 117–18, 123, 129, 181n66, 184n29, 188n95; as "habitations," 155n41; orchards on, 3, 99–100, 102–11, 138; ribbon, x; and settlers, 3–4, 12, 32–4; layout of, 36, 81; US government and French farms, 85–6, 89–90, 95–6, 182n84
fences, 28, 45, 90, 104–5, 107–9, 180n60, 180n61
Five Nations Iroquois, 10–12, 34
Fort de Buade (today's Saint Ignace, Michigan), 10, 14, 143n5, 145n18
Fort Detroit (Fort Pontchartrain; Fort Detroit), 3, 4, 7, 18, 31–2, 34–5, 55, 74, 80, 100, 103, 106; and Aboriginal attacks, 109, 131, 146n23, 157n59; American spy at, 40; British commanders at, 41–4, 46–7, 51, 58, 60, 68, 81, 84; Cadillac at, 11, 18–19, 21–4,

30, 100–2, 108, 137; and District of Hamtramck, 85; early urbanization, 7, 57, 110, 115, 138; French commanders at, 12, 23, 27–8, 30, 36, 40, 43–4, 47–9, 64, 68, 82, 106; residents, 31–4, 37, 39, 52, 102, 105, 117, 119, 165n67; and Treaty of Greenville, 83; and US government representatives, 85–6, 89, 110, 173n53; and War of 1812, 131
Fort Frontenac, 143n5
Fort Greenville, 82–3
Fort Meigs, 131
Fort Miami (British), 172n38, 173n38
Fort Miami (French), 7
Fort Pontchartrain. *See* Fort Detroit
Fort Saint Joseph (Dulhut Post, today's Port Huron, Michigan), 10, 100, 144n11
Fort Saint Joseph (today's Niles, Michigan), 144n11
French: loyalty to farms, 130
French farmers: and dissident narratives, 113; and imperialist narratives, 112
Fréton dit Nantais, Julien (1759 grantee), 160n33

Gage, Thomas (British commander-in-chief in North America), xiii, 44–54, 58–9, 63, 68, 69, 123
Gages, Horatio, 109
Gallatin, Albert (US secretary of the Treasury), 86, 88, 90–1, 93, 95
Gamelin, Laurent Eustache (1747 grantee), 32, 35, 67, 154n40, 160n33
Gaudet, Jacques, 37

Généreux, Joseph-Ambroise, 129
Gervais, Louis, 37
Gervais dit Ladéroute, François, 104
Gignac, Antoine, 37
Gladwin, Henry (British commander of Fort Detroit), 47, 109
Godefroy dit St-Georges, François, 104
Godet dit Marantette, François, 164n66
Godet dit Marantette, Jacques, 164n66
Godet dit Marantette, Joseph Charles, 164n66
Godfroy, Gabriel, 93
Godfroy, Gabriel Jacques (1780 Potawatomi deed recipient), 55, 105
Godfroy, Jacques (1760 grantee), 55, 105–6
Gouin, Claude (or Claude Jacques Thomas), 37, 160n33
Goulet, Clémence, 134
Goulet, Louis, 133
Goyau, Baptiste, 37
Goyau, Guillaume, 37
Goyau, Vital, 37
Greeley, Aaron (Michigan private claims surveyor), 92–5, 110
Griffard, Laurent, 93, 175n82
Grimard, Charles (1750 grantee), 37
Griswold, Stanley (secretary of Michigan Territory and Michigan private claims commissioner), 89, 93, 95, 115
Guignard dit Saint-Pierre, Pierre, 161n33
Guignard dit St-Étienne, Joseph, 161n33

Guillet dit Tourangeau, Jean Baptiste (1751 or 1752 grantee), 160n33
Guy, Antoine, 91

Haldimand, Frederick (governor of the Province of Quebec), 69, 75
Hamilton, Henry (lieutenant-governor of the District of Detroit), 69, 109–10
Hamtramck, Jean-François (US military officer), 84–5, 87, 92, 116, 173n53, 174n53
Harrison, William Henry (US military officer), 131
Heir and Devisee Commission (first and second), 80, 95, 117, 119
Hennepin, Louis (Recollet missionary), 100
Hocquart, Gilles (intendant of New France), 12, 26–8, 30
Hoffman, George (Michigan private claims commissioner), 88, 95
Huault de Montmagny, Charles (governor general of New France), 62
Hubbard, Bela (Detroit naturalist), 101, 112, 121, 139
Hull, Abijah (Michigan private claims surveyor), 93, 175n88
Hull, William (governor of Michigan Territory), 112, 181n78
Huron, 4, 11–12, 32, 35, 74, 76, 89, 103, 145n22, 153n26, 154n40, 157n59, 166n82
Huron Church Reserve, 74, 76
Huron mission, 35, 103, 157n59, 171n5

Indian Country (territory), 42–5, 47, 49, 53, 59, 68, 70, 73, 137
Indiana Territory, 86, 90, 118

Jacques, Étienne, 161n33
Jadot, Louis, 161n33
Janisse, François, 37
Jefferson, Thomas, 95, 113, 182n84
Johnson, William (British officer), 35, 167n97, 168n97
Jolibois, Marguerite, 120
Jouett, Charles (Indian agent), 86
Jubinville, François, 186n65
Jubinville, Joseph-Marie, 127

Labadie, Élizabeth, 128
Labadie dit Badichon, Joseph, 47
Laboursonière, Élisabeth, 106
La Butte, Pierre, 37
Lacelle, Nicholas, Jr (1780 Potawatomi deed recipient), 55
La Feuillade, Joseph, 37
Lake Erie, 3, 10, 73, 76, 84, 131, 145n22
Lakeshore (town), 76
Lake St Clair, 35, 73, 119
Lamarre, Charles, 37, 161
Landry, Michel, 37
Landry dit St-André, Claude (1750 grantee), 160n33
Languedoc, François, 37
L'Assomption (or L'Assomption de la Pointe de Montréal), 75, 78–9, 103. *See also* Côte du Sud
Laumet de Lamothe Cadillac, Antoine: and 1705 trip to Montreal, 18; as commander of Fort de Buade, 14; and founding of Detroit, 3, 11, 18, 25, 137; and fruit trees, 100, 102, 108; in

Louisiana, 22; and minister of the Marine, 14, 18–23; and seigneurialism and feudalism, 20–5, 27, 33–4, 67; and travels to France, 14
Lauzon, Cécile, 119
Lauzon, François, 118
Lauzon, François (or François Nicolas): at Detroit in 1730s, 105, 154n34
Lauzon, Jacques, 118
Lauzon, Léo, 134
Lavoie, Martin, 160n33
Lebeau, François (1749 grantee), 161n33
Lebeau, Jean Baptiste (1749 grantee), 161n33
Legrand, Gabriel (Detroit notary), 59, 170n40
Le Moyne de Longueuil, Paul-Joseph (Chevalier de Longueuil, commander of Fort Pontchartrain), 12
L'Esperance, Joseph, 37
Livernois, Angélique, 120
Livernois, Étienne (settled at Detroit before 1760), 160n33
livestock, 12, 18, 32–4, 36, 45, 61–2, 64, 68, 97, 102, 109
Lom d'Arce de Lahontan, Louis-Armand de (Baron de Lahontan), 100
London, 61, 120
Lootman dit Barrois, François, 104
Loranger dit Maisonville, Alexis (1765 Ottawa deed recipient), 52–3, 123, 165n72
Louis XIII, 17
Louis XIV, 10, 17, 26, 33, 100
Lower Canada, 99, 127, 130, 135

Loyalists, 69, 73–4, 96, 99

Macomb, William (British merchant), 70
Mailloux, Joseph, 37
Maisonville, Alexis (son of Alexis Loranger dit Maisonville), 123–4, 185n46
Mansfield, Jared (surveyor general of the United States), 93
Marchand, Geneviève, 129
Marest, Pierre-Gabriel (Jesuit missionary), 102
Marsac, François, Sr (1734 grantee), 46, 164n66
Maumee River, 55, 131–2
Maure, Laurent, 180n62
Maure, Louis, Sr, 106–8, 180n62
Mayne, William (British military officer), 81
McDougall, George (British military officer, 1765 Ottawa deed recipient, and 1768 Chippewa/Ottawa deed recipient (Belle Isle)), 44, 51, 63–5, 67–70
McKee, Alexander, 73
McNiff, Patrick (deputy-surveyor of the district of Hesse), 76
Meldrum, George (merchant), 105
Meloche, Jean-Baptiste, 117
Meloche, Pierre, Sr (1734 grantee), 117, 161n33
Ménard, Gabriel, 128
Miami River. See Maumee River
Michigan Territory, 86, 89, 119–20, 138; border issues, 123; cross-border migrations, 127–9; French orchards, 113; private claims commission, 93, 95, 97,

112, 117–19, 182n84; sale of public land, 97; and War of 1812, 108, 110, 117, 130–1; windmills, 121
Michipichy (Huron chief), 11
Monforton, Guillaume (Detroit notary), 106, 170n40
Montreal, 10; capitulation, 41, 47–8, 50; côtes, 62; founding of, 11, 36; fruit trees, 99–101; and transportation to Detroit, 30, 32–3, 103, 125–9, 154n41
Montreuil, Luc (or François-Luc), 121–2, 128, 186n70
Moran, Charles (or Claude Charles, 1734 grantee), 27, 37 101, 154n34
Moreau, Marie, 107
Morel, Olivier (Olivier Morel, Sieur de La Durantaye, commander of Fort de Buade), 10
Mornier dit Léveillé, Marie Félicité, 117
Mount Clemens, 3, 133, 158n71, 180n62
Murray, James (governor of the Province of Quebec), 50

Navarre, François (1785 Potawatomi deed recipient), 57, 82, 130–3
Navarre, Jacques (1785 Potawatomi deed recipient), 57, 188n95
Navarre, Marie-France, 70
Navarre, Peter (War of 1812 scout), 131
Navarre, Robert (Detroit royal notary and 1747 grantee), 26–30, 32, 37, 43, 47–9, 57–9, 63, 67–9, 82, 104, 160n33, 161n33, 170n40
Navarre, Robert, Jr (1771 Potawatomi deed recipient), 48, 52, 54, 56, 83
New England, ix, 126, 134, 138
New York (city), 40, 53, 61, 101, 123, 139
New York (state), 40, 110, 134, 138

Odawa. *See* Ottawa
Ohio valley, 83, 133
Ojibwa. *See* Chippewa
Orontony (Huron chief), 12
Ottawa, 4, 11–12, 35, 51–5, 63, 65, 67, 73–4, 89, 132, 145n18, 157n59, 164n65, 164n66, 166n82
Oüà-Oüi-attenne (Potawatomi chief), 57

Paillé dit Paillard, Léonard (windmill builder), 30
Paré, Jean-Baptiste, Sr, 119, 184n29
Payen de Noyan et de Chavoy, Pierre-Jacques (commander of Fort Pontchartrain), 32
Pelletier, Marie-France, 119
Pépin, Suzanne, 104–5
Petite Côte, 35, 37, 73–6, 78–9, 81, 103–4, 106, 110, 117–18, 120–1, 133, 184n33
Picard, Eulalie, 130
Picard, Joseph, 130
Picoté de Belestre, François-Marie (last commander of Fort Pontchartrain), 36, 48–9, 55, 83
Pilet, Joseph (1750 grantee), 161n33

Index

Pontiac (Ottawa chief), 41, 43, 51–4, 109, 157n59
Pontiac's War. *See* Pontiac
Potawatomi, 4, 11–12, 32, 35, 54–7, 74, 83–4, 89, 91, 130, 132, 164n65, 172n37, 188n95
Potier, Pierre-Philippe (Jesuit missionary), 103
Pradet dit Laforge, Louis, 106, 119
Proulx, Angélique, 127
Province of Quebec (1763–91), 43, 49–50, 53–4, 57–8, 64, 69–70, 73–5, 109
Prud'homme, François Xavier (1751 grantee), 104

Quebec (city), 4, 10–11, 17, 23–5, 33, 36, 61, 75, 99, 106–7, 129, 137, 141, 149n2, 165n67, 173n53, 180n62
Quebec Act, 53–4, 58–9, 69
Quintin, Michel (1750 grantee), 37

Rameau de Saint-Père, Edmé (French historian), 135
Rau, Jean Baptiste, 104
Raymond dit Toulouse, Gertrude, 134
Réaume, Charles (1776 Ottawa deed recipient), 54–5
Réaume, Hyacinthe (1750 grantee), 37, 54, 164n66, 165n66
Réaume, Louise, 128
Réaume, Marguerite, 127
Rigaud de Vaudreuil, Philippe de (Marquis de Vaudreuil, governor general of New France), 13, 25–6, 28, 48
Rivard, François, 91, 175n76
Rivard, Jean (1750 grantee), 37

River Canard, 73, 76
River Ecorse, 47–50, 55, 85
River Huron (Clinton River), 81, 83, 85, 91, 96, 106–7, 180n62
River Raisin, 55, 80–1, 96, 121, 132; and District of Sargent, 85, 131; militia, 131–2, 188n97; and Navarre family, 57, 82, 130–1, 188n95; and Ottawa, 55; Potawatomi at, 35, 132; and Potawatomi deed, 57, 82, 130; residents, 83, 91, 112–13, 117–18, 120, 128–9, 132–5; and Treaty of Greenville, 83; and Upper Canada, 132
River Rouge, 40, 44, 47, 48, 49, 50, 55, 78, 83, 85, 93, 121, 131, 162n41, 167n86, 167n87, 172n37
Rivière aux Écorces. *See* River Ecorse
Rivière aux Raisins. *See* River Raisin
Rivière Rouge. *See* River Rouge
Robert, Antoine, 37
Robert, Marie-Louise, 128, 130
Roy, Marie-Joseph, 118
Roy, Pierre, 7
Royal Proclamation (1763), 41, 43, 46, 50–1, 54, 57, 59, 61, 63, 70, 72–3, 96, 123, 137

Sabrevois, Jacques-Charles de (commander of Fort Pontchartrain), 23, 27
Saint Anne's parish or church, 119–20, 127, 129–30, 133–4, 184n33
Saint Antoine parish or church, 120, 128, 184n33, 188n97

Saint François de Sales parish or church, 134
Sandwich (town), 3, 110, 115, 132
Sargent, Winthrop (acting governor of the Northwest Territory), 83
Simcoe, John Graves (governor of Upper Canada), 75, 79, 81, 132, 172n38, 173n38
Soullière, Cécile, 129
Soullière, Jean-Baptiste, 117
St Clair, Arthur (American military officer), 84–5
St-Cosme, Pierre Laurent, 68
Sterling, James (Irish merchant), 59
Stevenson, James (British commander of Fort Detroit), 47–9, 51–3, 68
Suzor, Louis François, 106, 161n33

Talon, Jean (intendant of New France), 33
Tecumseh (Shawnee chief), 131
Tecumseh (town), 76, 79
Thibault, François, 93
Tonty, Alphonse de (Baron de Paludy, commander of Fort Pontchartrain), 27, 30, 64, 100
Treaty of Paris (1763), 42, 125
Treaty of Paris (1783), 69, 72, 74, 82
Tremblay, Ambroise (1750 grantee), 37
Tremblay, Archange, 133
Tremblay, Louis, Jr (1750 grantee), 37

Tremblay, Pierre (1750 grantee), 37
Tremblay, Pierre, Jr (1750 grantee), 37
Tremblay, Thérèse, 106
Trois-Rivières, ix, 33–4, 62–3, 129
Turnbull, George (British commander of Fort Detroit), 45–6, 48, 50–1, 63–4

Upper Canada, 3, 6, 75–6, 80–1, 93, 95, 99, 110, 115, 117, 119–20, 127, 129–30, 132, 134, 168n104, 172n38, 188n97

Versailles, 4, 17–21, 23–5
Villers dit St-Louis, Louis, Sr (1750 grantee), 161n33
voyageurs, 27, 30, 36, 112, 125–9, 186n57

Walkerville, 3, 75, 122, 124
Walpole Island, 74
Wayne, Anthony (American military officer), 82, 89, 133
Williams, Thomas (Detroit notary), 59, 105, 170n40
windmills, 3, 20, 30, 97, 120–5, 138, 184n41
Windsor, x, xiii, 3, 7, 15–16, 31, 74, 111, 123, 135–6, 139, 184n41
Woodward, Augustus (Michigan Territory's first chief justice), 86, 95, 138
Wyandot. *See* Huron